STARCRAFT
SCAVENGERS

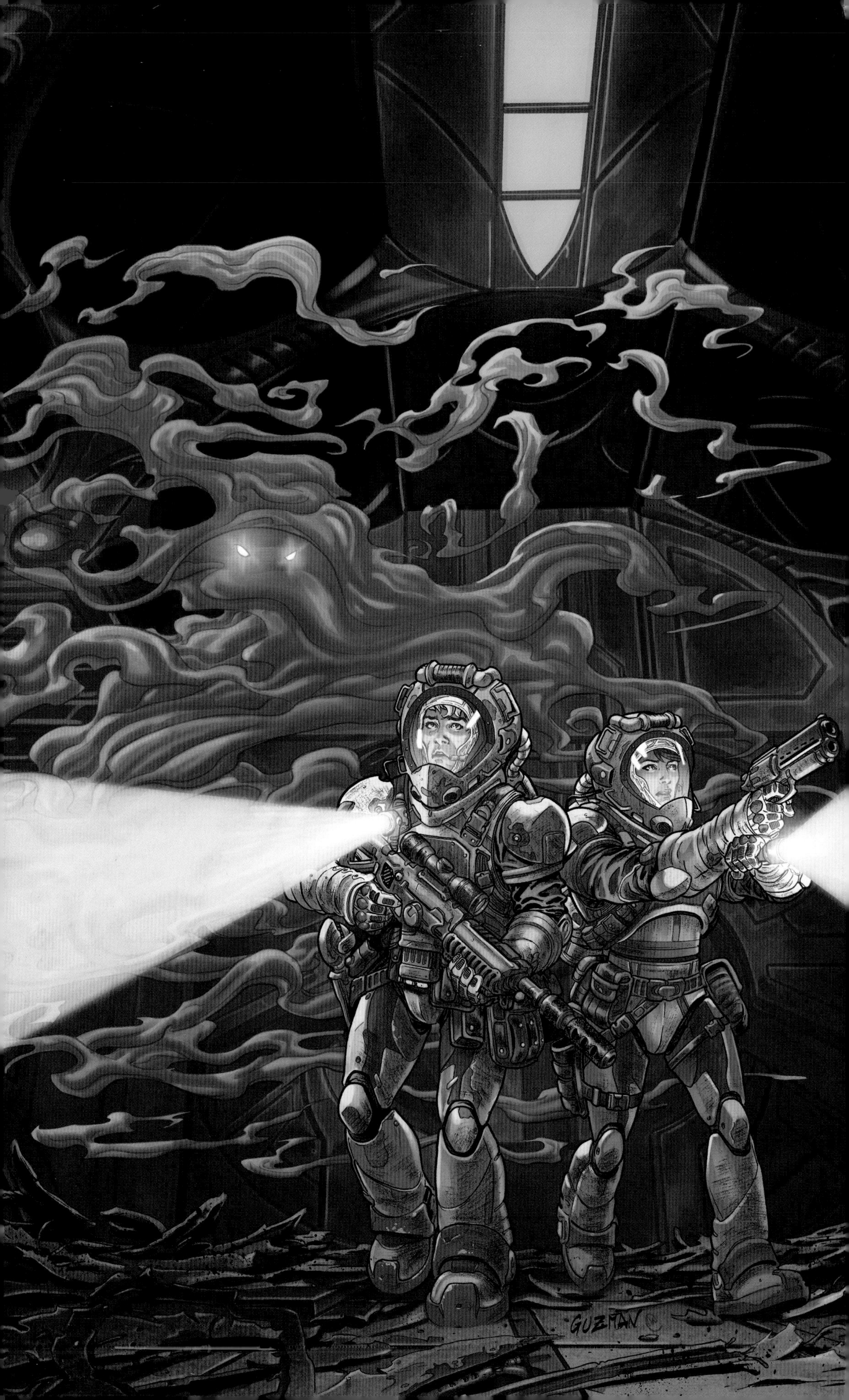
GUZMAN

STARCRAFT®
SCAVENGERS

SCRIPT
JODY HOUSER

COVER & LINE ART
GABRIEL GUZMÁN

COLORS
MICHAEL ATIYEH

LETTERING
STEVE DUTRO

LICENSED
BLIZZARD
ENTERTAINMENT
PRODUCT

DARK HORSE BOOKS®

PRESIDENT & PUBLISHER
MIKE RICHARDSON

SENIOR EDITOR
PHILIP R. SIMON

COLLECTION DESIGNER
LIN HUANG

ASSOCIATE EDITOR
MEGAN WALKER

DIGITAL ART TECHNICIAN
ADAM PRUETT

Special thanks to Dustin Browder, Sean Copeland, Allen Dilling, Cate Gary, Allison Irons, George Krstic, Brianne M Loftis, Paul Morrissey, Justin Parker, Byron Parnell, Andrew R. Robinson, Derek Rosenberg, Ralph Sanchez, and everyone at Blizzard Entertainment.

LICENSED
BLIZZARD
ENTERTAINMENT
PRODUCT

This volume collects issues #1 through #4 of the Dark Horse Comics series *StarCraft: Scavengers* and is Dark Horse's first collection in a series of StarCraft graphic novels.

Published by Dark Horse Books
A division of Dark Horse Comics, Inc.
10956 SE Main Street, Milwaukie, OR 97222

DarkHorse.com | Blizzard.com

Facebook.com/DarkHorseComics
Twitter.com/DarkHorseComics

To find a comics shop in your area, visit comicshoplocator.com

First edition: February 2019 | ISBN 978-1-50670-755-6

1 3 5 7 9 10 8 6 4 2
Printed in China

Library of Congress Cataloging-in-Publication Data

Names: Houser, Jody, author. | Guzman, Gabriel, 1975- artist. | Atiyeh,
   Michael, colourist. | Dutro, Steve, letterer.
Title: Scavengers / script, Jody Houser ; cover and line art, Gabriel Guzman
   ; colors, Michael Atiyeh ; lettering, Steve Dutro.
Description: First edition. | Milwaukie, OR : Dark Horse Books, February
   2019. | Series: StarCraft ; Volume 1 | "This volume collects issues #1
   through #4 of the Dark Horse Comics series StarCraft: Scavengers and is
   Dark Horse's first collection in a series of StarCraft graphic novels."
Identifiers: LCCN 2018042029 | ISBN 9781506707556 (paperback)
Subjects: LCSH: Comic books, strips, etc. | BISAC: COMICS & GRAPHIC NOVELS /
   Media Tie-In. | COMICS & GRAPHIC NOVELS / Science Fiction. | COMICS &
   GRAPHIC NOVELS / Fantasy.
Classification: LCC PN6728.S68186 H68 2019 | DDC 741.5/973–dc23
LC record available at https://lccn.loc.gov/2018042029

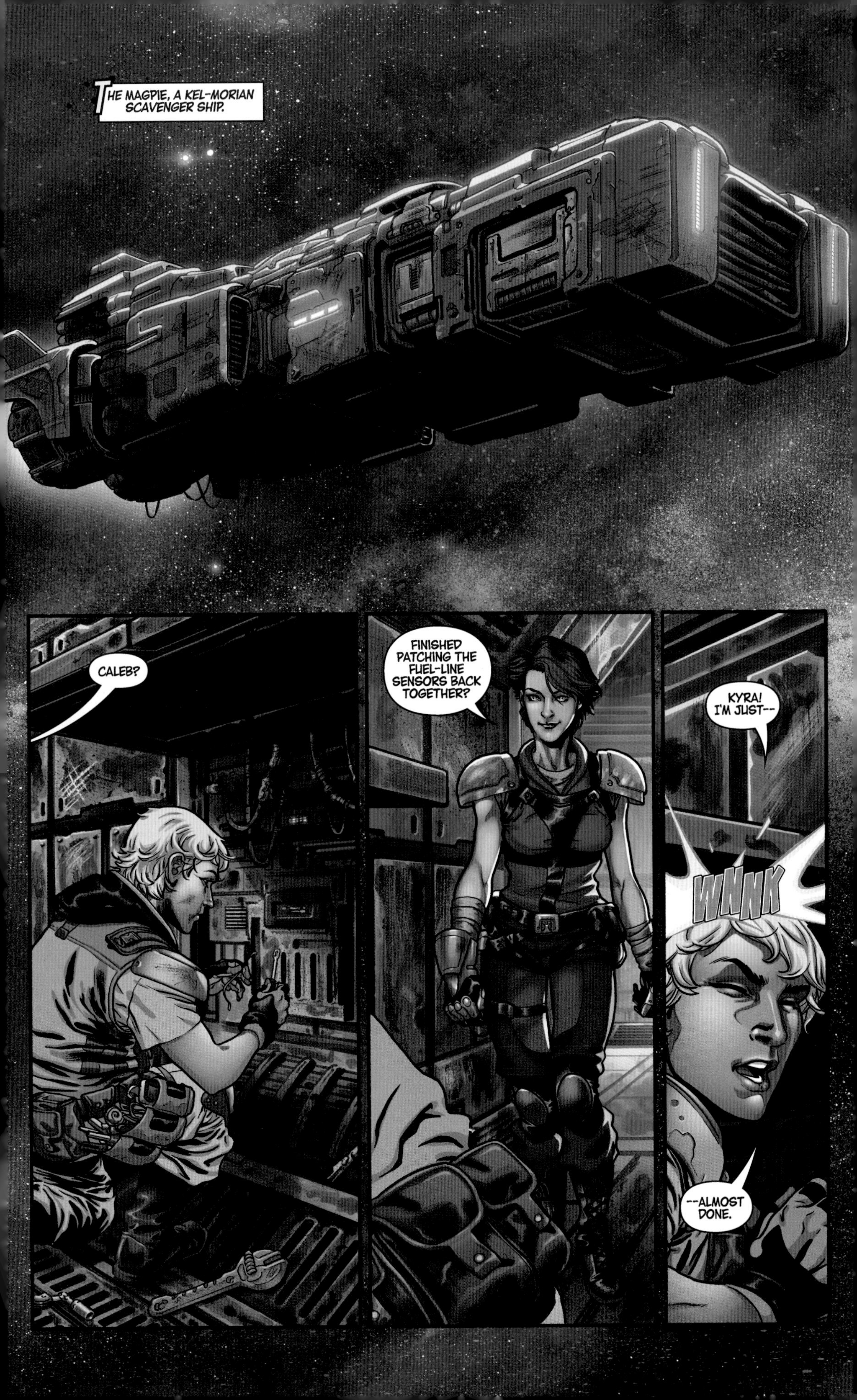
THE MAGPIE, A KEL-MORIAN SCAVENGER SHIP.
CALEB?
FINISHED PATCHING THE FUEL-LINE SENSORS BACK TOGETHER?
KYRA! I'M JUST--
WNNK
--ALMOST DONE.

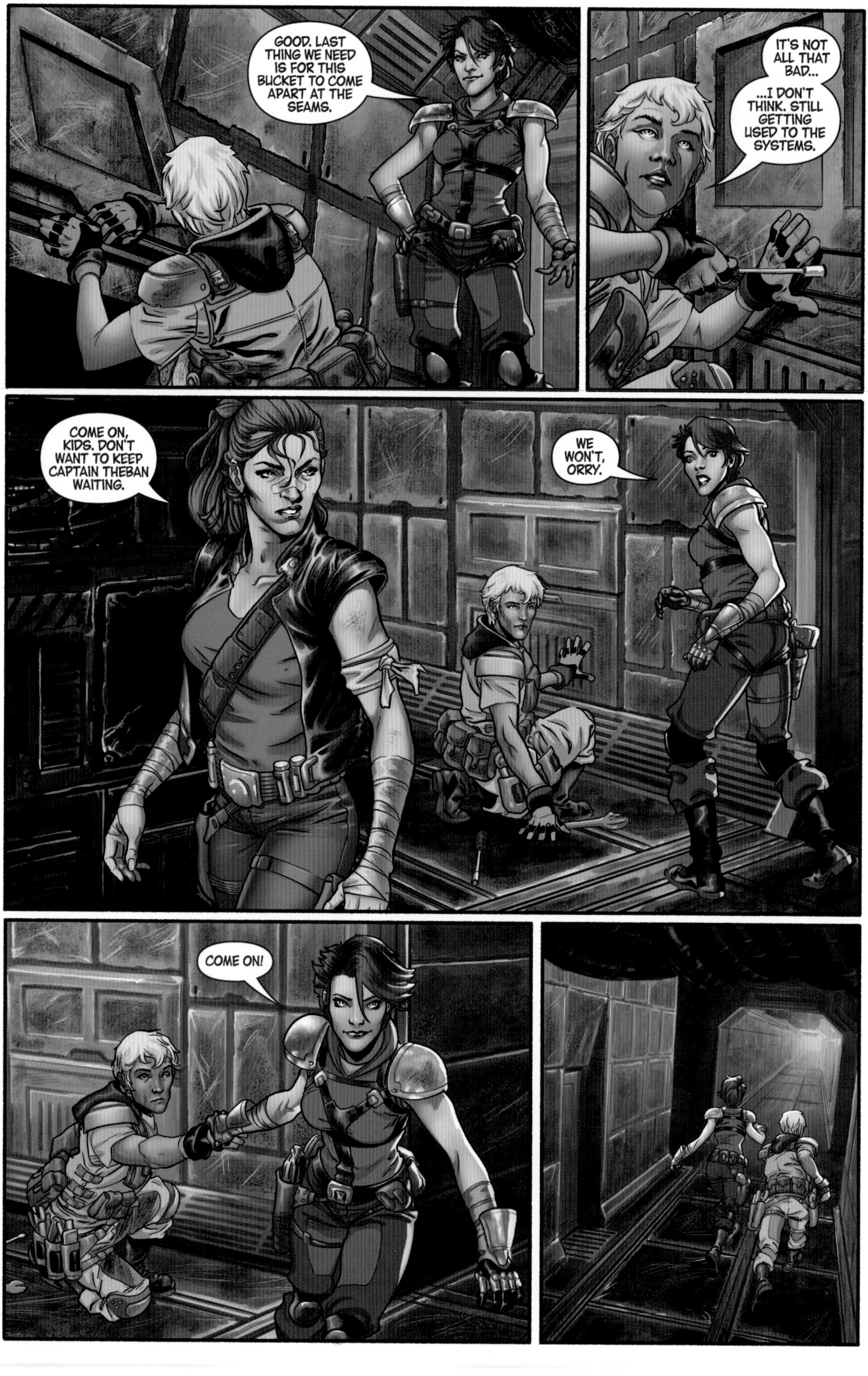
GOOD. LAST THING WE NEED IS FOR THIS BUCKET TO COME APART AT THE SEAMS.
IT'S NOT ALL THAT BAD...
...I DON'T THINK. STILL GETTING USED TO THE SYSTEMS.
COME ON, KIDS. DON'T WANT TO KEEP CAPTAIN THEBAN WAITING.
WE WON'T, ORRY.
COME ON!

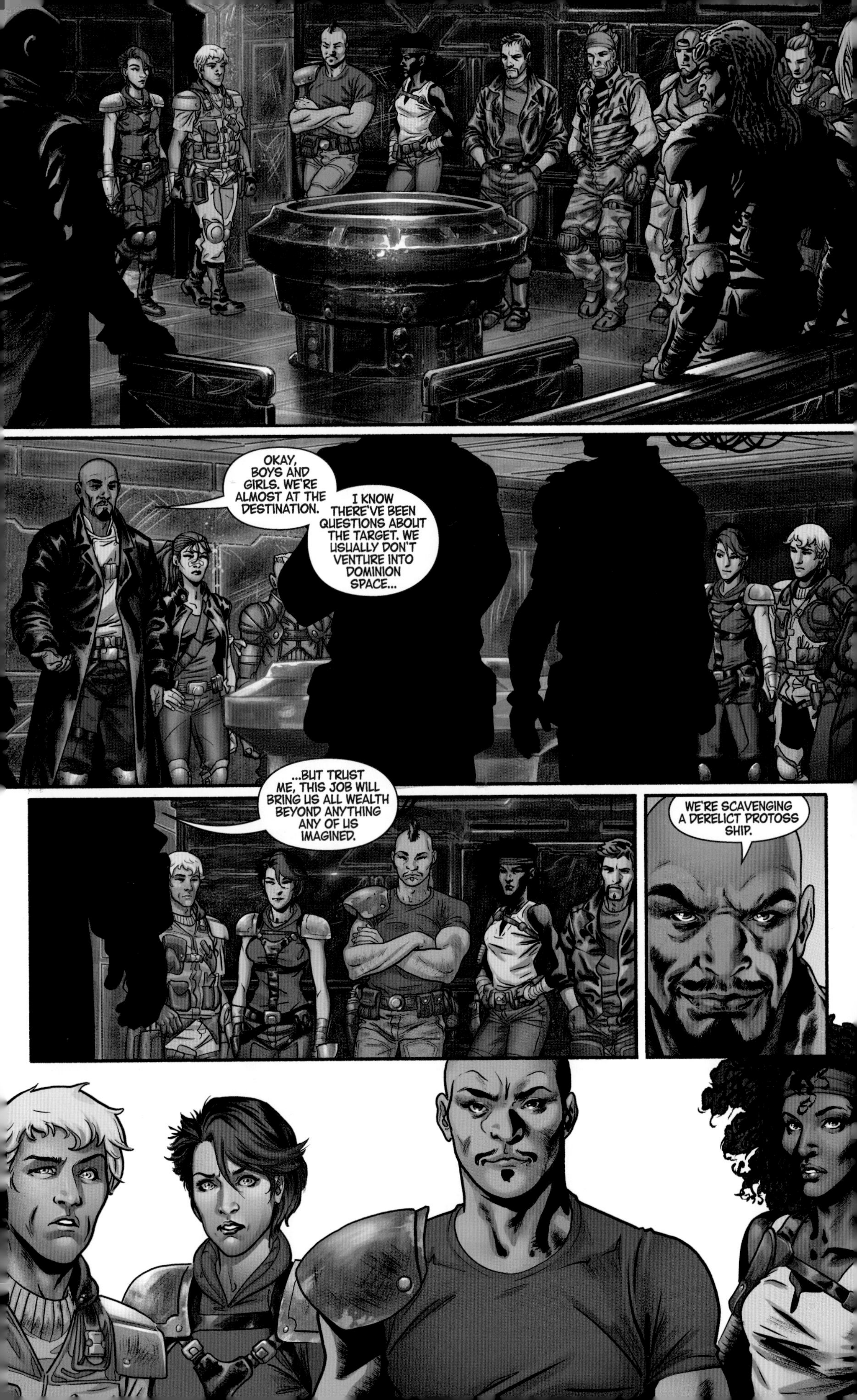
OKAY, BOYS AND GIRLS. WE'RE ALMOST AT THE DESTINATION.
I KNOW THERE'VE BEEN QUESTIONS ABOUT THE TARGET. WE USUALLY DON'T VENTURE INTO DOMINION SPACE...
...BUT TRUST ME, THIS JOB WILL BRING US ALL WEALTH BEYOND ANYTHING ANY OF US IMAGINED.
WE'RE SCAVENGING A DERELICT PROTOSS SHIP.

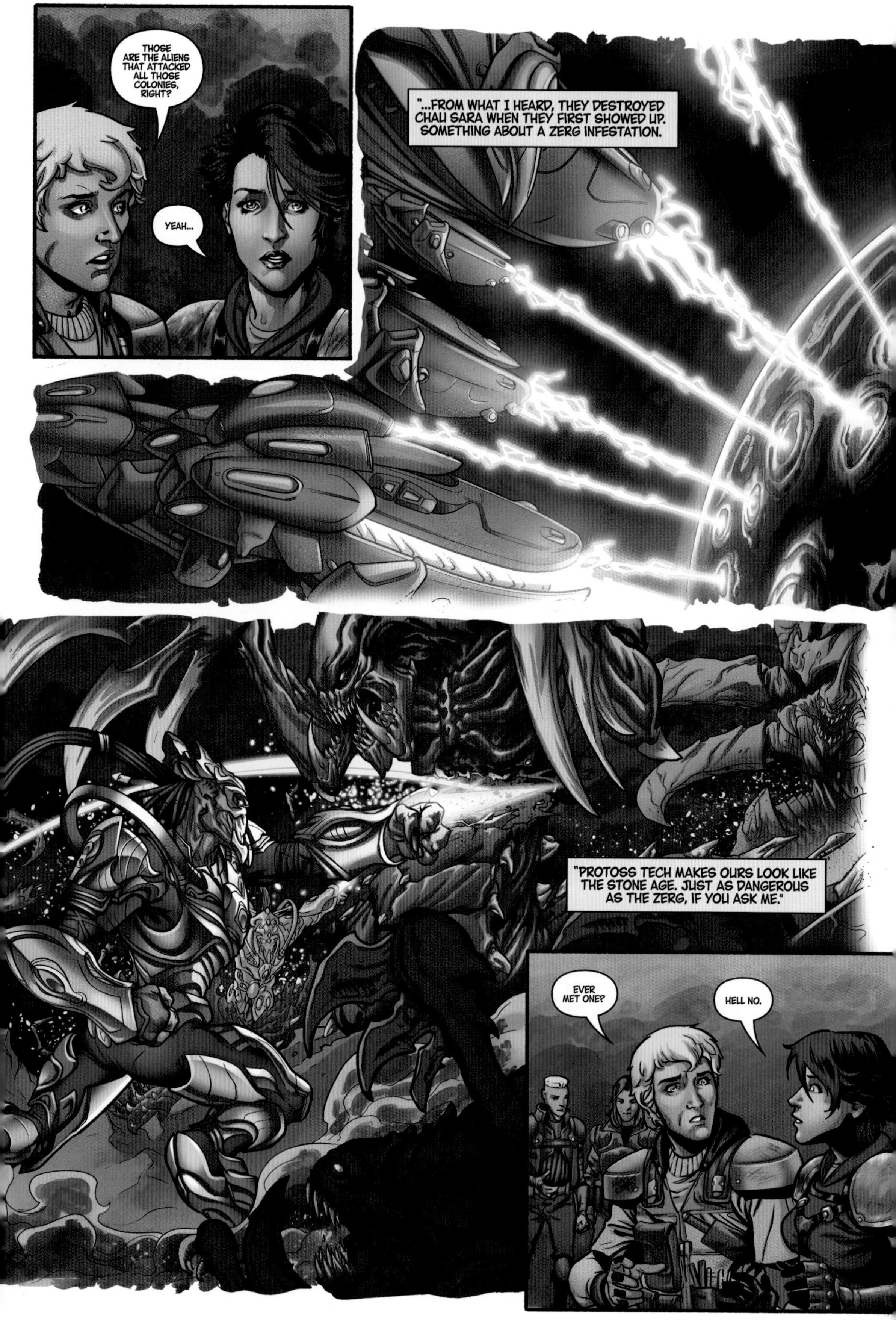
THOSE ARE THE ALIENS THAT ATTACKED ALL THOSE COLONIES, RIGHT?
YEAH...
"...FROM WHAT I HEARD, THEY DESTROYED CHAU SARA WHEN THEY FIRST SHOWED UP. SOMETHING ABOUT A ZERG INFESTATION.
"PROTOSS TECH MAKES OURS LOOK LIKE THE STONE AGE. JUST AS DANGEROUS AS THE ZERG, IF YOU ASK ME."
EVER MET ONE?
HELL NO.

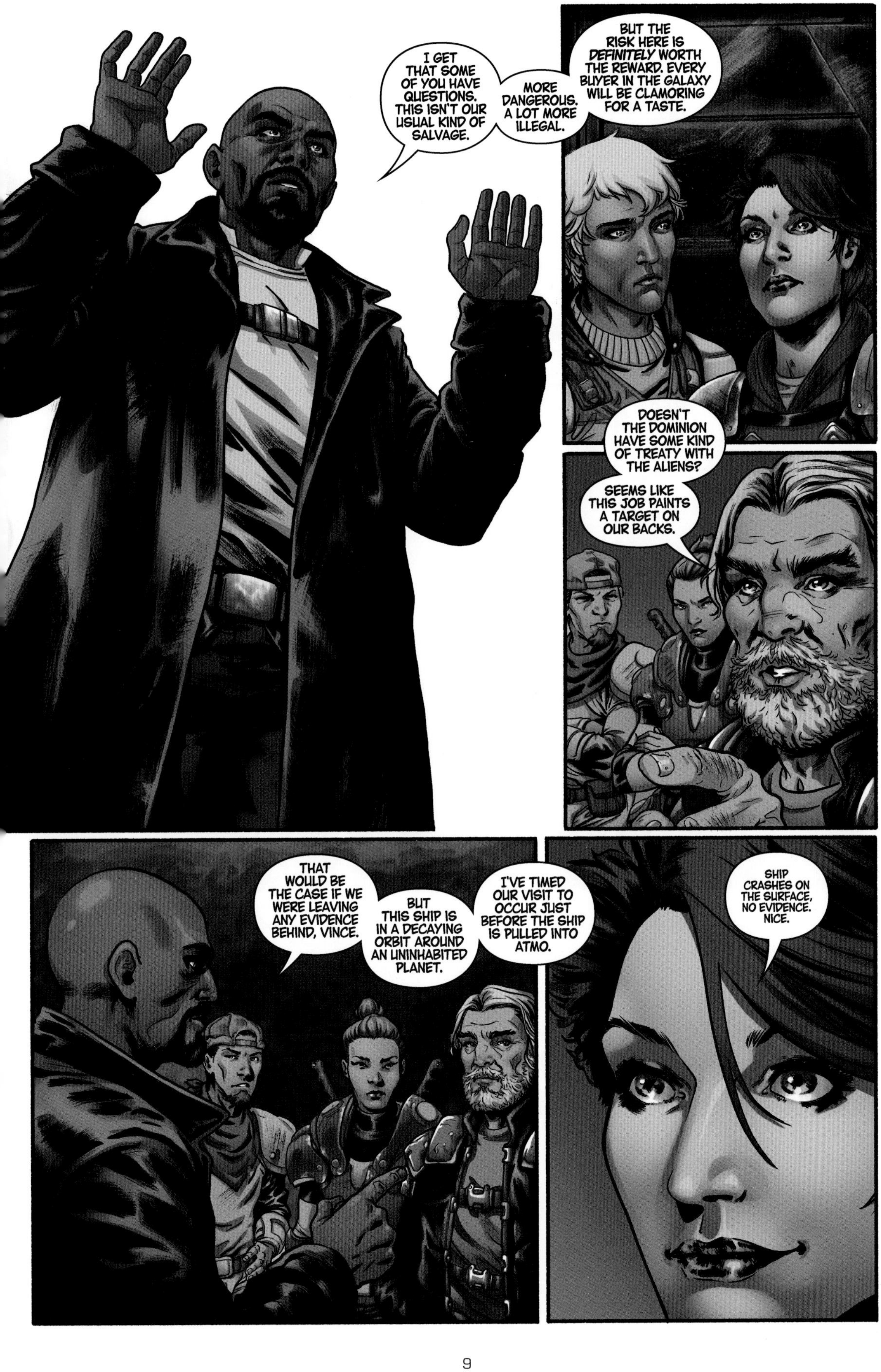
I GET THAT SOME OF YOU HAVE QUESTIONS. THIS ISN'T OUR USUAL KIND OF SALVAGE.
MORE DANGEROUS. A LOT MORE ILLEGAL.
BUT THE RISK HERE IS DEFINITELY WORTH THE REWARD. EVERY BUYER IN THE GALAXY WILL BE CLAMORING FOR A TASTE.
DOESN'T THE DOMINION HAVE SOME KIND OF TREATY WITH THE ALIENS?
SEEMS LIKE THIS JOB PAINTS A TARGET ON OUR BACKS.
THAT WOULD BE THE CASE IF WE WERE LEAVING ANY EVIDENCE BEHIND, VINCE.
BUT THIS SHIP IS IN A DECAYING ORBIT AROUND AN UNINHABITED PLANET.
I'VE TIMED OUR VISIT TO OCCUR JUST BEFORE THE SHIP IS PULLED INTO ATMO.
SHIP CRASHES ON THE SURFACE, NO EVIDENCE. NICE.

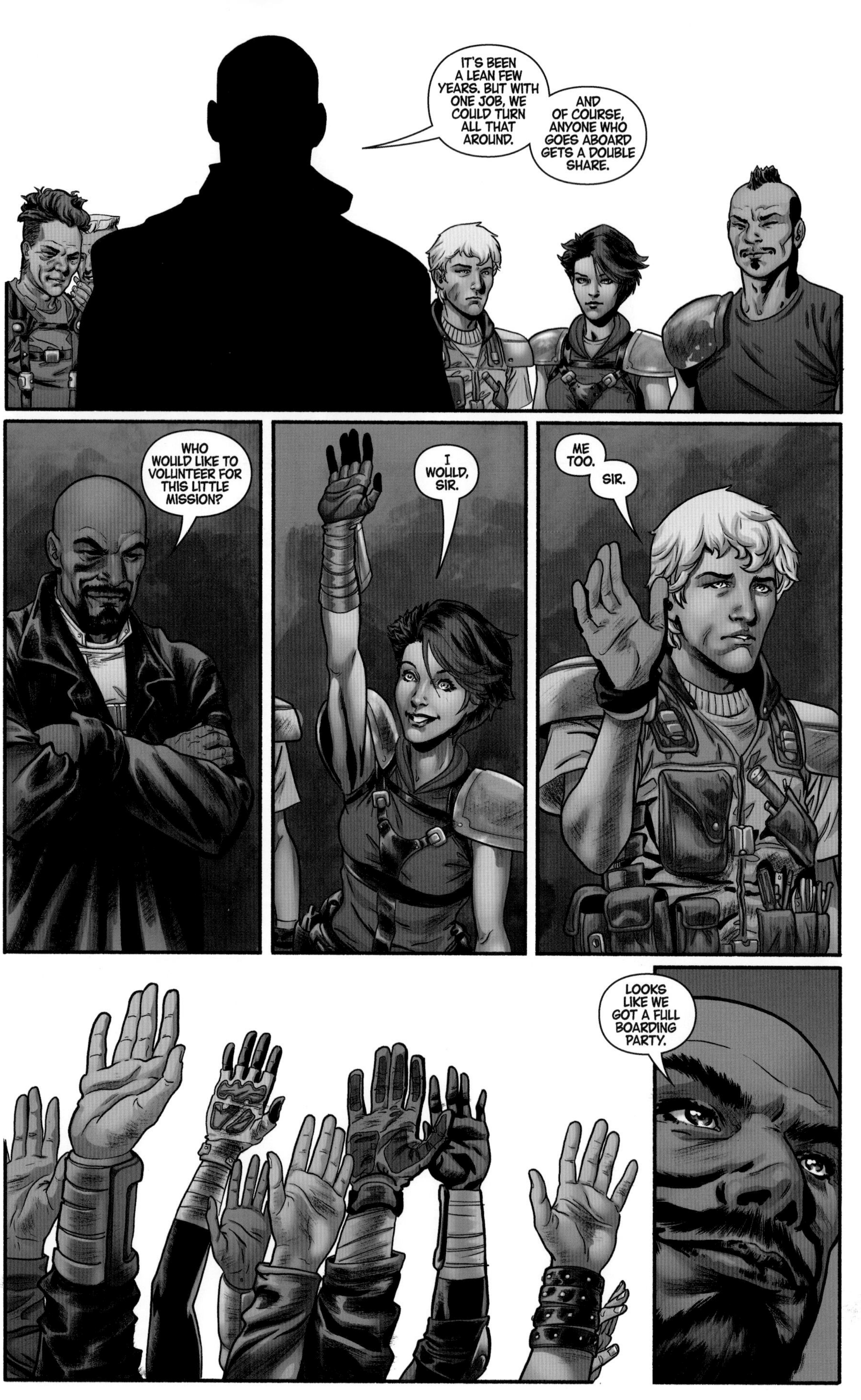
IT'S BEEN A LEAN FEW YEARS. BUT WITH ONE JOB, WE COULD TURN ALL THAT AROUND.
AND OF COURSE, ANYONE WHO GOES ABOARD GETS A DOUBLE SHARE.
WHO WOULD LIKE TO VOLUNTEER FOR THIS LITTLE MISSION?
I WOULD, SIR.
ME TOO.
SIR.
LOOKS LIKE WE GOT A FULL BOARDING PARTY.

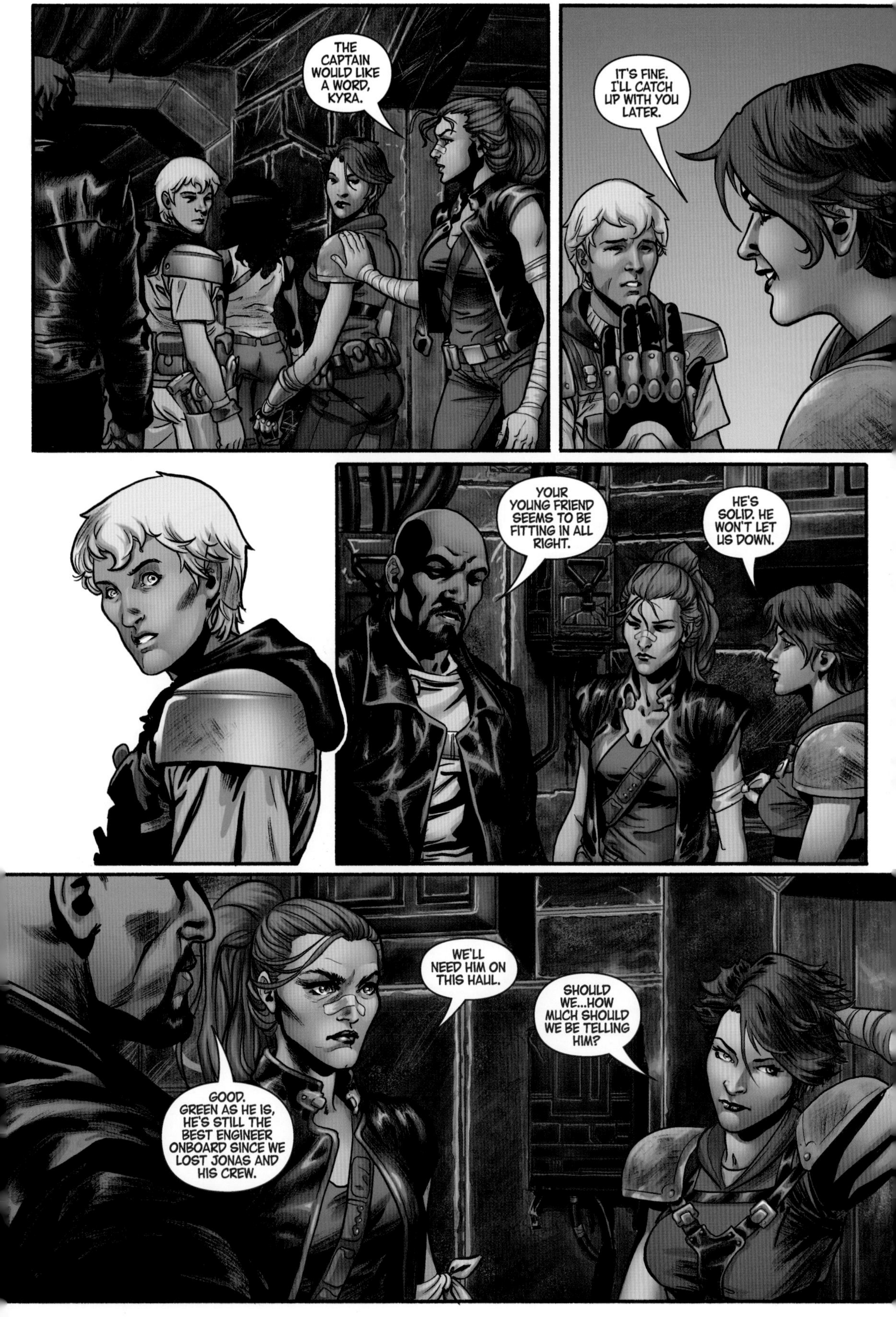
THE CAPTAIN WOULD LIKE A WORD, KYRA.
IT'S FINE. I'LL CATCH UP WITH YOU LATER.
YOUR YOUNG FRIEND SEEMS TO BE FITTING IN ALL RIGHT.
HE'S SOLID. HE WON'T LET US DOWN.
GOOD. GREEN AS HE IS, HE'S STILL THE BEST ENGINEER ONBOARD SINCE WE LOST JONAS AND HIS CREW.
WE'LL NEED HIM ON THIS HAUL.
SHOULD WE...HOW MUCH SHOULD WE BE TELLING HIM?

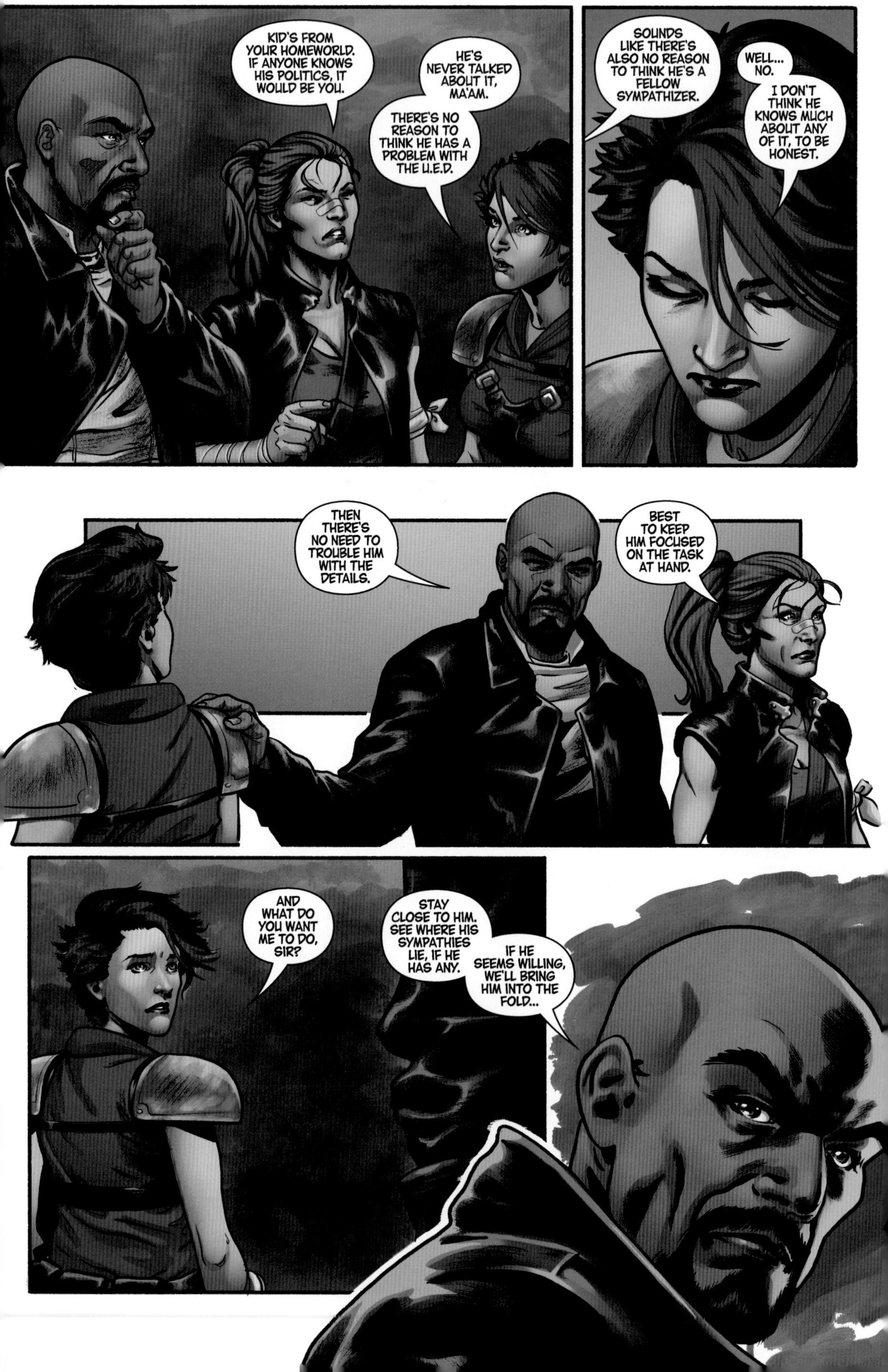
KID'S FROM YOUR HOMEWORLD. IF ANYONE KNOWS HIS POLITICS, IT WOULD BE YOU.
HE'S NEVER TALKED ABOUT IT, MA'AM.
THERE'S NO REASON TO THINK HE HAS A PROBLEM WITH THE U.E.D.
SOUNDS LIKE THERE'S ALSO NO REASON TO THINK HE'S A FELLOW SYMPATHIZER.
WELL... NO.
I DON'T THINK HE KNOWS MUCH ABOUT ANY OF IT, TO BE HONEST.
THEN THERE'S NO NEED TO TROUBLE HIM WITH THE DETAILS.
BEST TO KEEP HIM FOCUSED ON THE TASK AT HAND.
AND WHAT DO YOU WANT ME TO DO, SIR?
STAY CLOSE TO HIM. SEE WHERE HIS SYMPATHIES LIE, IF HE HAS ANY.
IF HE SEEMS WILLING, WE'LL BRING HIM INTO THE FOLD...

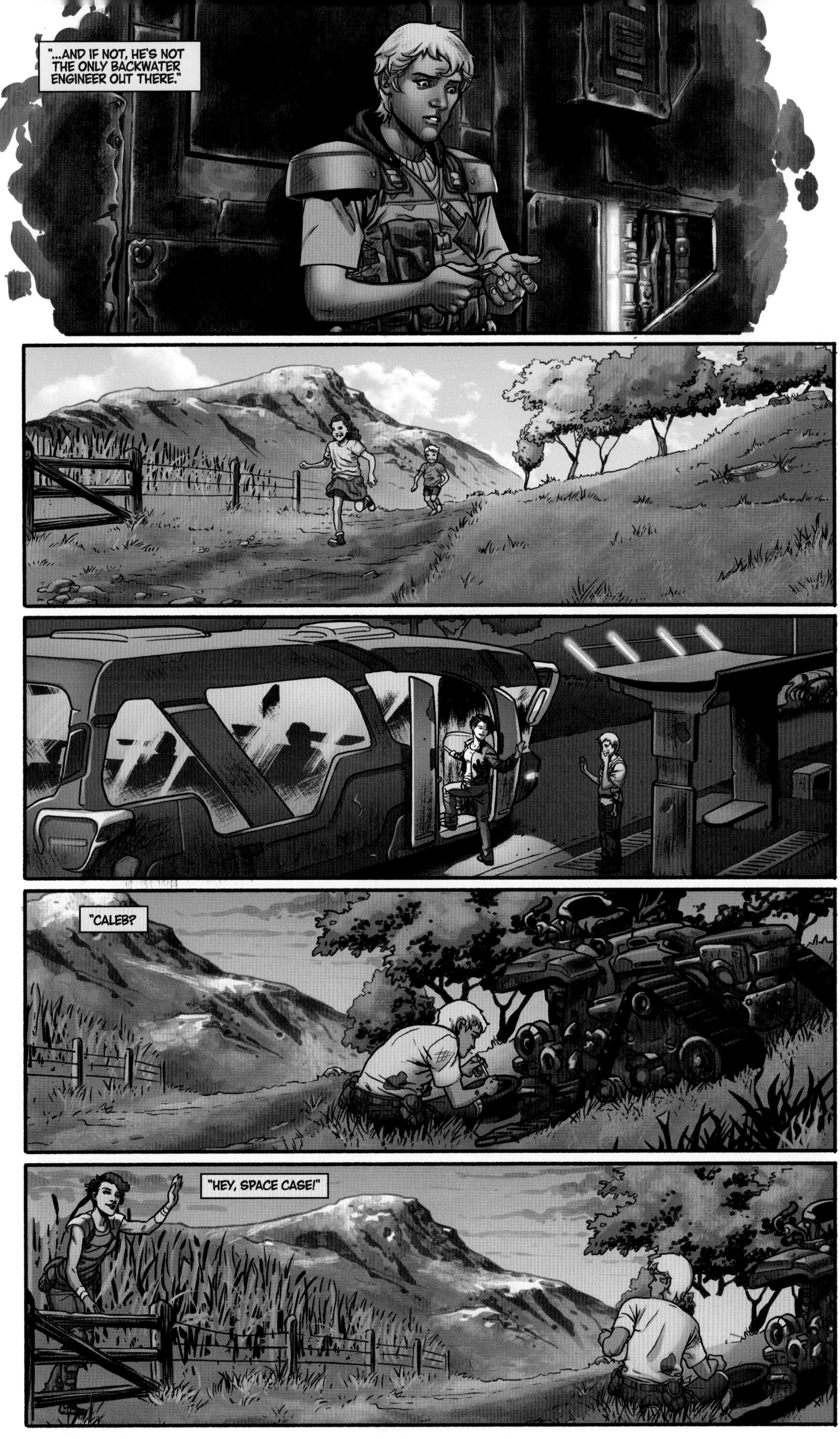
"...AND IF NOT, HE'S NOT THE ONLY BACKWATER ENGINEER OUT THERE."
"CALEB?
"HEY, SPACE CASE!"

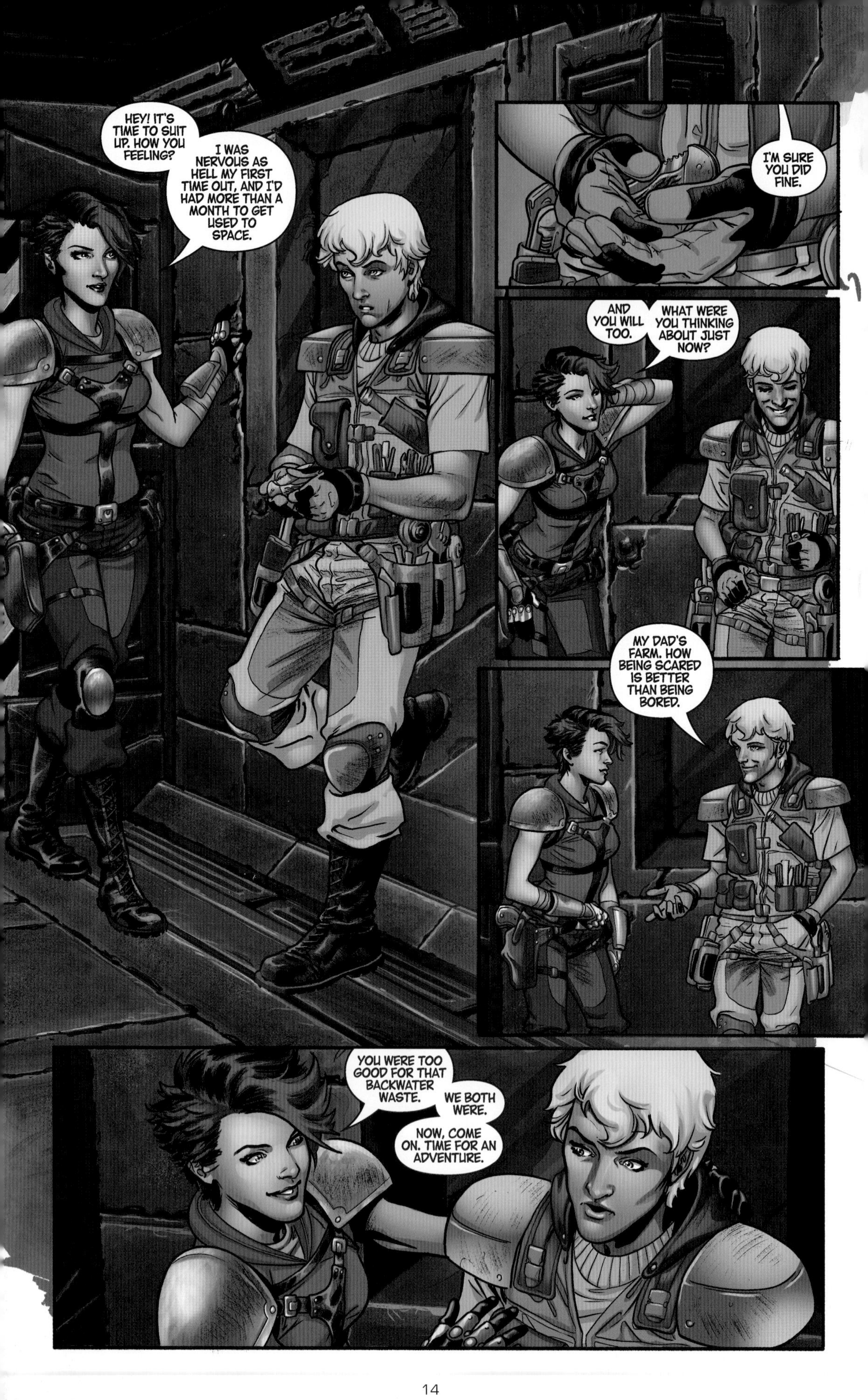
HEY! IT'S TIME TO SUIT UP. HOW YOU FEELING?
I WAS NERVOUS AS HELL MY FIRST TIME OUT, AND I'D HAD MORE THAN A MONTH TO GET USED TO SPACE.
I'M SURE YOU DID FINE.
AND YOU WILL TOO.
WHAT WERE YOU THINKING ABOUT JUST NOW?
MY DAD'S FARM. HOW BEING SCARED IS BETTER THAN BEING BORED.
YOU WERE TOO GOOD FOR THAT BACKWATER WASTE.
WE BOTH WERE.
NOW, COME ON. TIME FOR AN ADVENTURE.

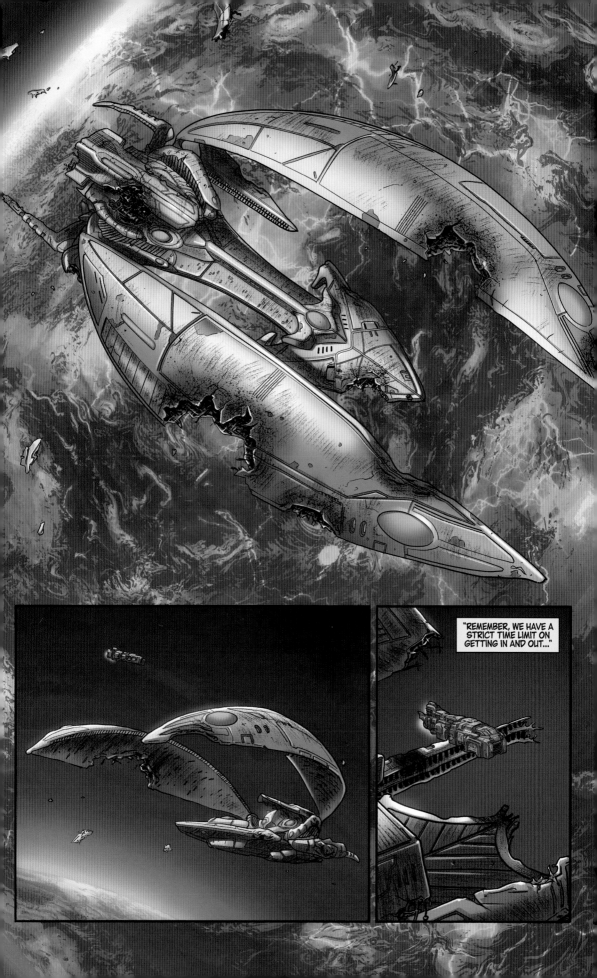

"REMEMBER, WE HAVE A STRICT TIME LIMIT ON GETTING IN AND OUT..."

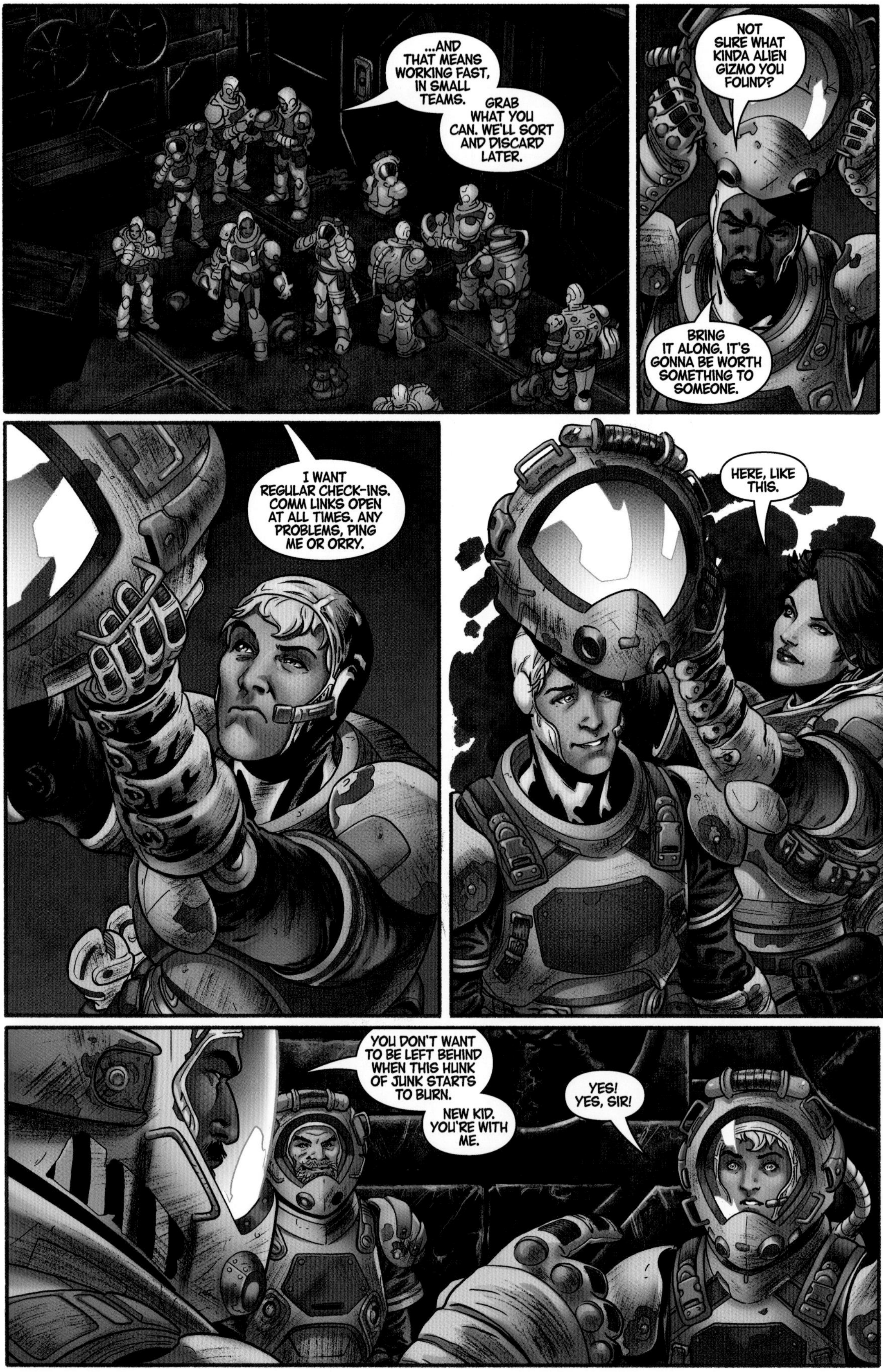
...AND THAT MEANS WORKING FAST, IN SMALL TEAMS.
GRAB WHAT YOU CAN. WE'LL SORT AND DISCARD LATER.
NOT SURE WHAT KINDA ALIEN GIZMO YOU FOUND?
BRING IT ALONG. IT'S GONNA BE WORTH SOMETHING TO SOMEONE.
I WANT REGULAR CHECK-INS. COMM LINKS OPEN AT ALL TIMES. ANY PROBLEMS, PING ME OR ORRY.
HERE, LIKE THIS.
YOU DON'T WANT TO BE LEFT BEHIND WHEN THIS HUNK OF JUNK STARTS TO BURN.
NEW KID. YOU'RE WITH ME.
YES! YES, SIR!

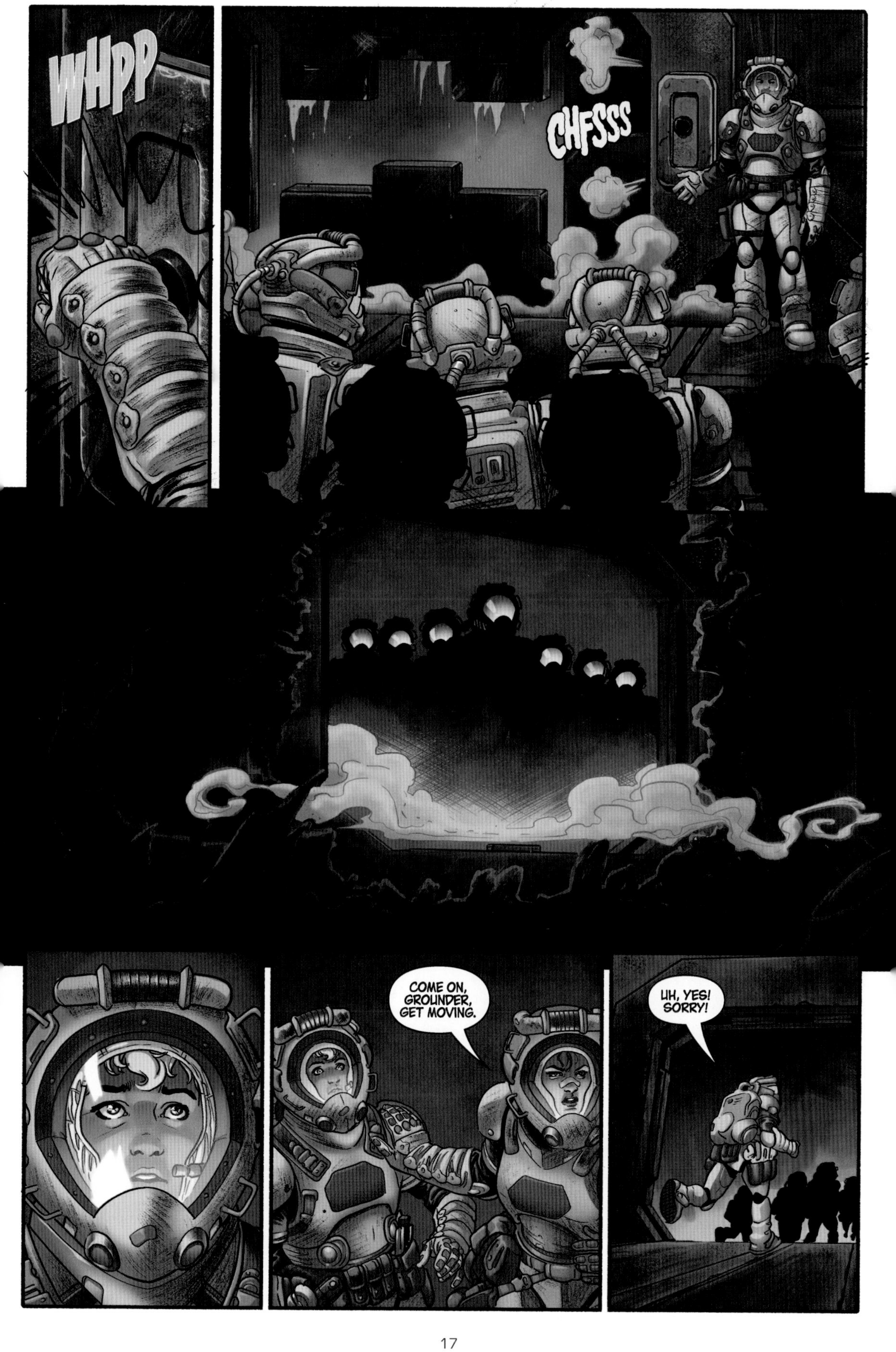
WHPP
CHFSSS
COME ON, GROUNDER, GET MOVING.
UH, YES! SORRY!

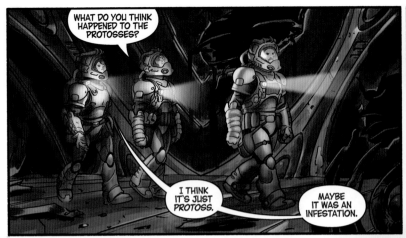

WHAT DO YOU THINK HAPPENED TO THE PROTOSSES?

I THINK IT'S JUST PROTOSS.

MAYBE IT WAS AN INFESTATION.

WHAT EXACTLY DOES THAT MEAN?

"THE ZERG SWARMS... THEY CAN CONSUME WHOLE SETTLEMENTS. WHOLE PLANETS.

"EVEN HEARD THEY CAN TURN PEOPLE INTO MORE OF THEM.

"MAYBE THAT'S WHAT HAPPENED TO THE PROTOSS HERE."

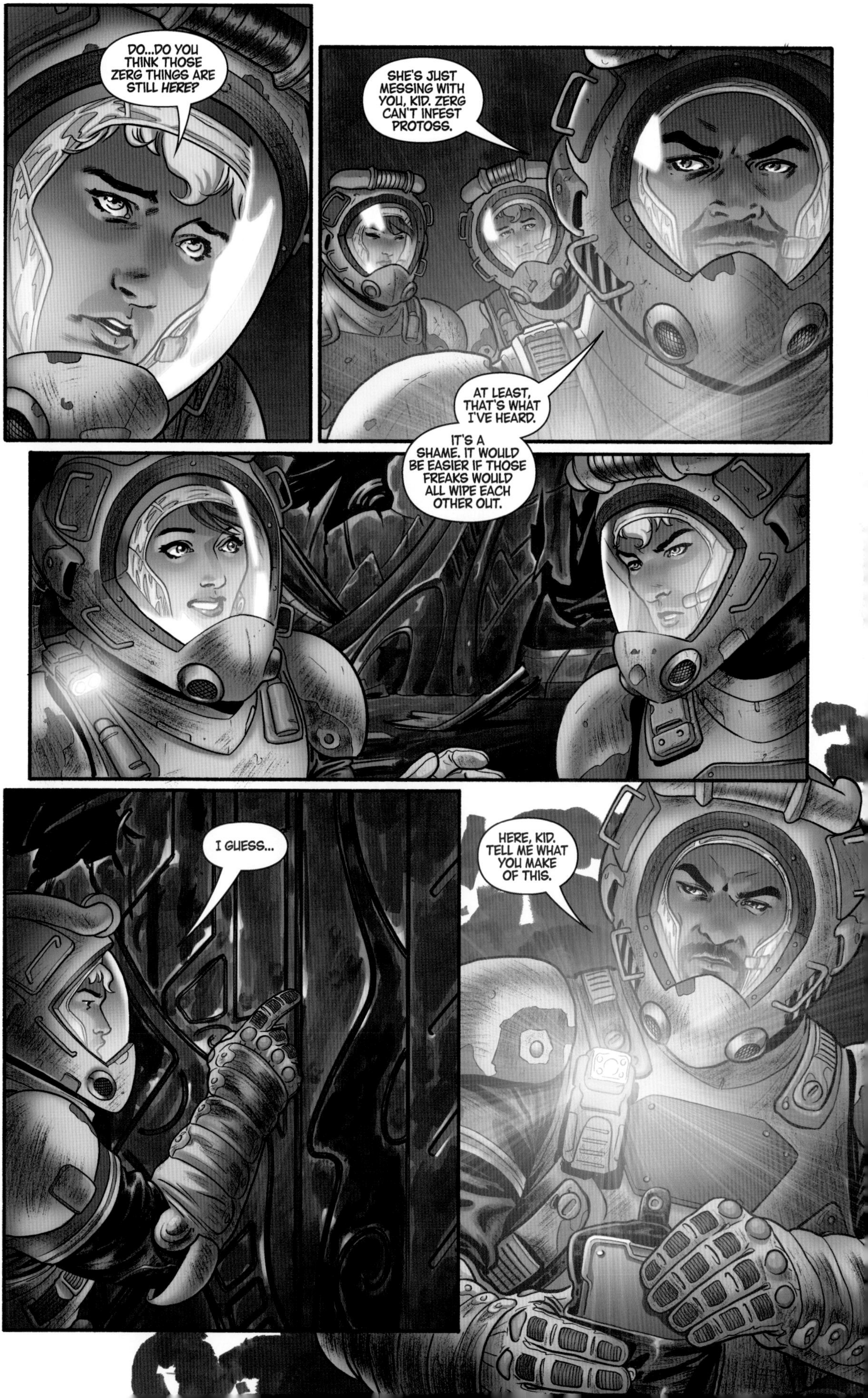
DO...DO YOU THINK THOSE ZERG THINGS ARE STILL HERE?
SHE'S JUST MESSING WITH YOU, KID. ZERG CAN'T INFEST PROTOSS.
AT LEAST, THAT'S WHAT I'VE HEARD.
IT'S A SHAME. IT WOULD BE EASIER IF THOSE FREAKS WOULD ALL WIPE EACH OTHER OUT.
I GUESS...
HERE, KID. TELL ME WHAT YOU MAKE OF THIS.

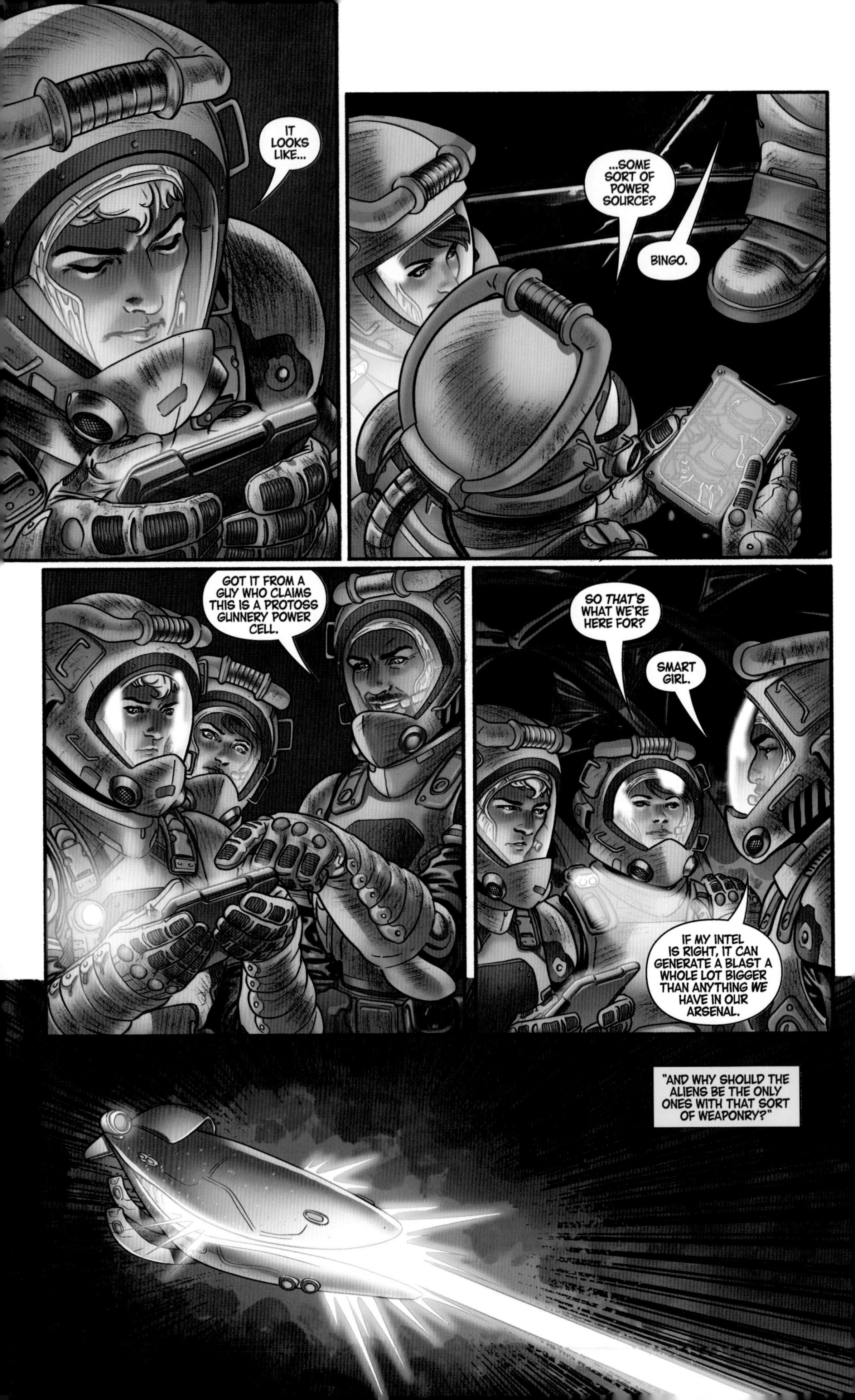
IT LOOKS LIKE...
...SOME SORT OF POWER SOURCE?
BINGO.
GOT IT FROM A GUY WHO CLAIMS THIS IS A PROTOSS GUNNERY POWER CELL.
SO *THAT'S* WHAT WE'RE HERE FOR?
SMART GIRL.
IF MY INTEL IS RIGHT, IT CAN GENERATE A BLAST A WHOLE LOT BIGGER THAN ANYTHING *WE* HAVE IN OUR ARSENAL.
"AND WHY SHOULD THE ALIENS BE THE ONLY ONES WITH THAT SORT OF WEAPONRY?"

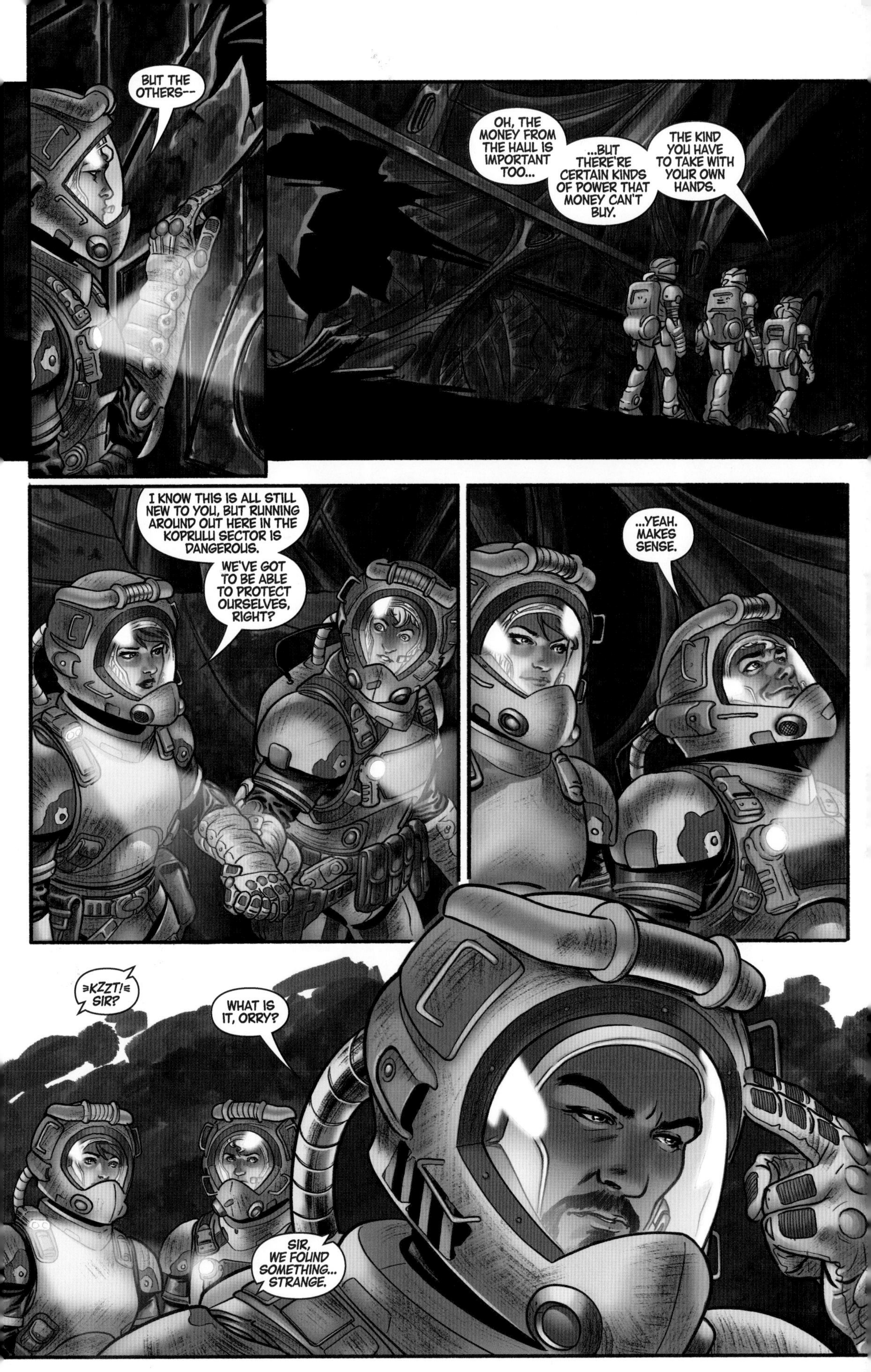
BUT THE OTHERS--
OH, THE MONEY FROM THE HAUL IS IMPORTANT TOO...
...BUT THERE'RE CERTAIN KINDS OF POWER THAT MONEY CAN'T BUY.
THE KIND YOU HAVE TO TAKE WITH YOUR OWN HANDS.
I KNOW THIS IS ALL STILL NEW TO YOU, BUT RUNNING AROUND OUT HERE IN THE KOPRULU SECTOR IS DANGEROUS.
WE'VE GOT TO BE ABLE TO PROTECT OURSELVES, RIGHT?
...YEAH. MAKES SENSE.
KZZT! SIR?
WHAT IS IT, ORRY?
SIR, WE FOUND SOMETHING... STRANGE.

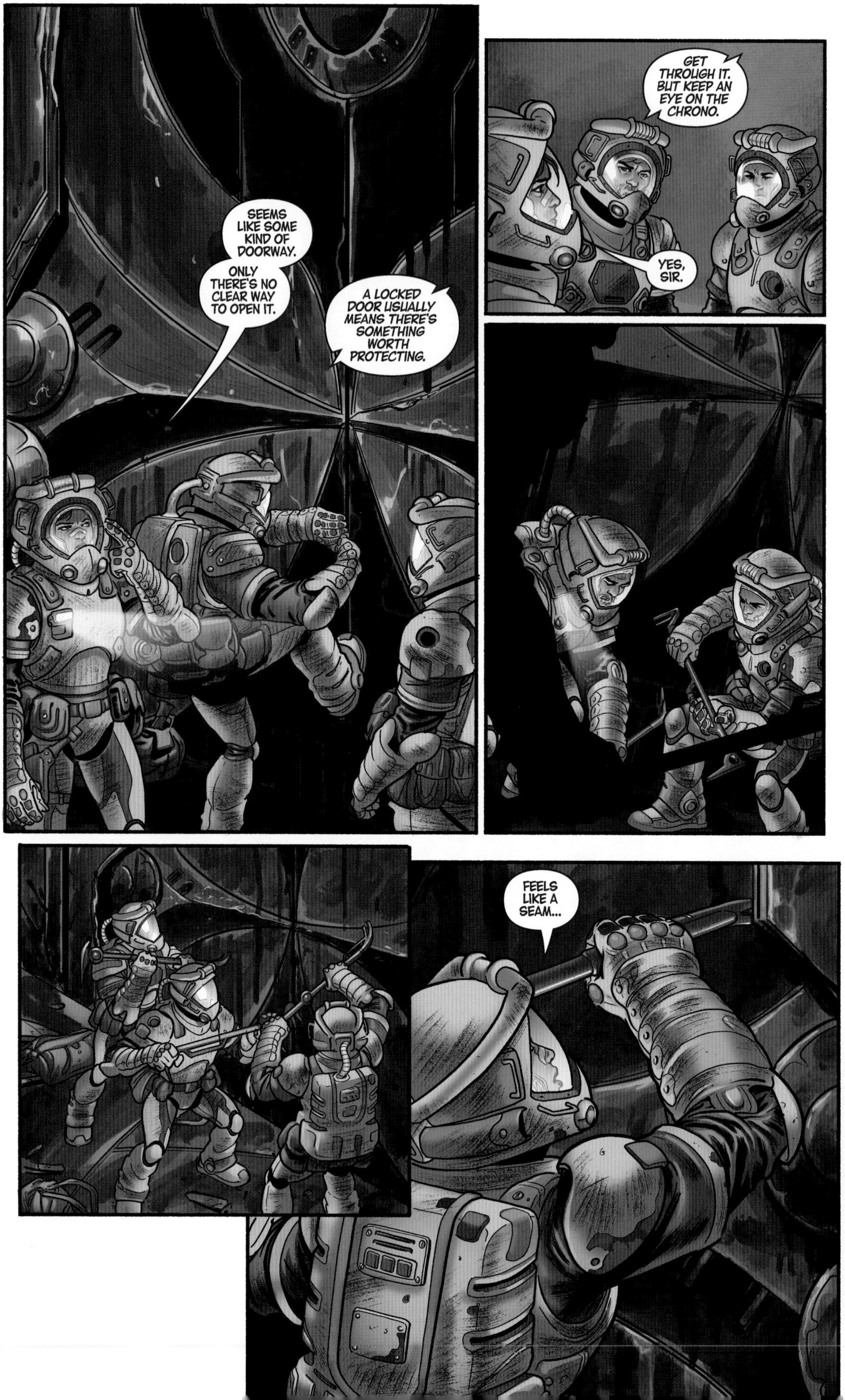
SEEMS LIKE SOME KIND OF DOORWAY.
ONLY THERE'S NO CLEAR WAY TO OPEN IT.
A LOCKED DOOR USUALLY MEANS THERE'S SOMETHING WORTH PROTECTING.
GET THROUGH IT. BUT KEEP AN EYE ON THE CHRONO.
YES, SIR.
FEELS LIKE A SEAM...

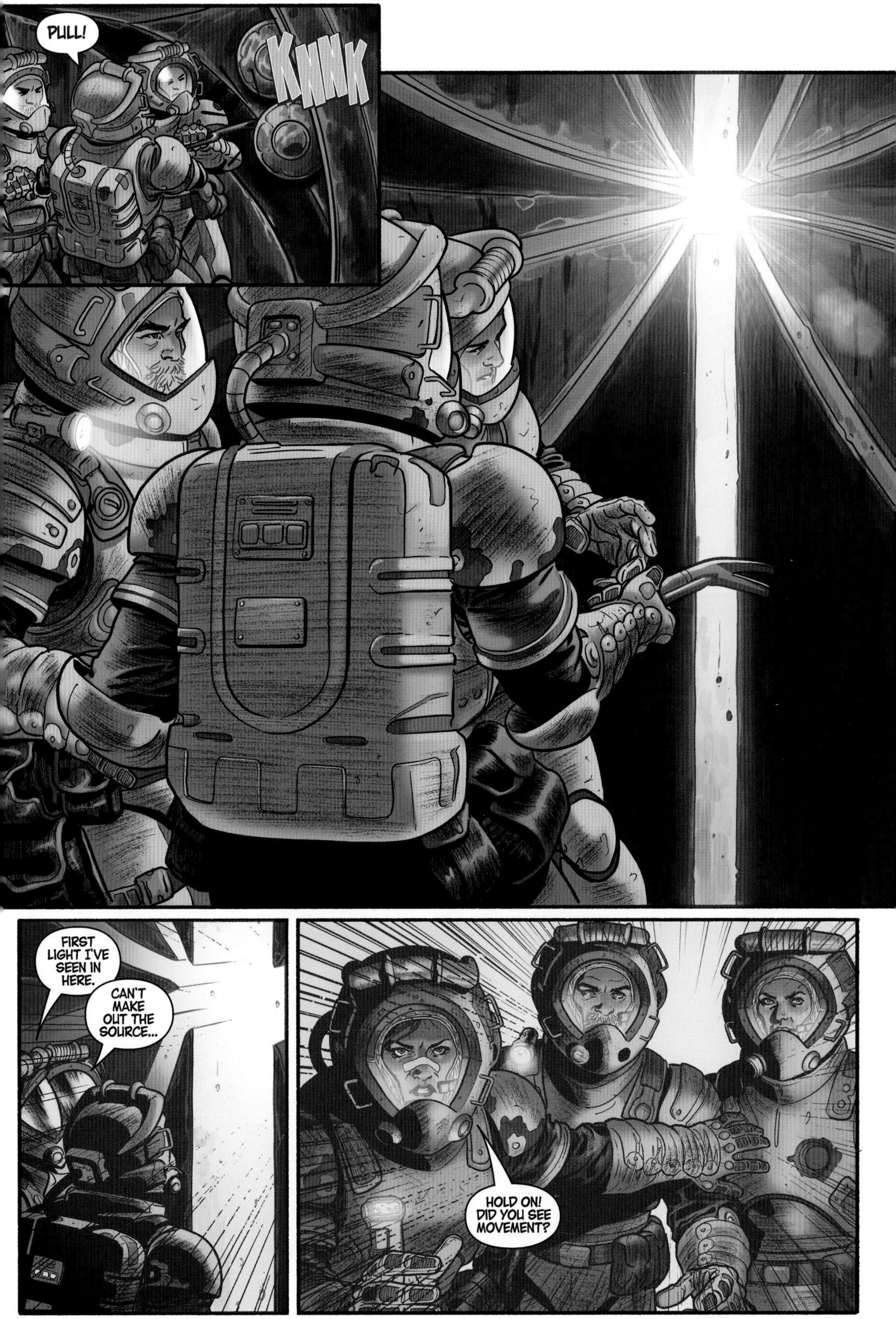
PULL!
KNNK
FIRST LIGHT I'VE SEEN IN HERE.
CAN'T MAKE OUT THE SOURCE...
HOLD ON! DID YOU SEE MOVEMENT?

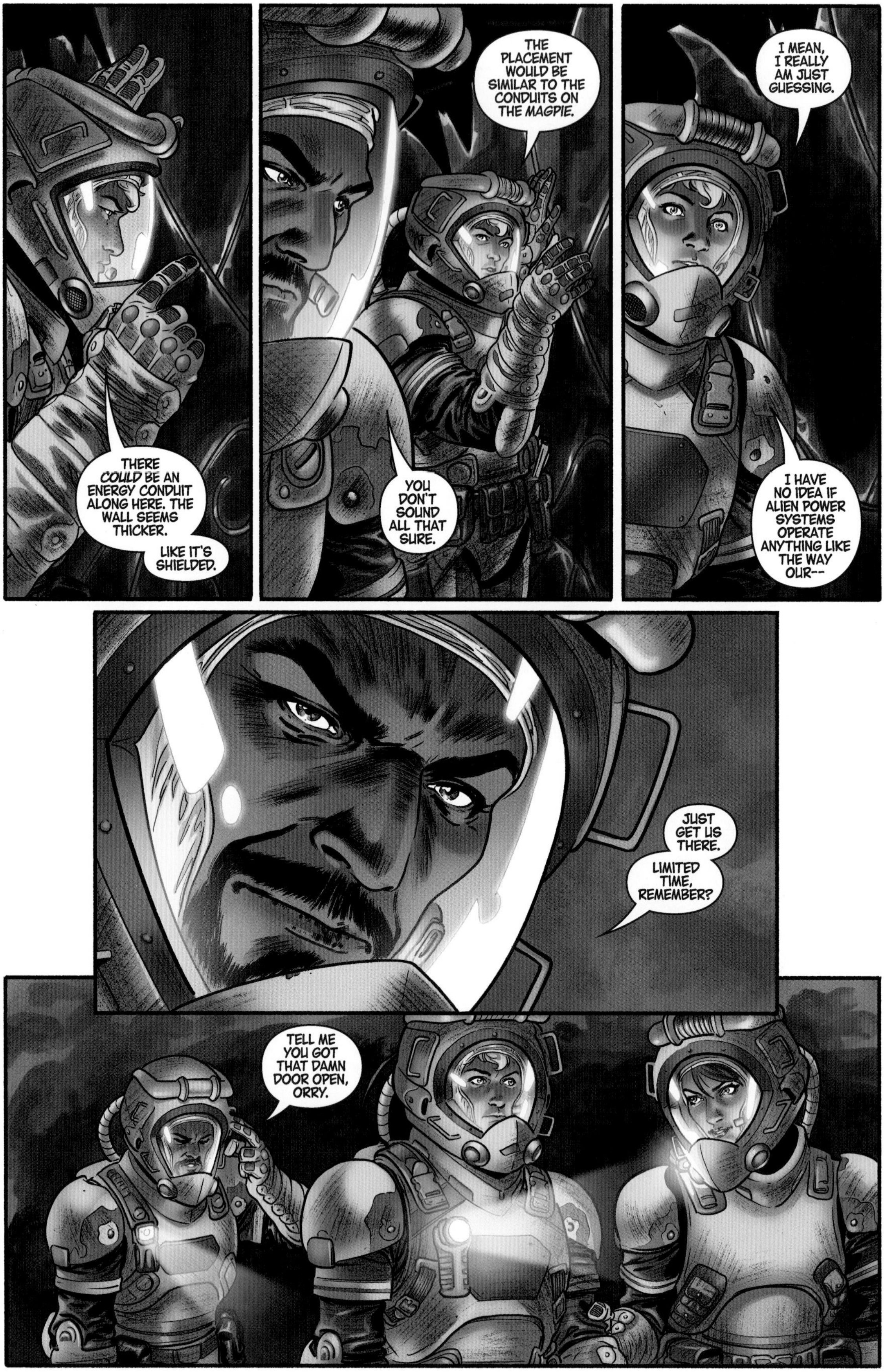
THERE COULD BE AN ENERGY CONDUIT ALONG HERE. THE WALL SEEMS THICKER.
LIKE IT'S SHIELDED.
YOU DON'T SOUND ALL THAT SURE.
THE PLACEMENT WOULD BE SIMILAR TO THE CONDUITS ON THE MAGPIE.
I MEAN, I REALLY AM JUST GUESSING.
I HAVE NO IDEA IF ALIEN POWER SYSTEMS OPERATE ANYTHING LIKE THE WAY OUR--
JUST GET US THERE.
LIMITED TIME, REMEMBER?
TELL ME YOU GOT THAT DAMN DOOR OPEN, ORRY.

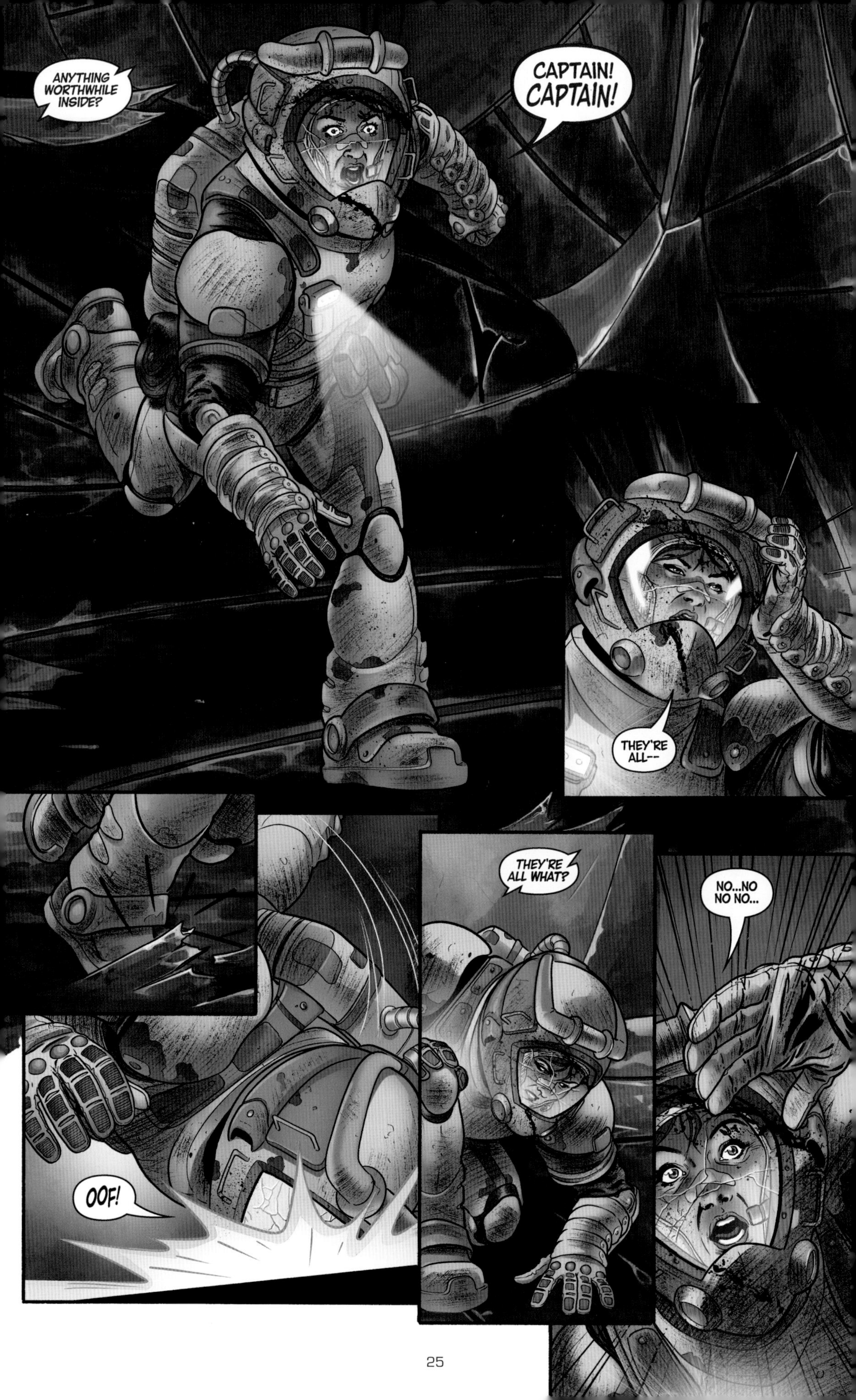
ANYTHING WORTHWHILE INSIDE?
CAPTAIN! CAPTAIN!
THEY'RE ALL--
OOF!
THEY'RE ALL WHAT?
NO...NO NO NO...

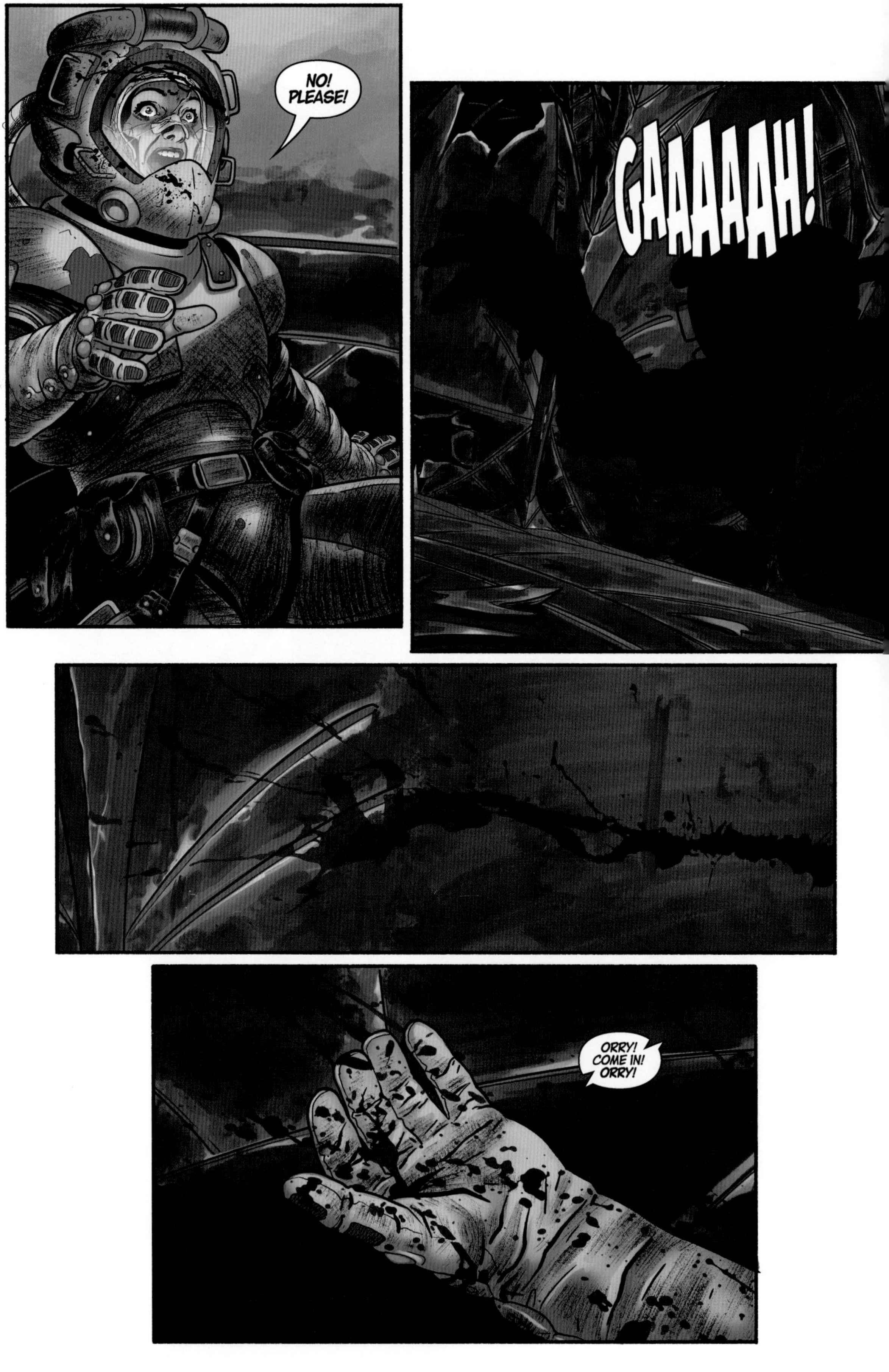
NO! PLEASE!
GAAAAH!
ORRY! COME IN! ORRY!

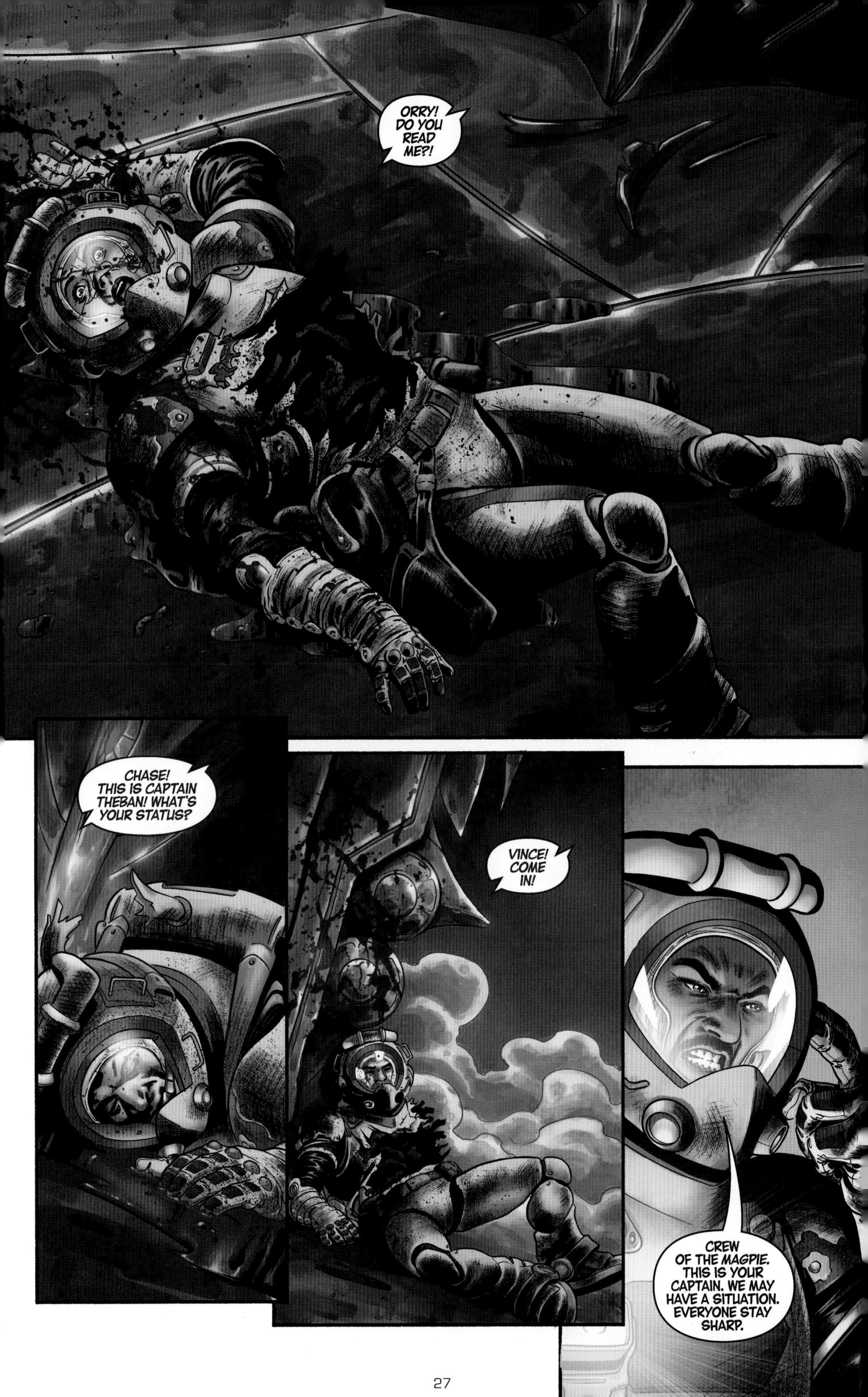
ORRY! DO YOU READ ME?!
CHASE! THIS IS CAPTAIN THEBAN! WHAT'S YOUR STATUS?
VINCE! COME IN!
CREW OF THE MAGPIE. THIS IS YOUR CAPTAIN. WE MAY HAVE A SITUATION. EVERYONE STAY SHARP.

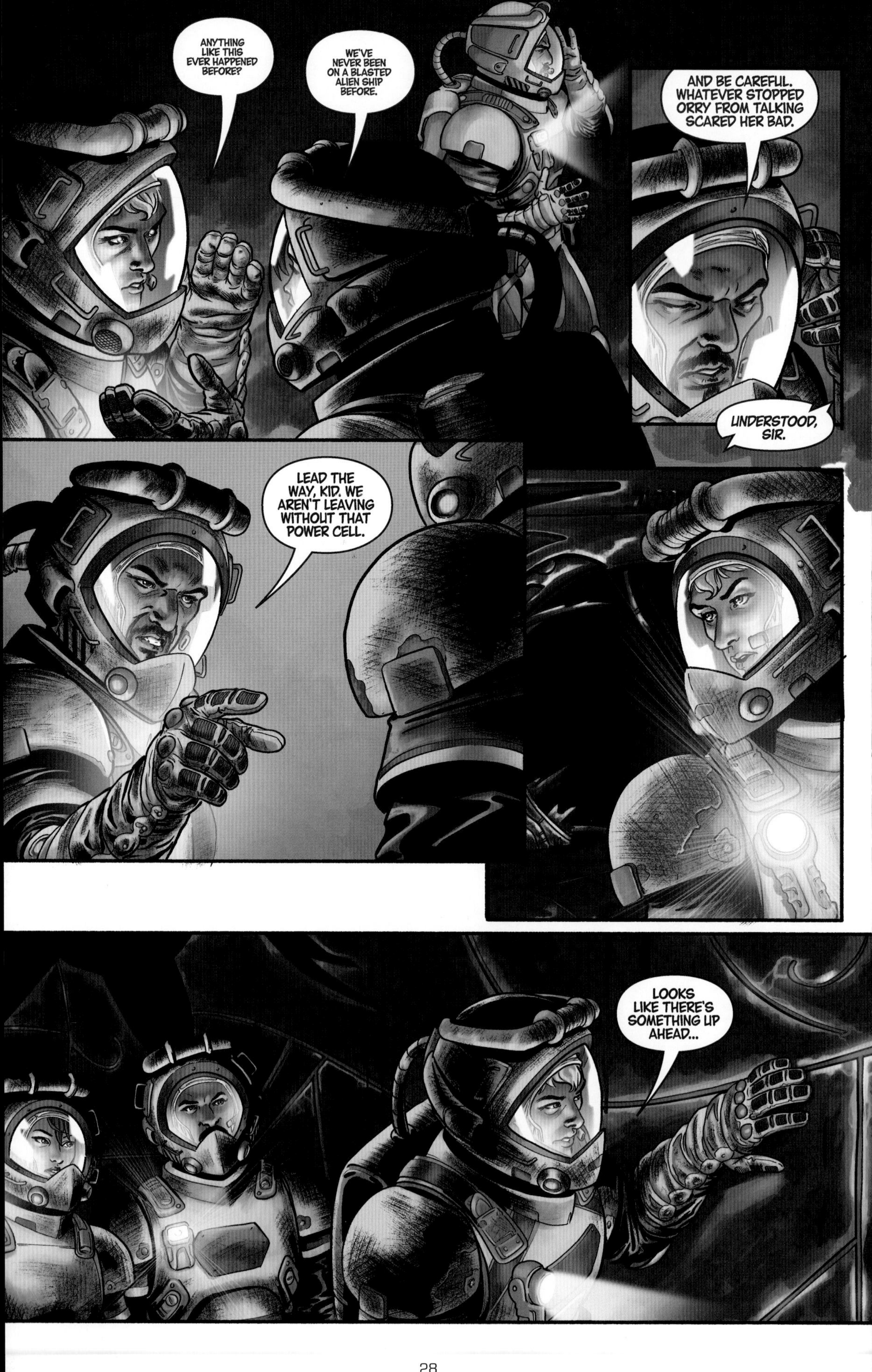
ANYTHING LIKE THIS EVER HAPPENED BEFORE?
WE'VE NEVER BEEN ON A BLASTED ALIEN SHIP BEFORE.
AND BE CAREFUL. WHATEVER STOPPED ORRY FROM TALKING SCARED HER BAD.
UNDERSTOOD, SIR.
LEAD THE WAY, KID. WE AREN'T LEAVING WITHOUT THAT POWER CELL.
LOOKS LIKE THERE'S SOMETHING UP AHEAD...

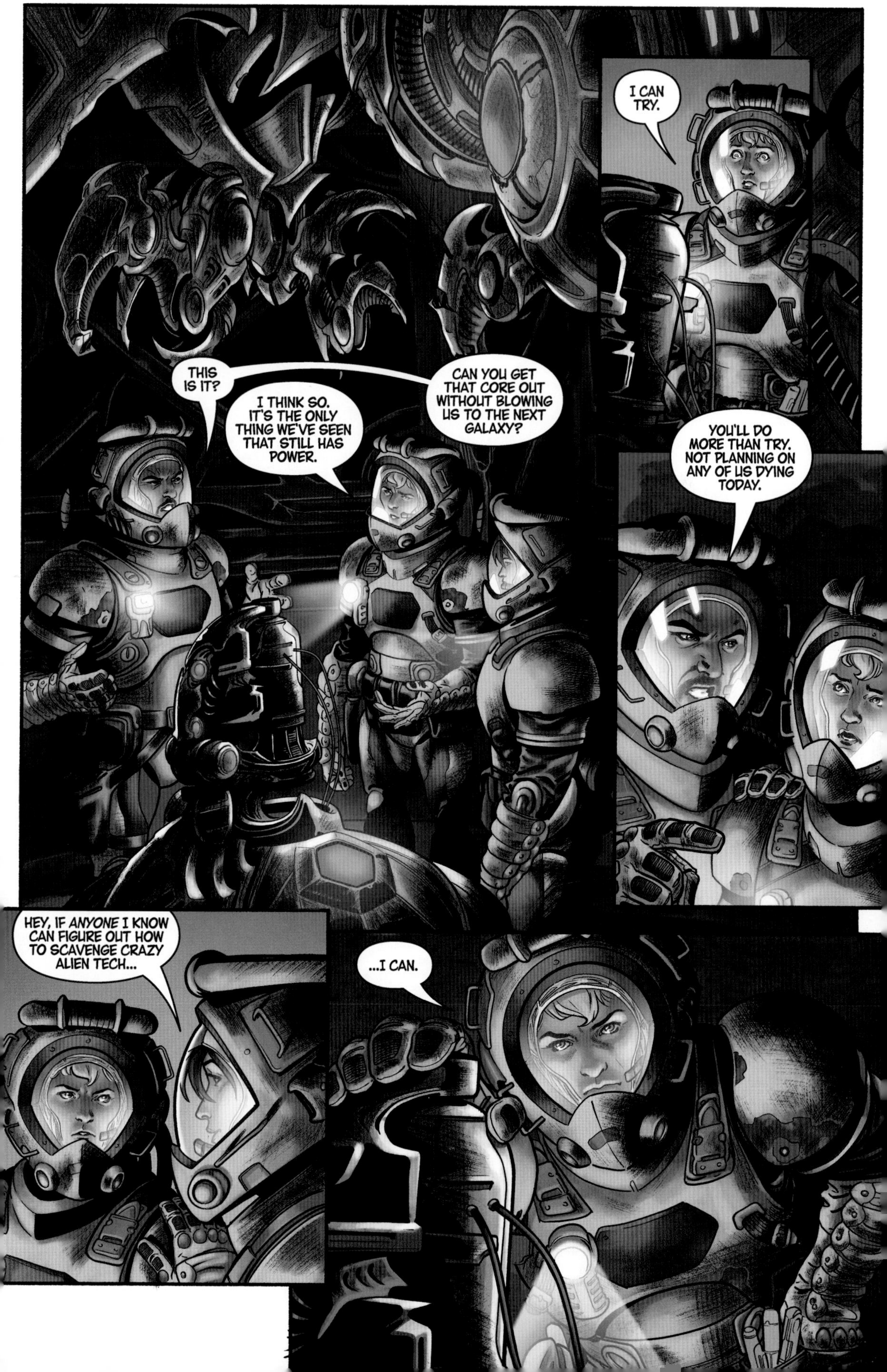
THIS IS IT?
I THINK SO. IT'S THE ONLY THING WE'VE SEEN THAT STILL HAS POWER.
CAN YOU GET THAT CORE OUT WITHOUT BLOWING US TO THE NEXT GALAXY?
I CAN TRY.
YOU'LL DO MORE THAN TRY. NOT PLANNING ON ANY OF US DYING TODAY.
HEY, IF ANYONE I KNOW CAN FIGURE OUT HOW TO SCAVENGE CRAZY ALIEN TECH...
...I CAN.

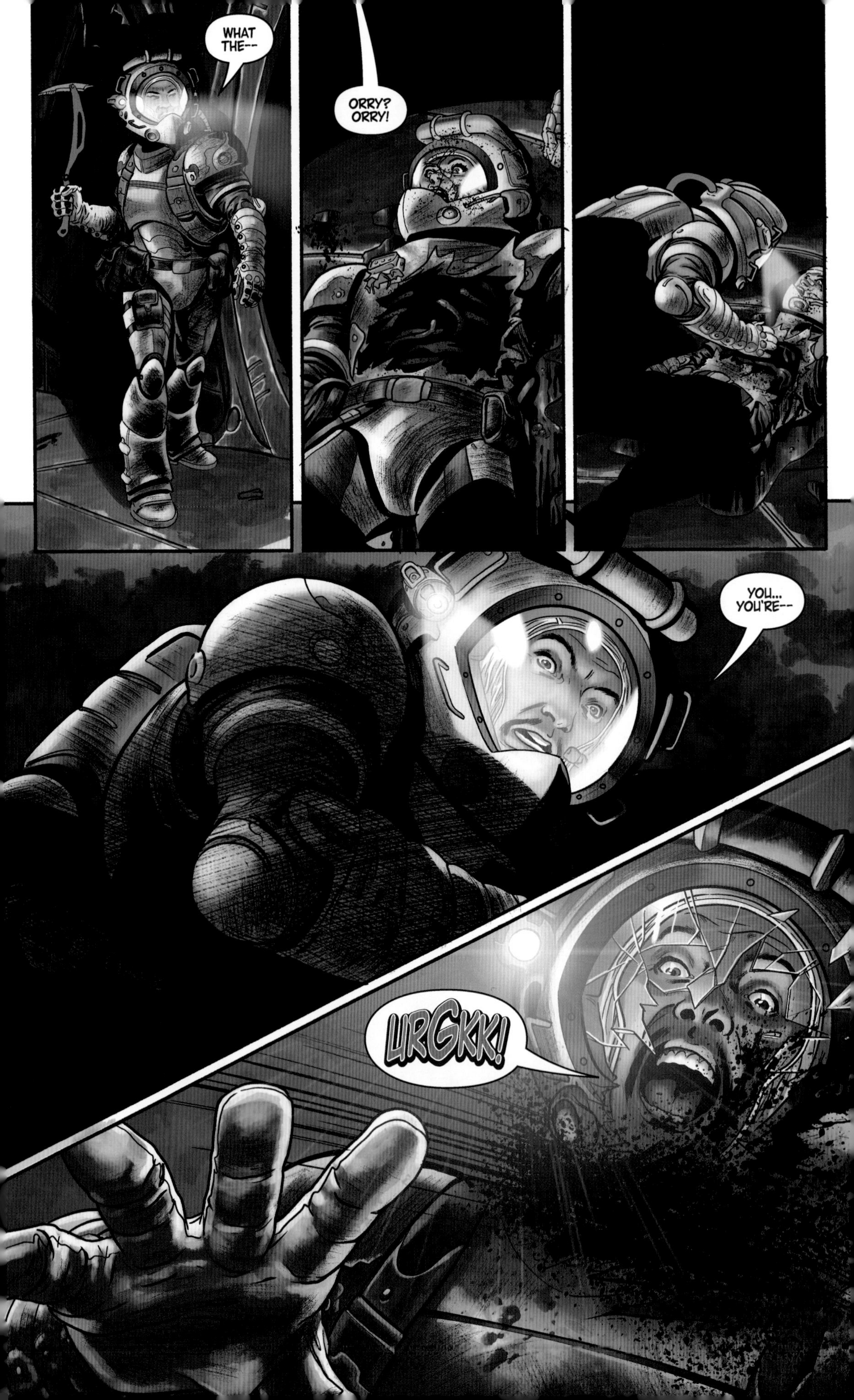
WHAT THE--
ORRY? ORRY!
YOU... YOU'RE--
URGKK!

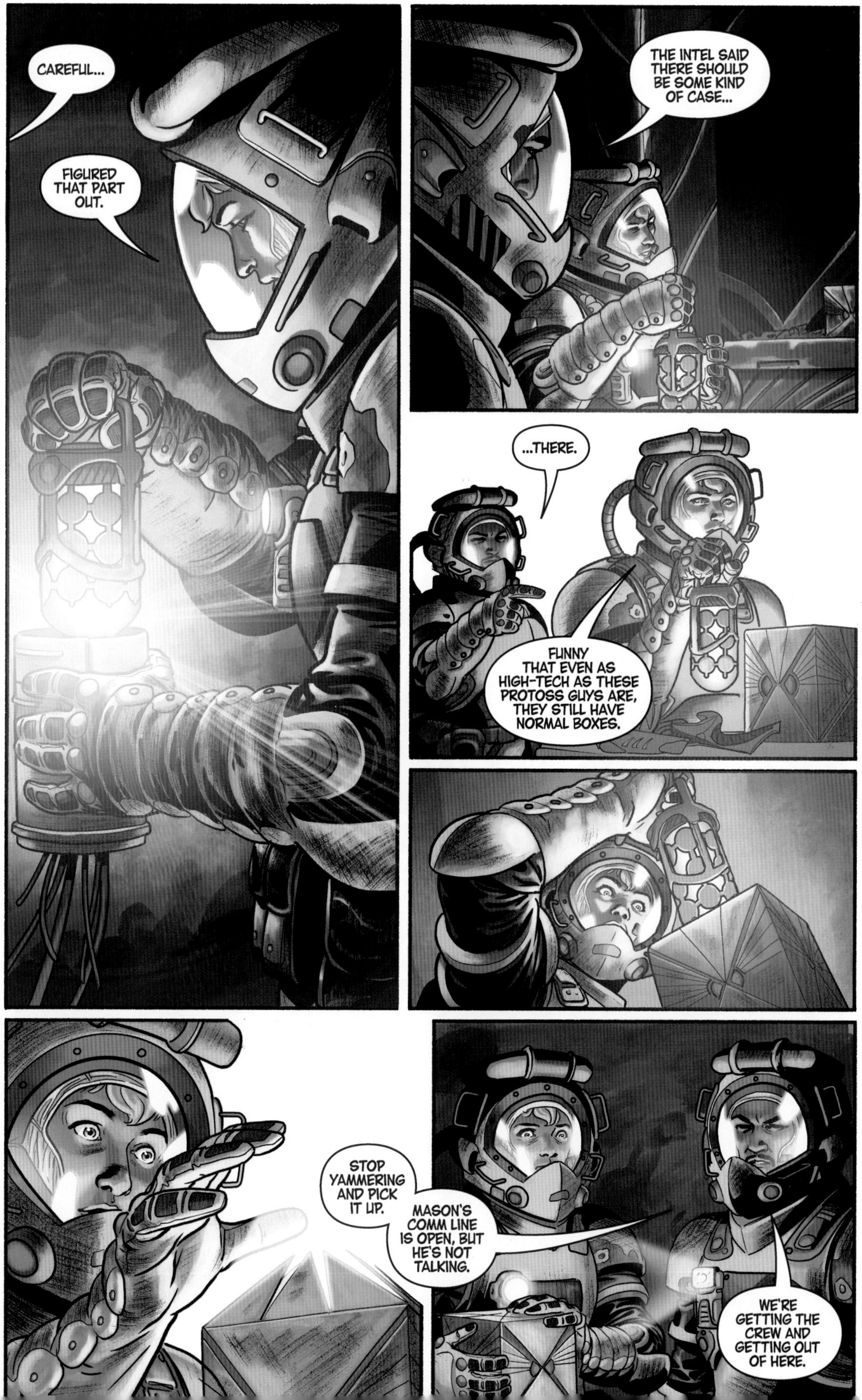
CAREFUL...
FIGURED THAT PART OUT.
THE INTEL SAID THERE SHOULD BE SOME KIND OF CASE...
...THERE.
FUNNY THAT EVEN AS HIGH-TECH AS THESE PROTOSS GUYS ARE, THEY STILL HAVE NORMAL BOXES.
STOP YAMMERING AND PICK IT UP.
MASON'S COMM LINE IS OPEN, BUT HE'S NOT TALKING.
WE'RE GETTING THE CREW AND GETTING OUT OF HERE.

CREW OF THE MAGPIE. SEEMS LIKE WE MIGHT NOT BE ALONE ON THIS WRECK.

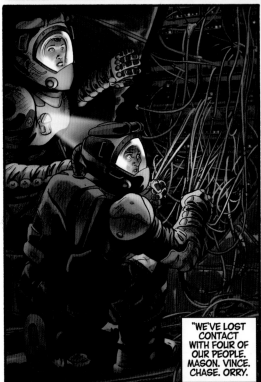

"AND LAST I HEARD FROM ORRY, IT SOUNDED LIKE SHE WAS GETTING ATTACKED BY SOMETHING."

"WE'VE LOST CONTACT WITH FOUR OF OUR PEOPLE. MASON. VINCE. CHASE. ORRY.

RUN!

"GRAB WHAT YOU CAN AND HEAD FOR THE MEETING POINT NOW.

"THIS SALVAGE IS OVER. WE'RE NOT LOSING ANYONE ELSE."

SHARON!

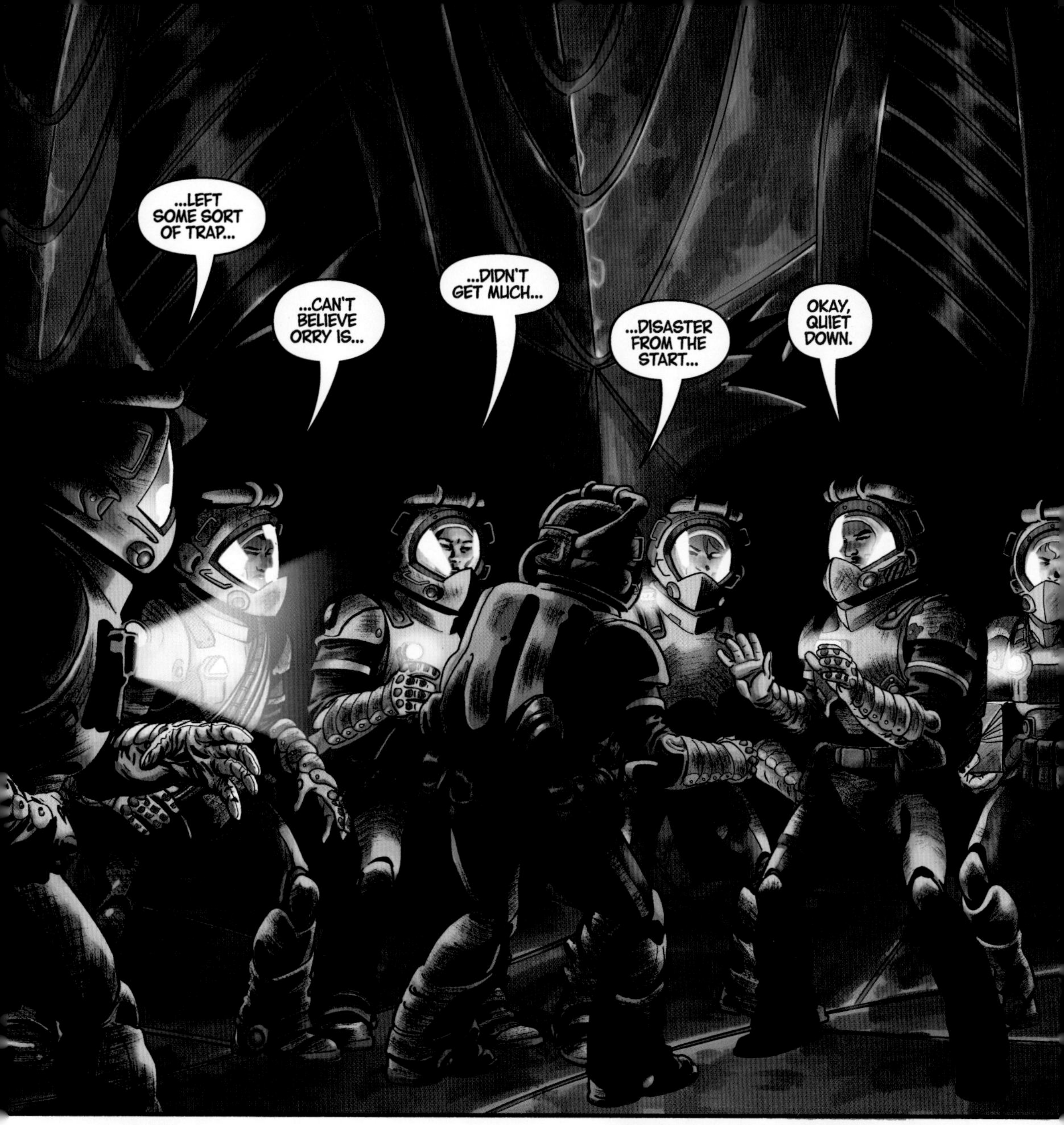
...LEFT SOME SORT OF TRAP...
...CAN'T BELIEVE ORRY IS...
...DIDN'T GET MUCH...
...DISASTER FROM THE START...
OKAY, QUIET DOWN.

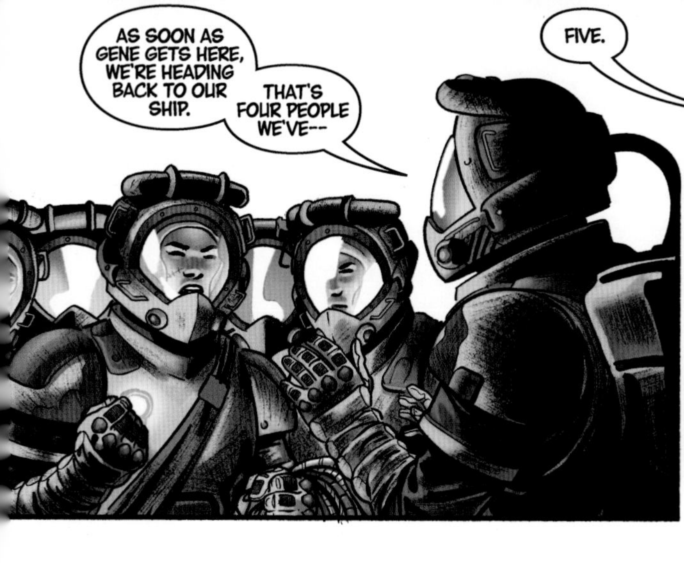
AS SOON AS GENE GETS HERE, WE'RE HEADING BACK TO OUR SHIP.
THAT'S FOUR PEOPLE WE'VE--
FIVE.

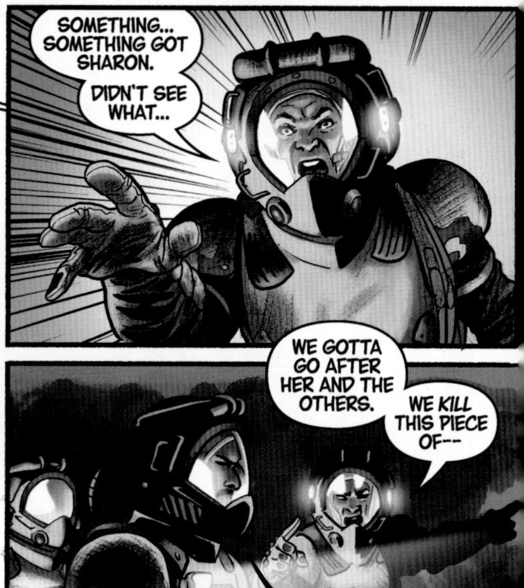
SOMETHING... SOMETHING GOT SHARON.
DIDN'T SEE WHAT...

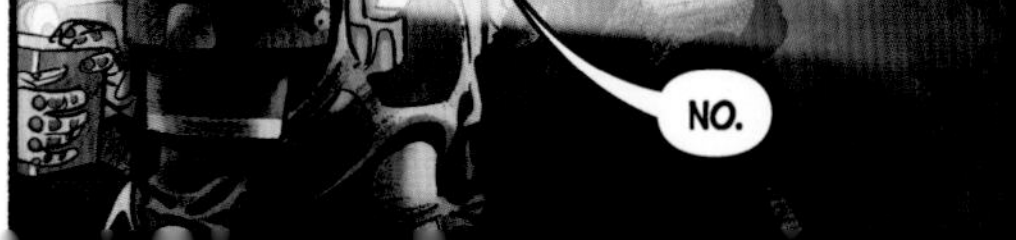
WE GOTTA GO AFTER HER AND THE OTHERS.
WE KILL THIS PIECE OF--
NO.

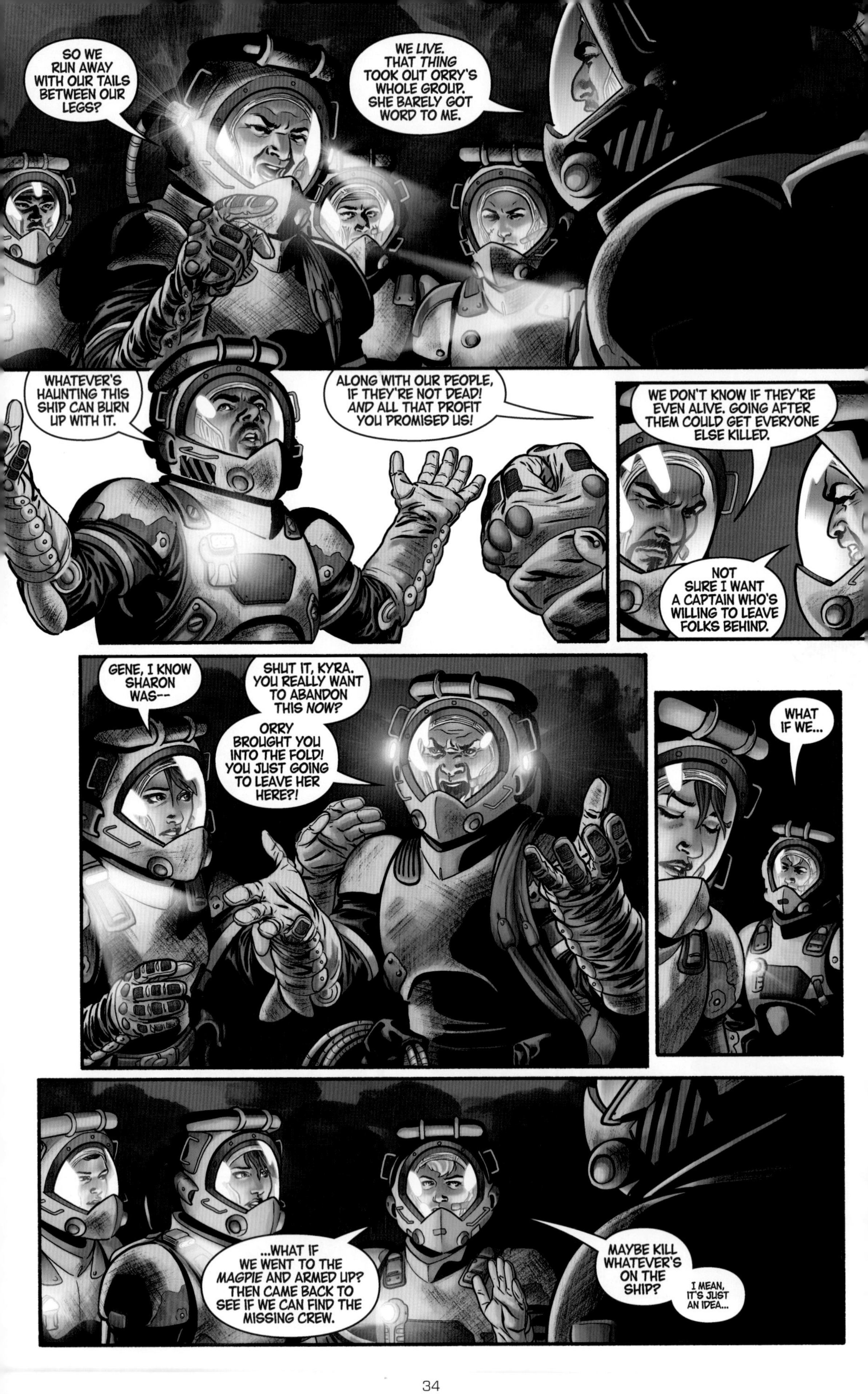
SO WE RUN AWAY WITH OUR TAILS BETWEEN OUR LEGS?
WE LIVE. THAT THING TOOK OUT ORRY'S WHOLE GROUP. SHE BARELY GOT WORD TO ME.
WHATEVER'S HAUNTING THIS SHIP CAN BURN UP WITH IT.
ALONG WITH OUR PEOPLE, IF THEY'RE NOT DEAD! AND ALL THAT PROFIT YOU PROMISED US!
WE DON'T KNOW IF THEY'RE EVEN ALIVE. GOING AFTER THEM COULD GET EVERYONE ELSE KILLED.
NOT SURE I WANT A CAPTAIN WHO'S WILLING TO LEAVE FOLKS BEHIND.
GENE, I KNOW SHARON WAS--
SHUT IT, KYRA. YOU REALLY WANT TO ABANDON THIS NOW?
ORRY BROUGHT YOU INTO THE FOLD! YOU JUST GOING TO LEAVE HER HERE?!
WHAT IF WE...
...WHAT IF WE WENT TO THE MAGPIE AND ARMED UP? THEN CAME BACK TO SEE IF WE CAN FIND THE MISSING CREW.
MAYBE KILL WHATEVER'S ON THE SHIP?
I MEAN, IT'S JUST AN IDEA...

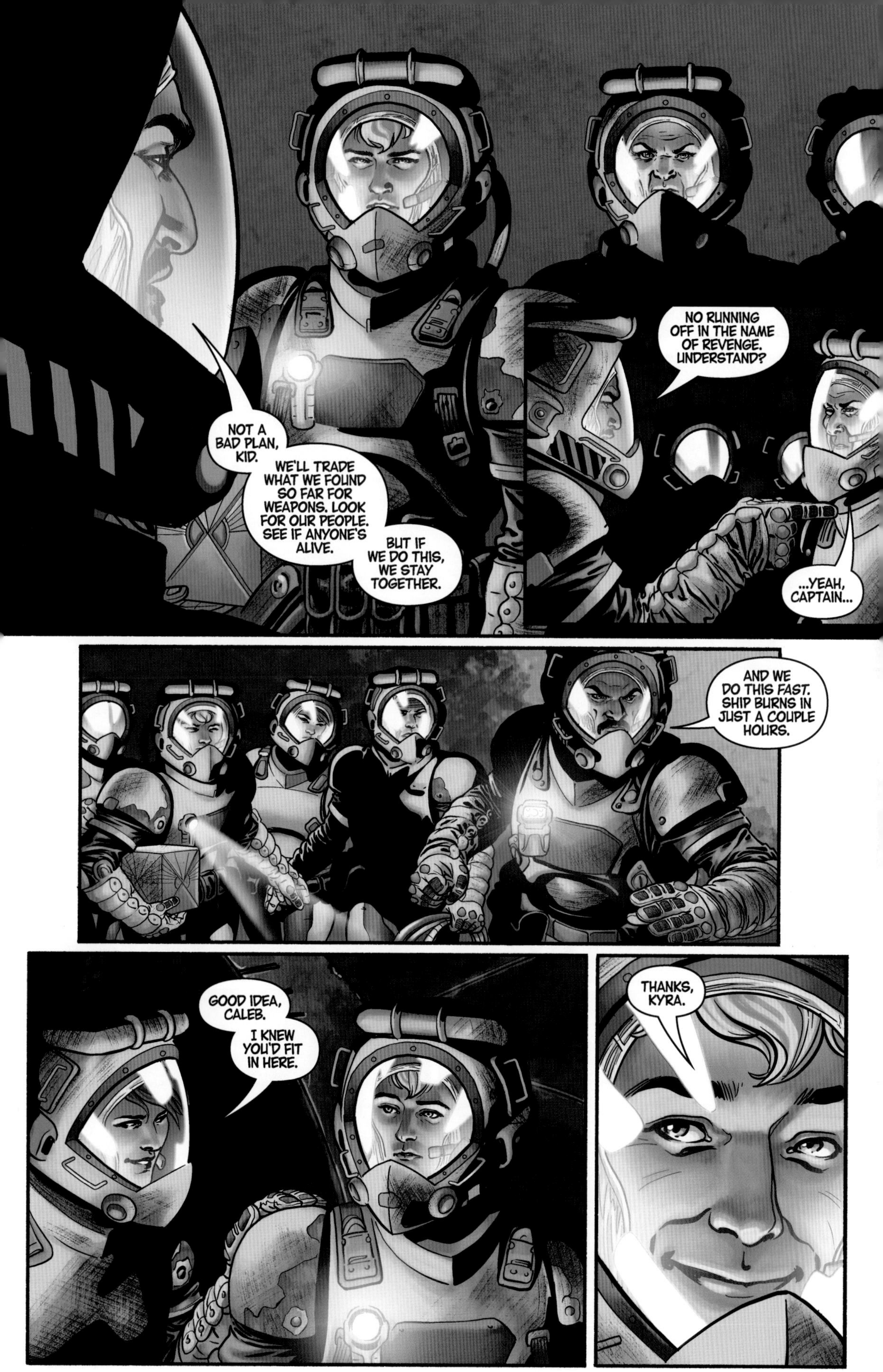
NOT A BAD PLAN, KID.
WE'LL TRADE WHAT WE FOUND SO FAR FOR WEAPONS. LOOK FOR OUR PEOPLE. SEE IF ANYONE'S ALIVE.
BUT IF WE DO THIS, WE STAY TOGETHER.
NO RUNNING OFF IN THE NAME OF REVENGE. UNDERSTAND?
...YEAH, CAPTAIN...
AND WE DO THIS FAST. SHIP BURNS IN JUST A COUPLE HOURS.
GOOD IDEA, CALEB.
I KNEW YOU'D FIT IN HERE.
THANKS, KYRA.

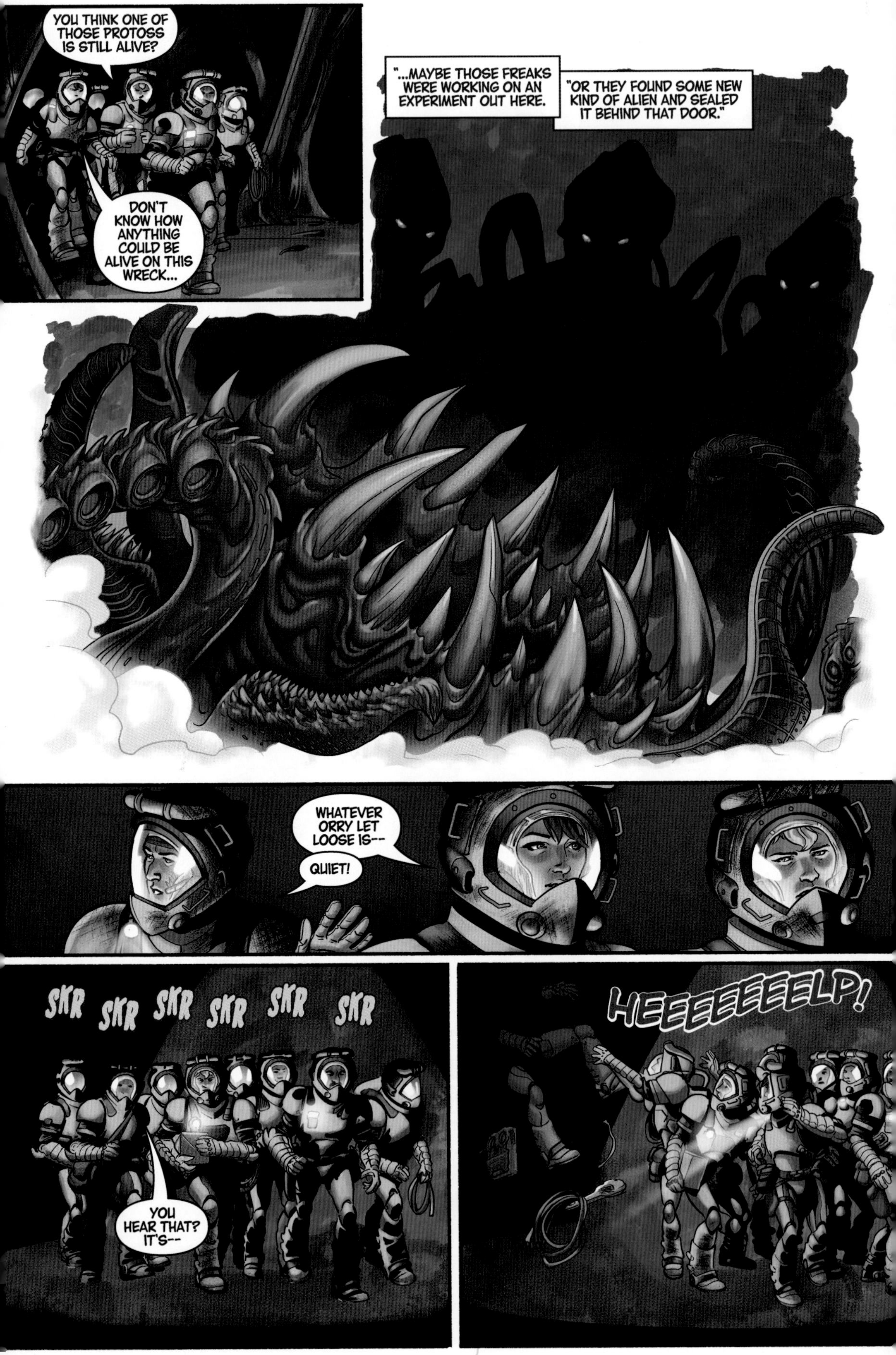
YOU THINK ONE OF THOSE PROTOSS IS STILL ALIVE?
DON'T KNOW HOW ANYTHING COULD BE ALIVE ON THIS WRECK...
"...MAYBE THOSE FREAKS WERE WORKING ON AN EXPERIMENT OUT HERE.
"OR THEY FOUND SOME NEW KIND OF ALIEN AND SEALED IT BEHIND THAT DOOR."
WHATEVER ORRY LET LOOSE IS--
QUIET!
SKR SKR SKR SKR SKR SKR
YOU HEAR THAT? IT'S--
HEEEEEEEELP!

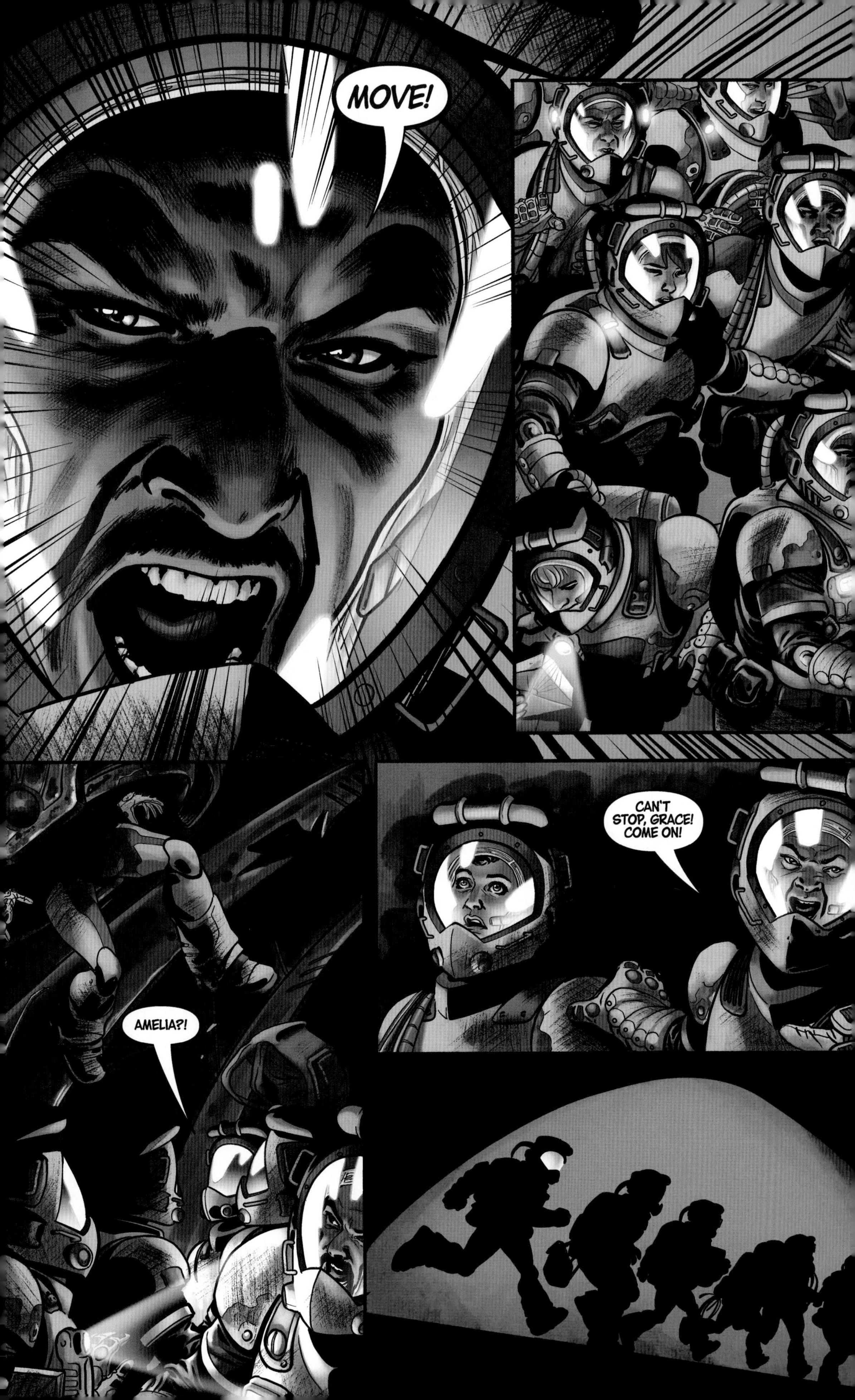
MOVE!
AMELIA?!
CAN'T STOP, GRACE! COME ON!

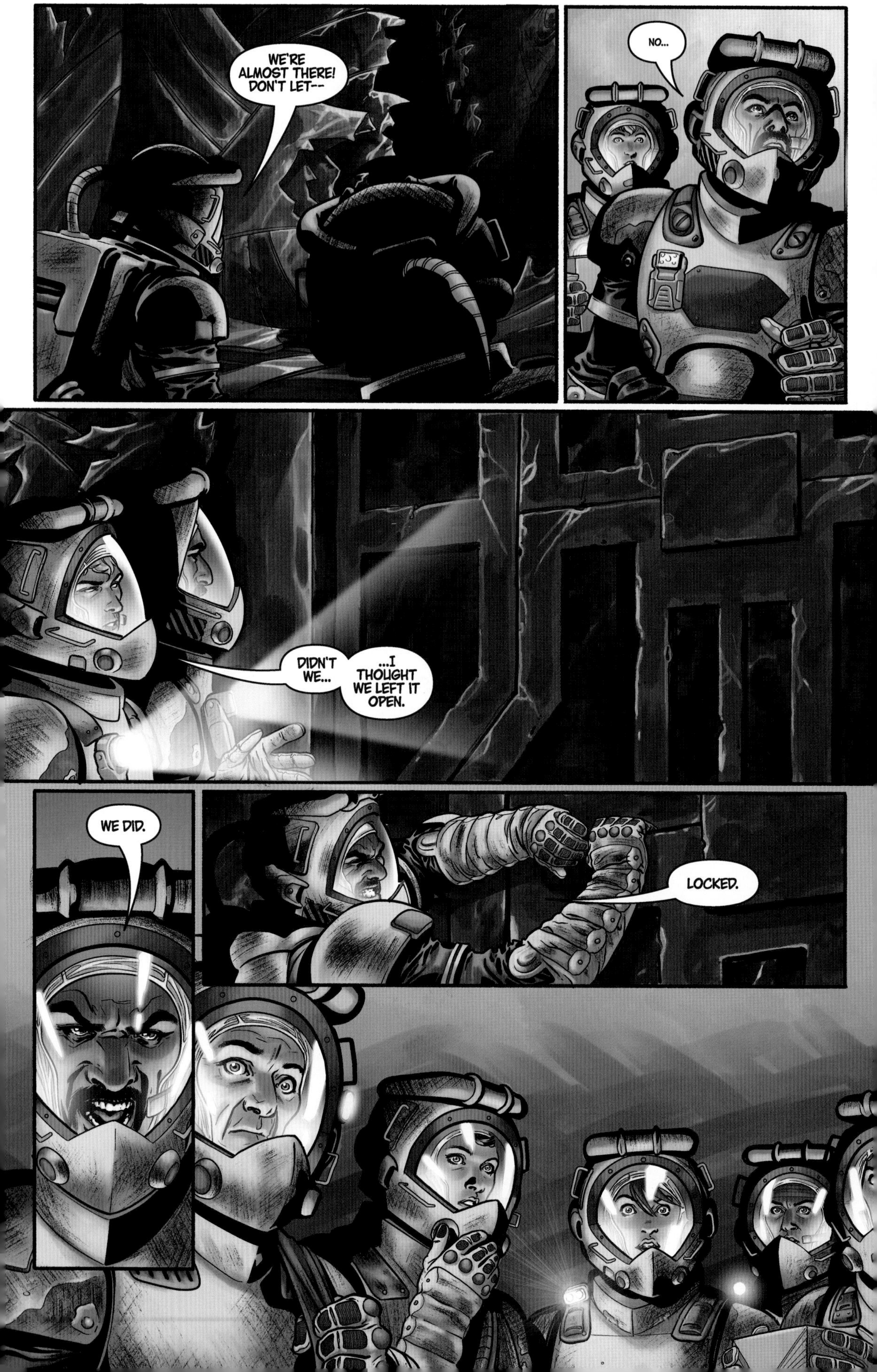
WE'RE ALMOST THERE! DON'T LET--
NO...
DIDN'T WE...
...I THOUGHT WE LEFT IT OPEN.
WE DID.
LOCKED.

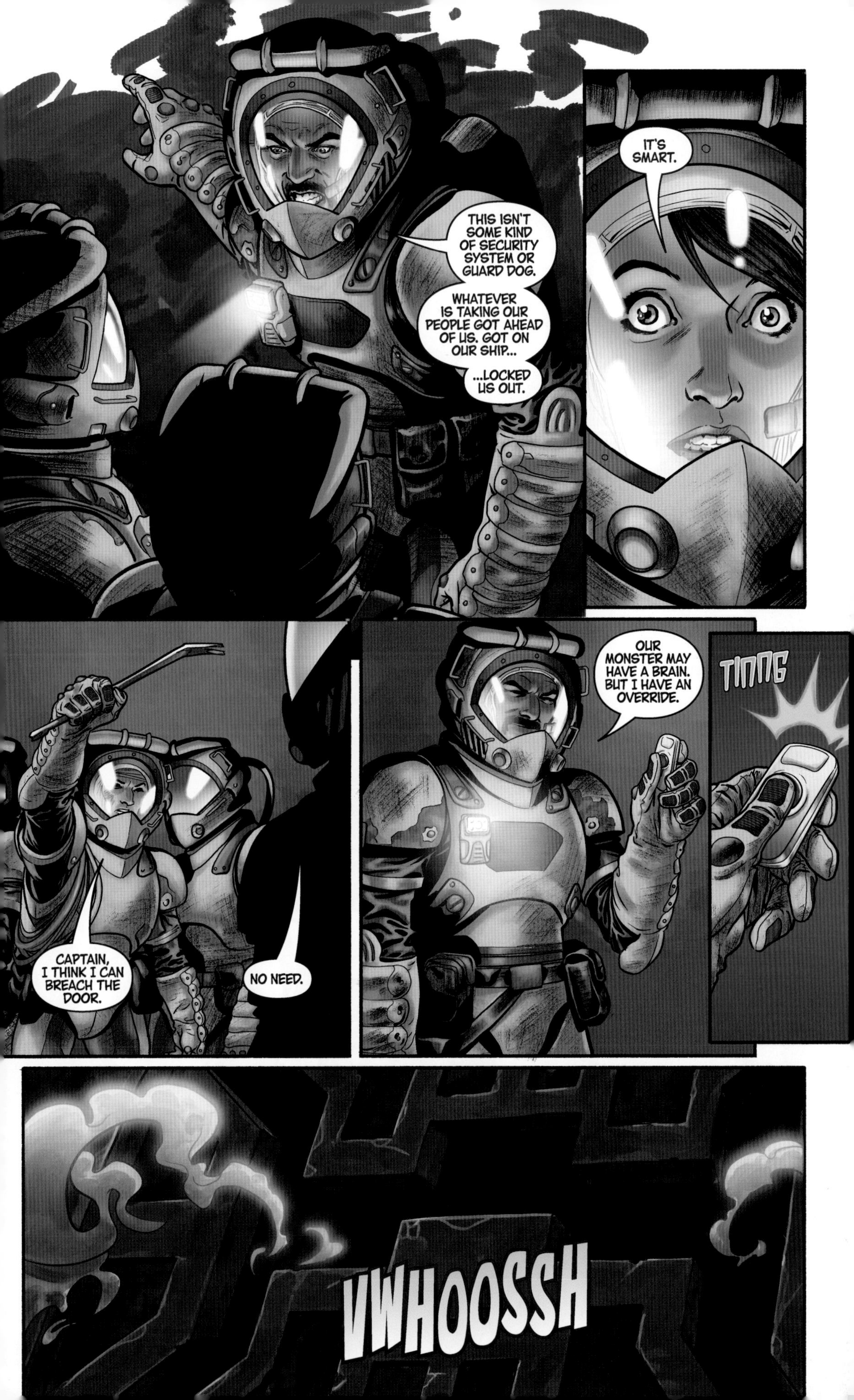
THIS ISN'T SOME KIND OF SECURITY SYSTEM OR GUARD DOG.
WHATEVER IS TAKING OUR PEOPLE GOT AHEAD OF US. GOT ON OUR SHIP...
...LOCKED US OUT.
IT'S SMART.
CAPTAIN, I THINK I CAN BREACH THE DOOR.
NO NEED.
OUR MONSTER MAY HAVE A BRAIN. BUT I HAVE AN OVERRIDE.
TINNG
VWHOOSSH

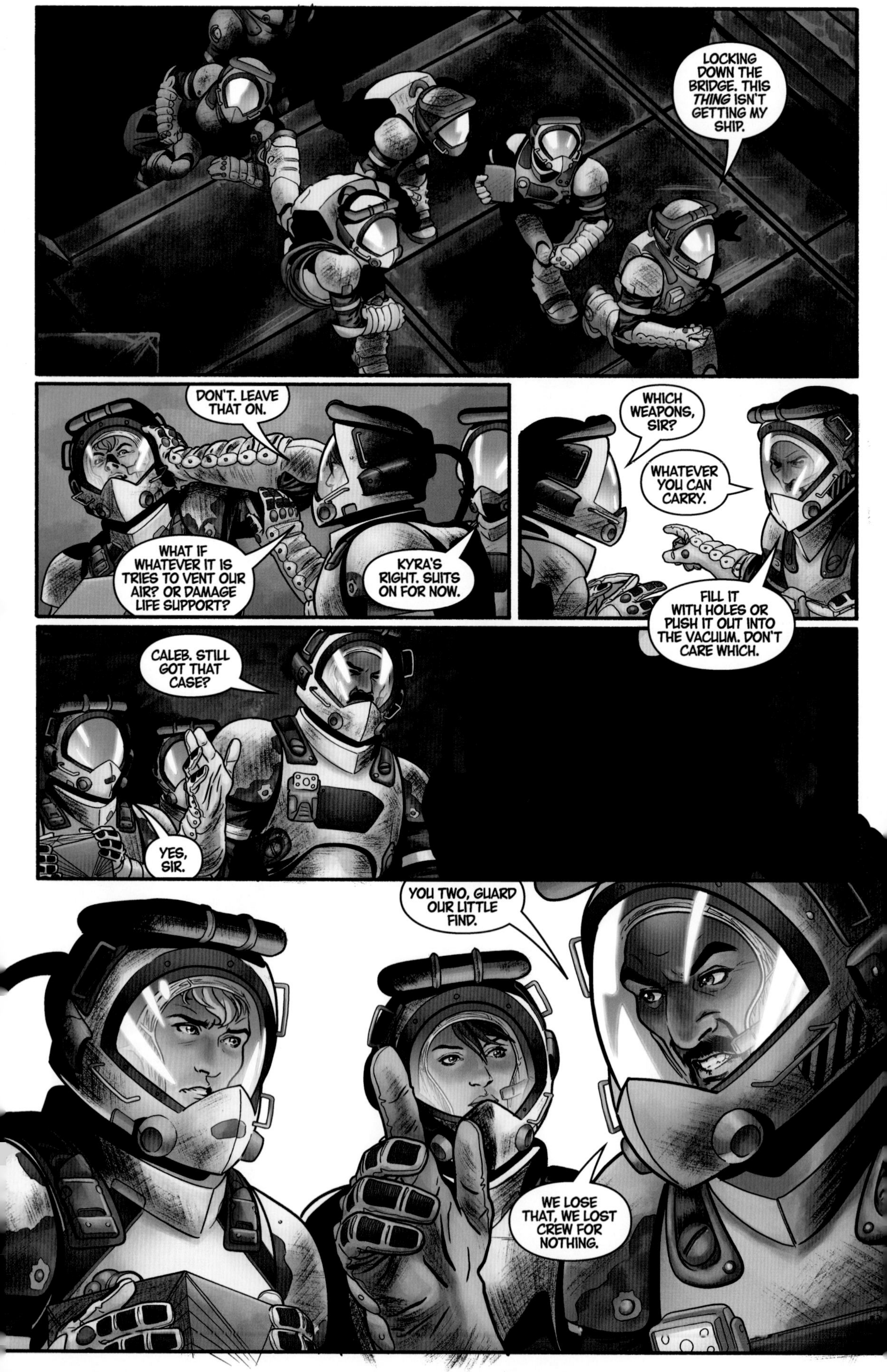
LOCKING DOWN THE BRIDGE. THIS *THING* ISN'T GETTING MY SHIP.
DON'T. LEAVE THAT ON.
WHAT IF WHATEVER IT IS TRIES TO VENT OUR AIR? OR DAMAGE LIFE SUPPORT?
KYRA'S RIGHT. SUITS ON FOR NOW.
WHICH WEAPONS, SIR?
WHATEVER YOU CAN CARRY.
FILL IT WITH HOLES OR PUSH IT OUT INTO THE VACUUM. DON'T CARE WHICH.
CALEB. STILL GOT THAT CASE?
YES, SIR.
YOU TWO, GUARD OUR LITTLE FIND.
WE LOSE THAT, WE LOST CREW FOR NOTHING.

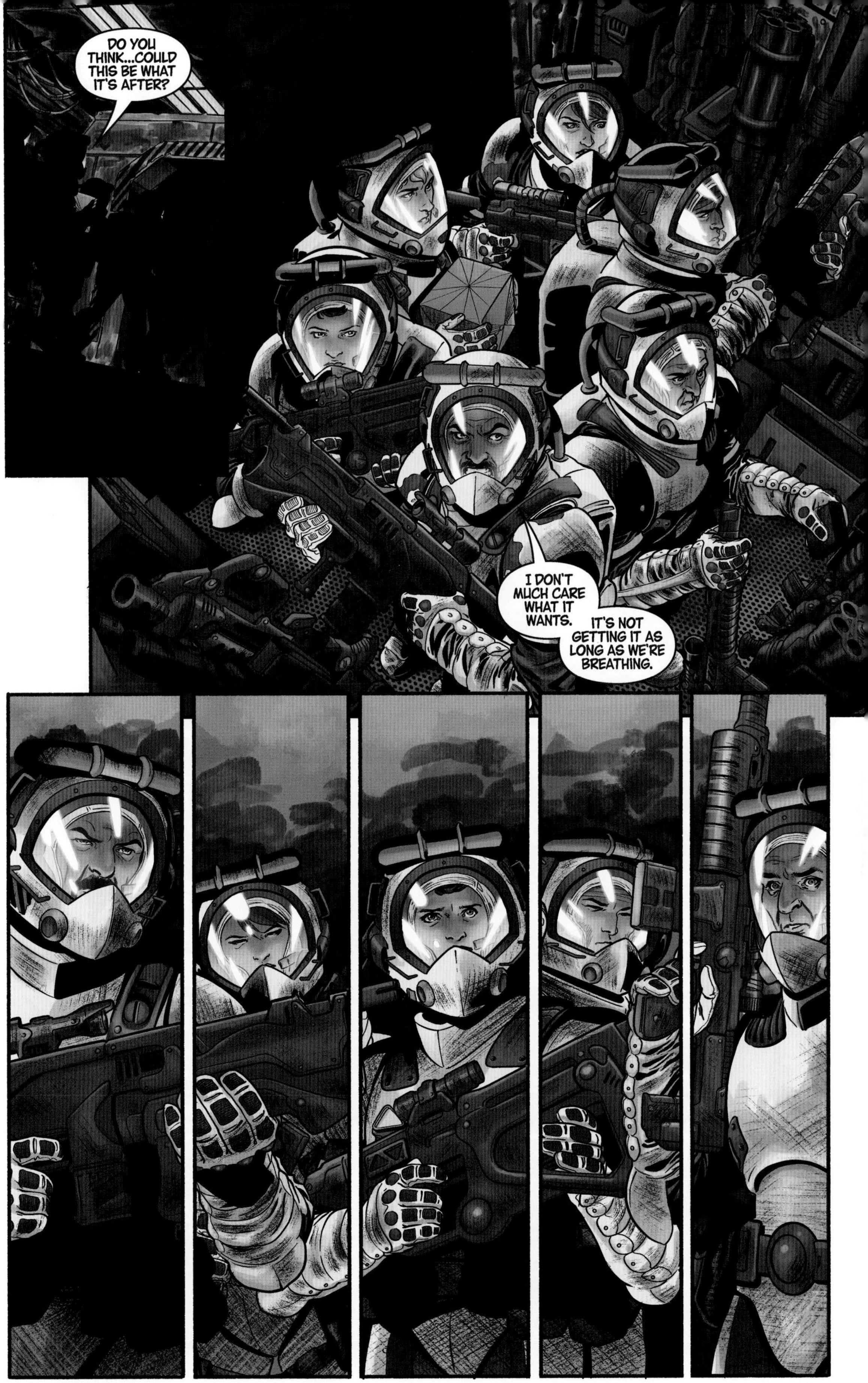
DO YOU THINK...COULD THIS BE WHAT IT'S AFTER?
I DON'T MUCH CARE WHAT IT WANTS.
IT'S NOT GETTING IT AS LONG AS WE'RE BREATHING.

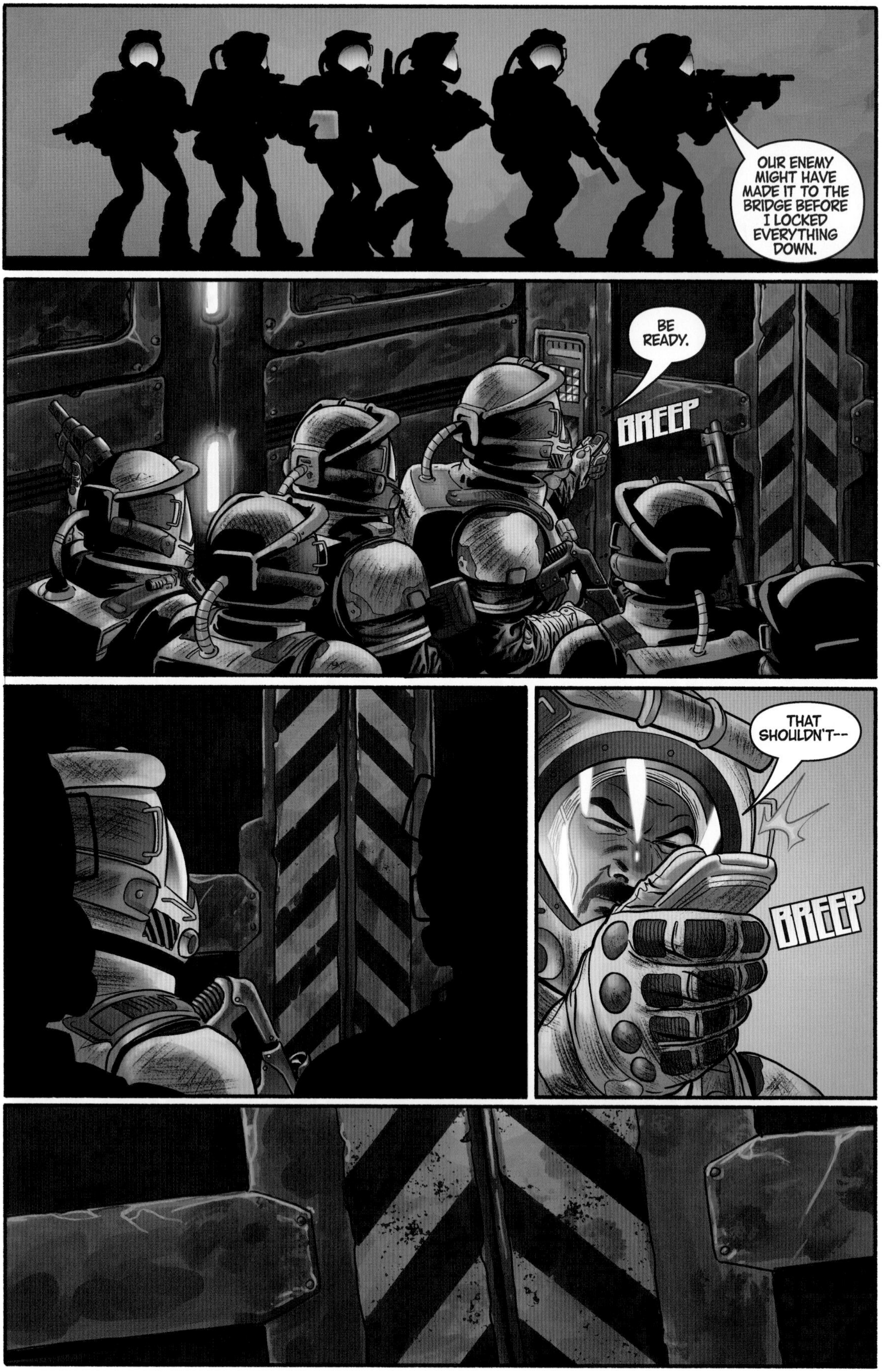
OUR ENEMY MIGHT HAVE MADE IT TO THE BRIDGE BEFORE I LOCKED EVERYTHING DOWN.
BE READY.
BREEP
THAT SHOULDN'T--
BREEP

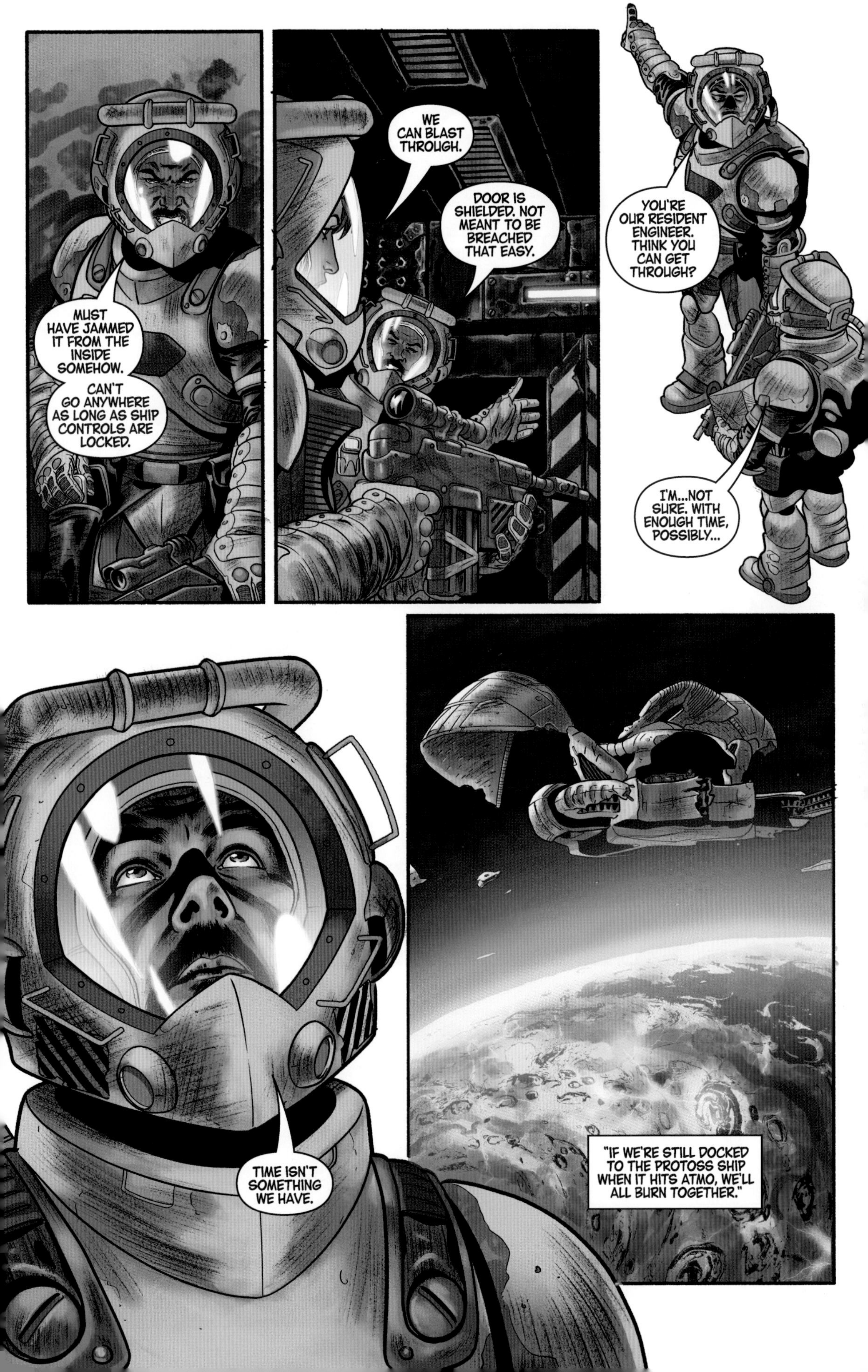
MUST HAVE JAMMED IT FROM THE INSIDE SOMEHOW.
CAN'T GO ANYWHERE AS LONG AS SHIP CONTROLS ARE LOCKED.
WE CAN BLAST THROUGH.
DOOR IS SHIELDED. NOT MEANT TO BE BREACHED THAT EASY.
YOU'RE OUR RESIDENT ENGINEER. THINK YOU CAN GET THROUGH?
I'M...NOT SURE. WITH ENOUGH TIME, POSSIBLY...
TIME ISN'T SOMETHING WE HAVE.
"IF WE'RE STILL DOCKED TO THE PROTOSS SHIP WHEN IT HITS ATMO, WE'LL ALL BURN TOGETHER."

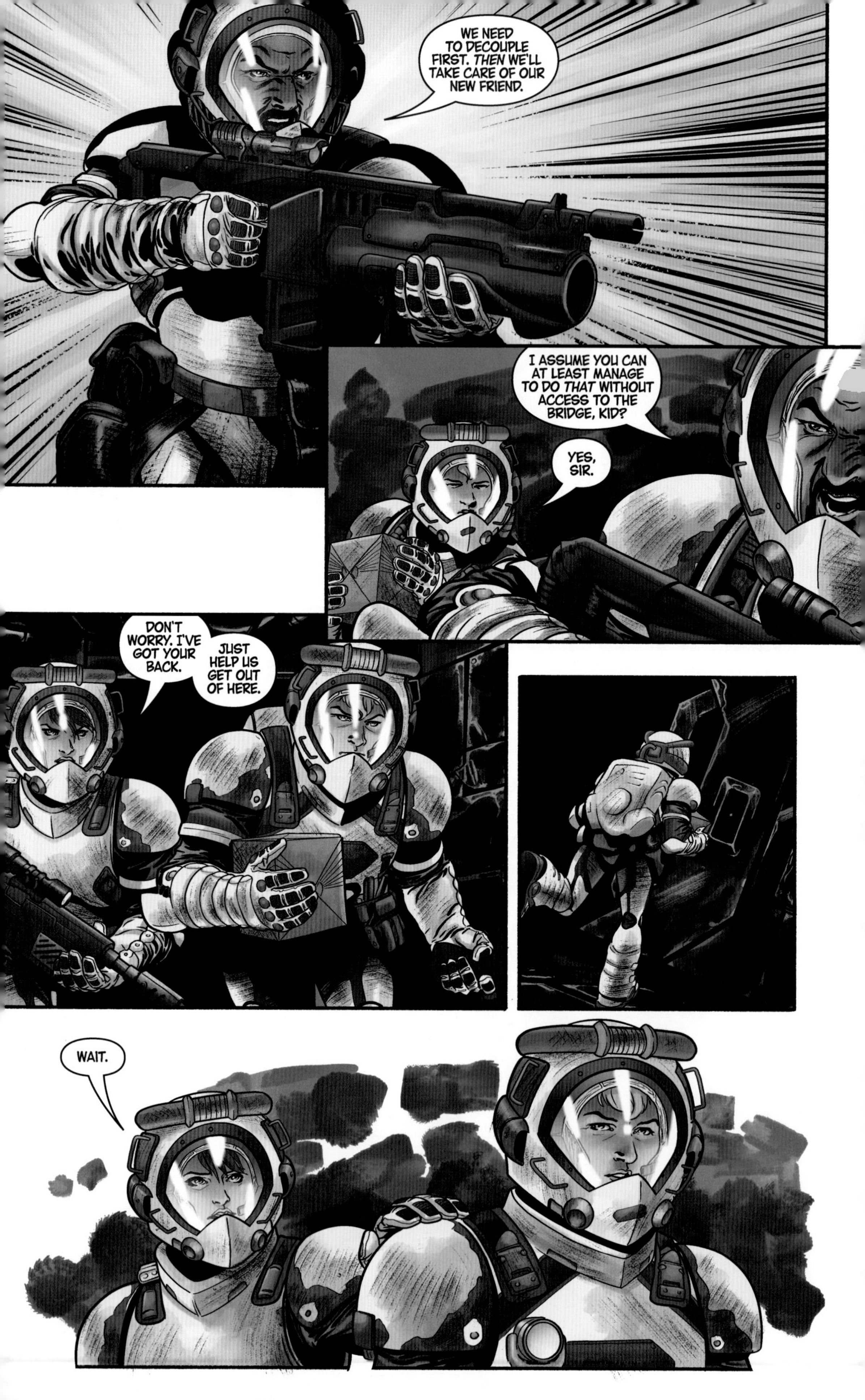
WE NEED TO DECOUPLE FIRST. *THEN* WE'LL TAKE CARE OF OUR NEW FRIEND.
I ASSUME YOU CAN AT LEAST MANAGE TO DO *THAT* WITHOUT ACCESS TO THE BRIDGE, KID?
YES, SIR.
DON'T WORRY. I'VE GOT YOUR BACK.
JUST HELP US GET OUT OF HERE.
WAIT.

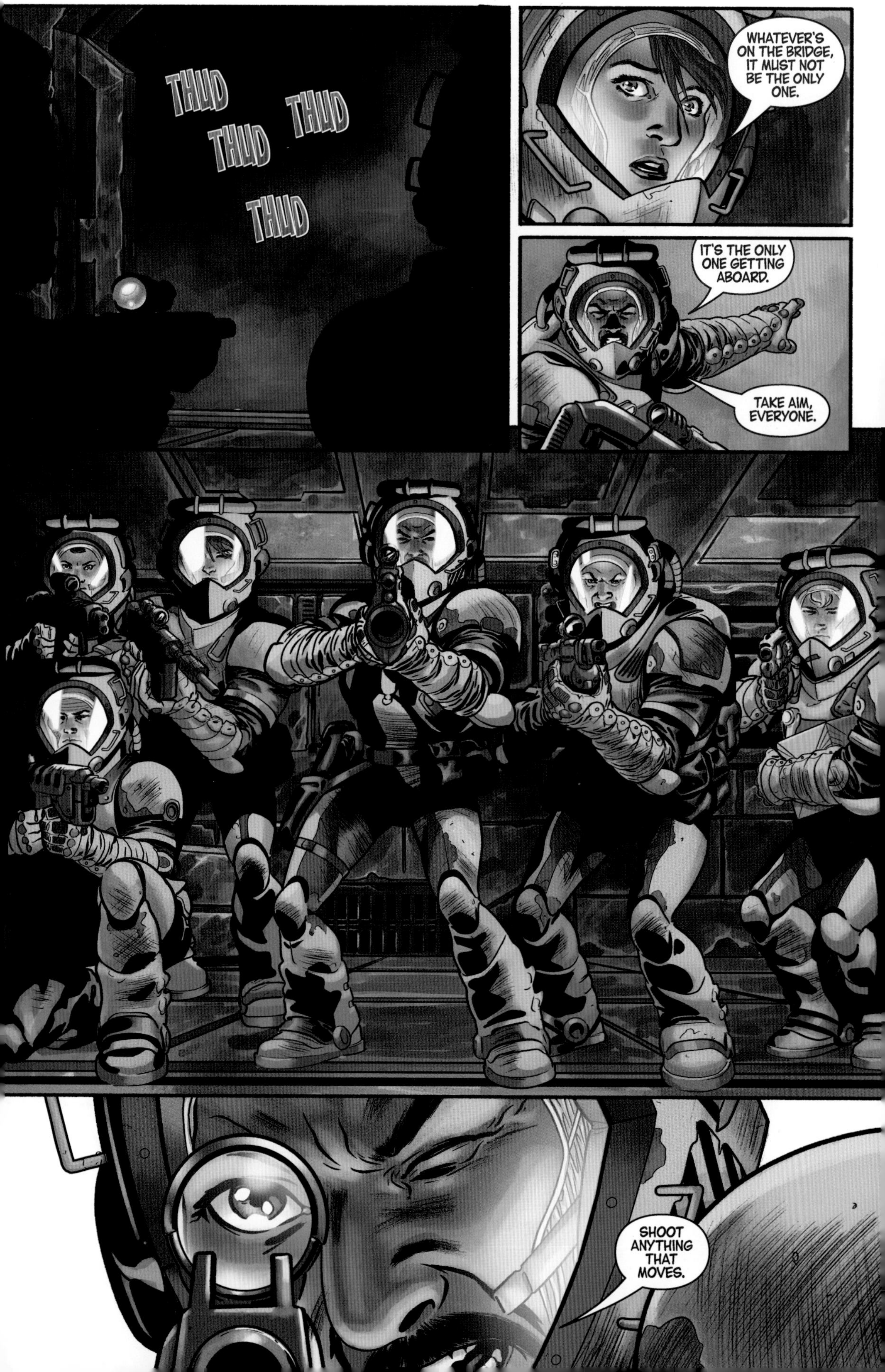
THUD
THUD
THUD
THUD
WHATEVER'S ON THE BRIDGE, IT MUST NOT BE THE ONLY ONE.
IT'S THE ONLY ONE GETTING ABOARD.
TAKE AIM, EVERYONE.
SHOOT ANYTHING THAT MOVES.

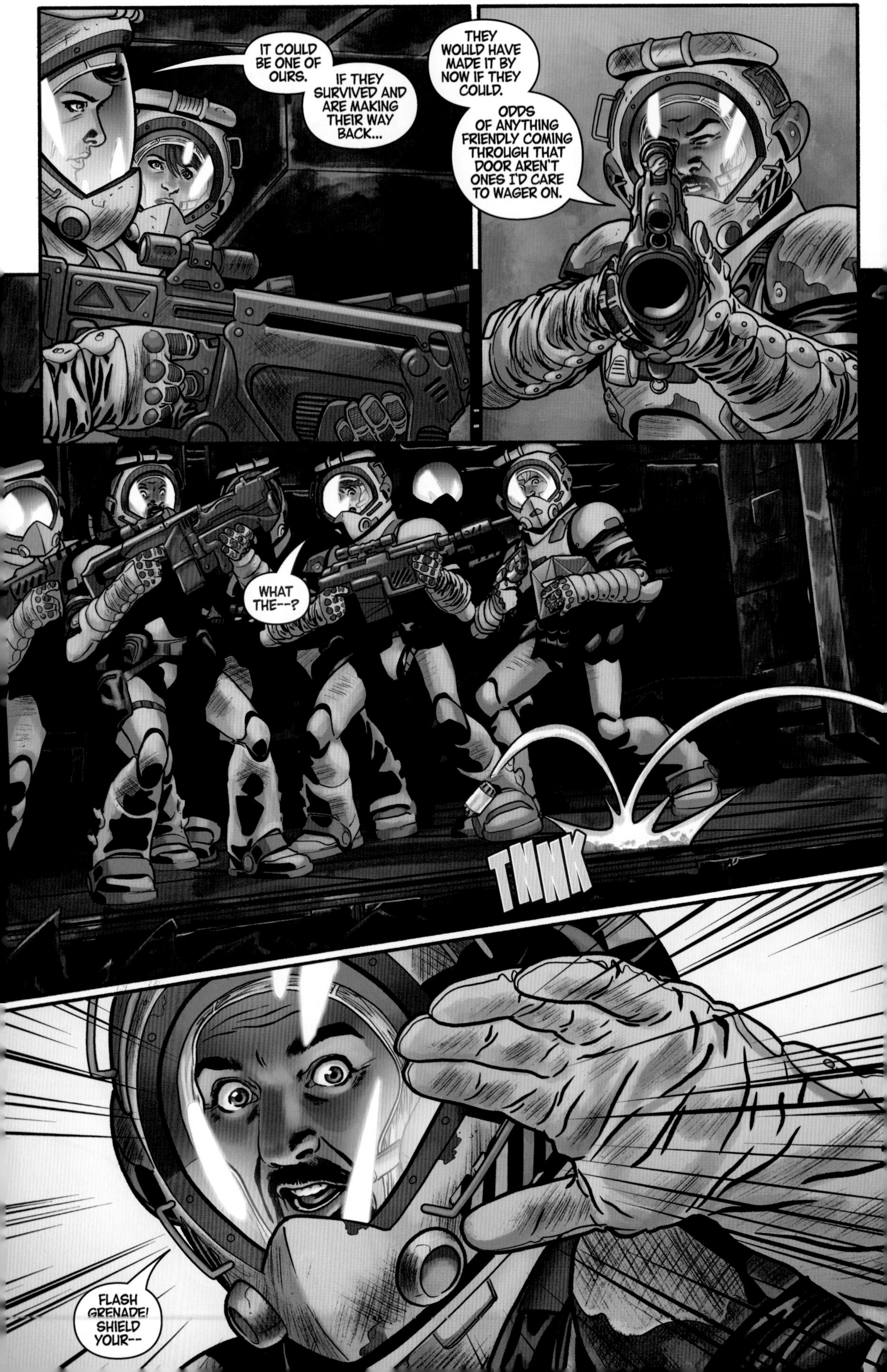
IT COULD BE ONE OF OURS.
IF THEY SURVIVED AND ARE MAKING THEIR WAY BACK...
THEY WOULD HAVE MADE IT BY NOW IF THEY COULD.
ODDS OF ANYTHING FRIENDLY COMING THROUGH THAT DOOR AREN'T ONES I'D CARE TO WAGER ON.
WHAT THE--?
TNNK
FLASH GRENADE! SHIELD YOUR--

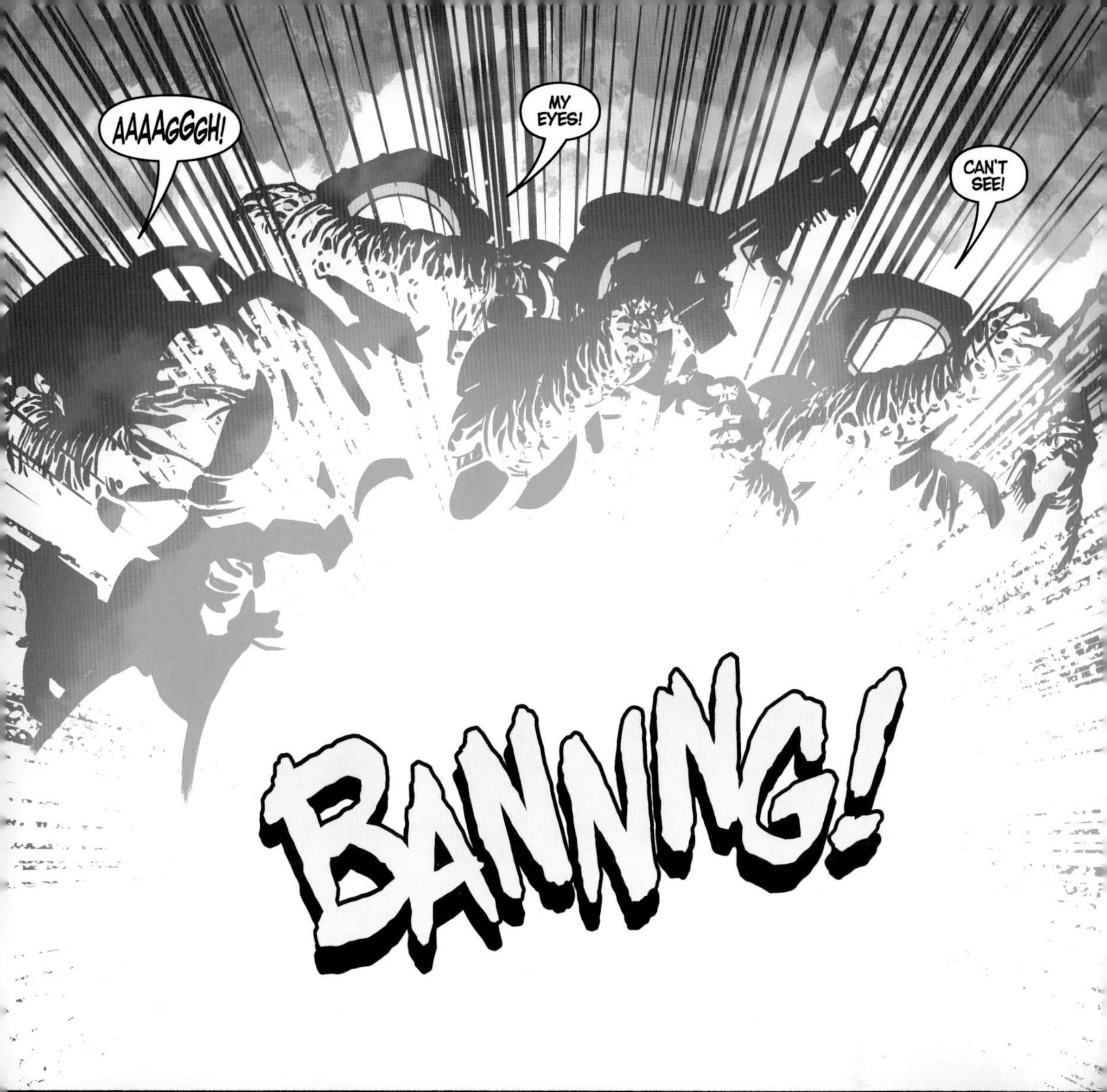
AAAAGGGH!
MY EYES!
CAN'T SEE!
BANNNG!

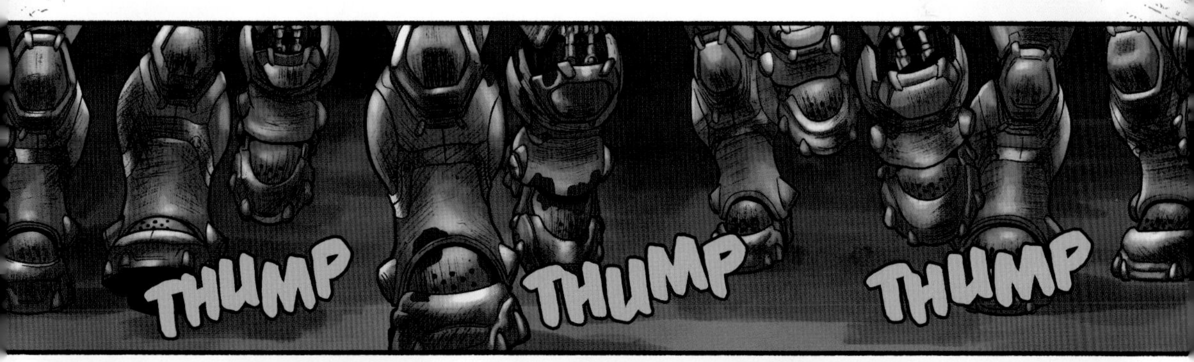
THUMP
THUMP
THUMP

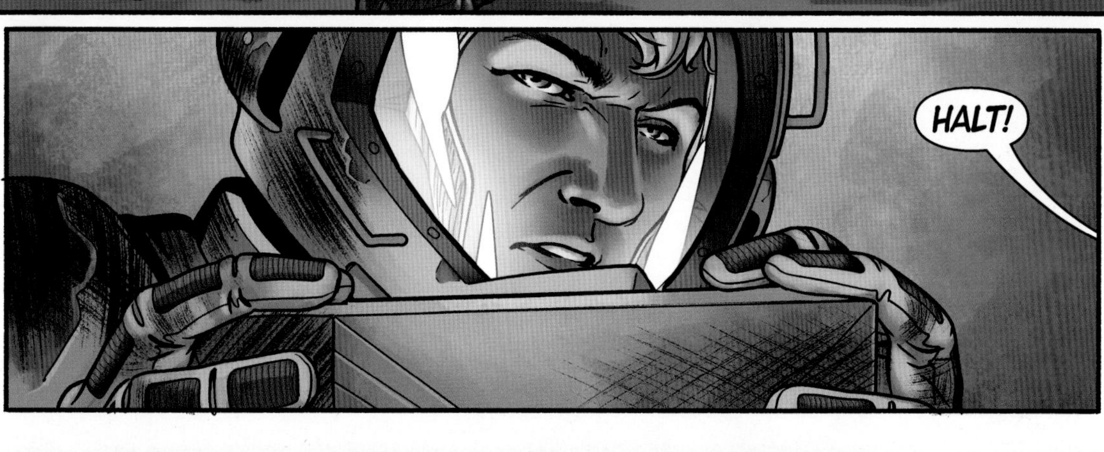
HALT!

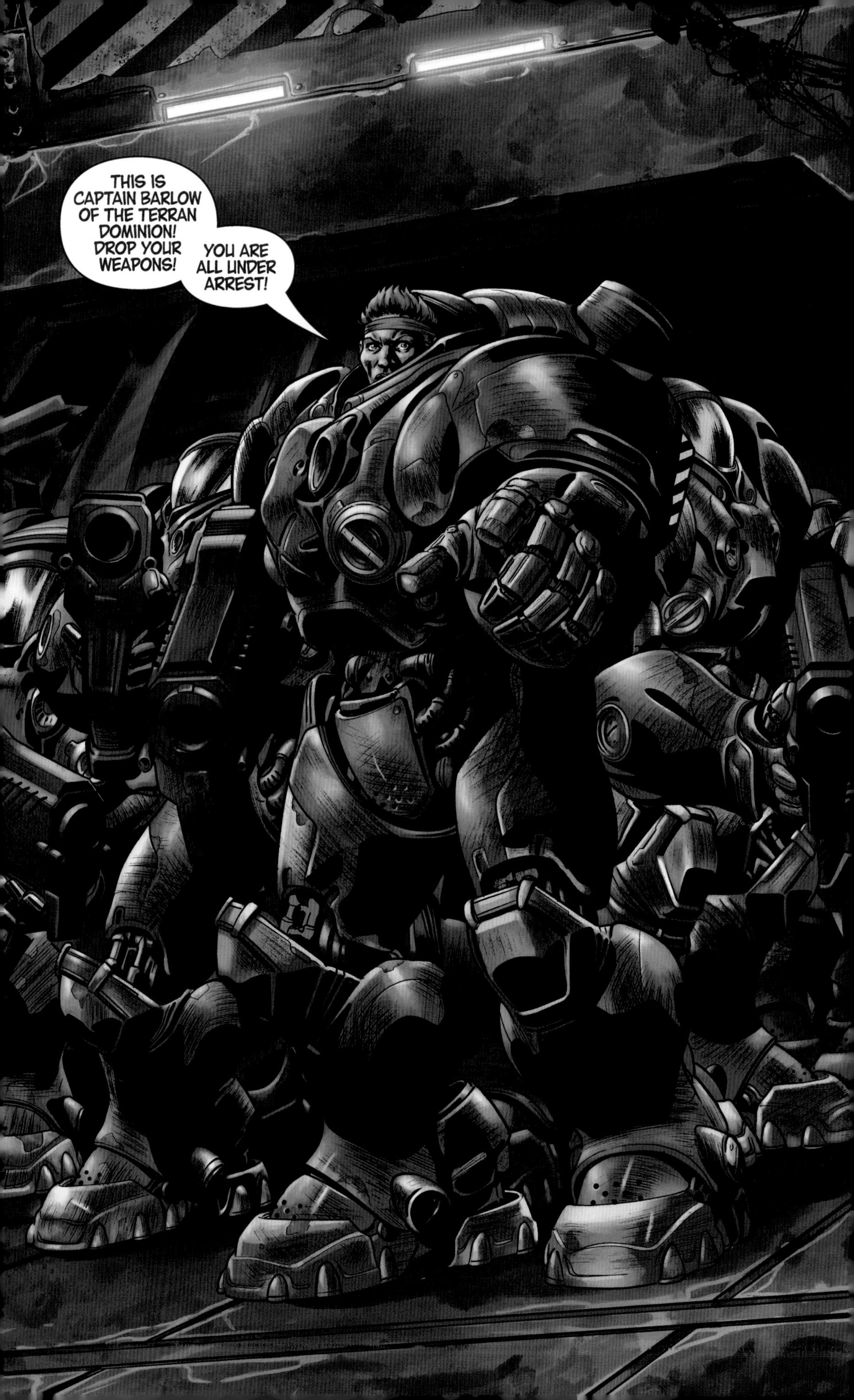
THIS IS CAPTAIN BARLOW OF THE TERRAN DOMINION! DROP YOUR WEAPONS!
YOU ARE ALL UNDER ARREST!

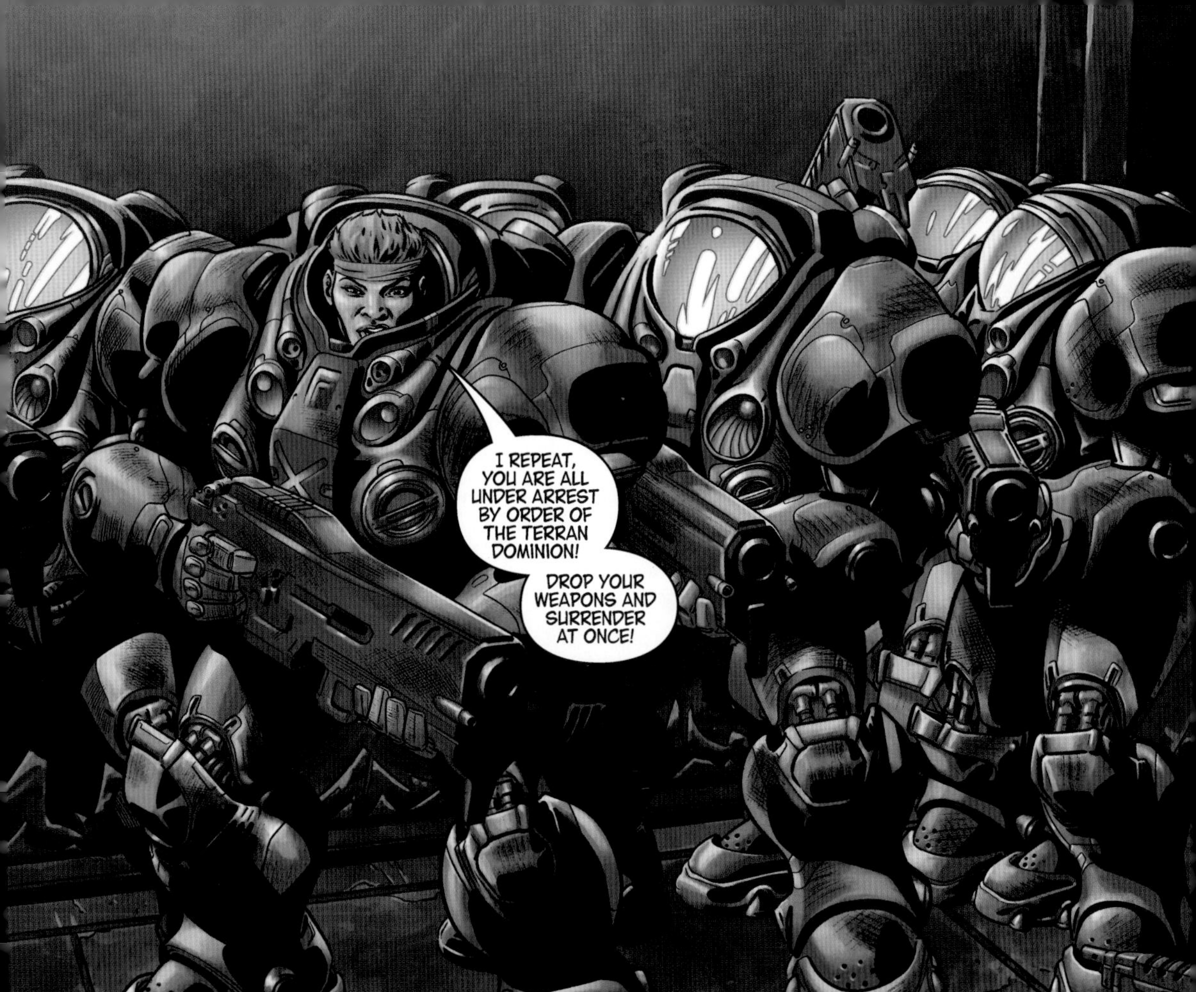
I REPEAT, YOU ARE ALL UNDER ARREST BY ORDER OF THE TERRAN DOMINION!
DROP YOUR WEAPONS AND SURRENDER AT ONCE!

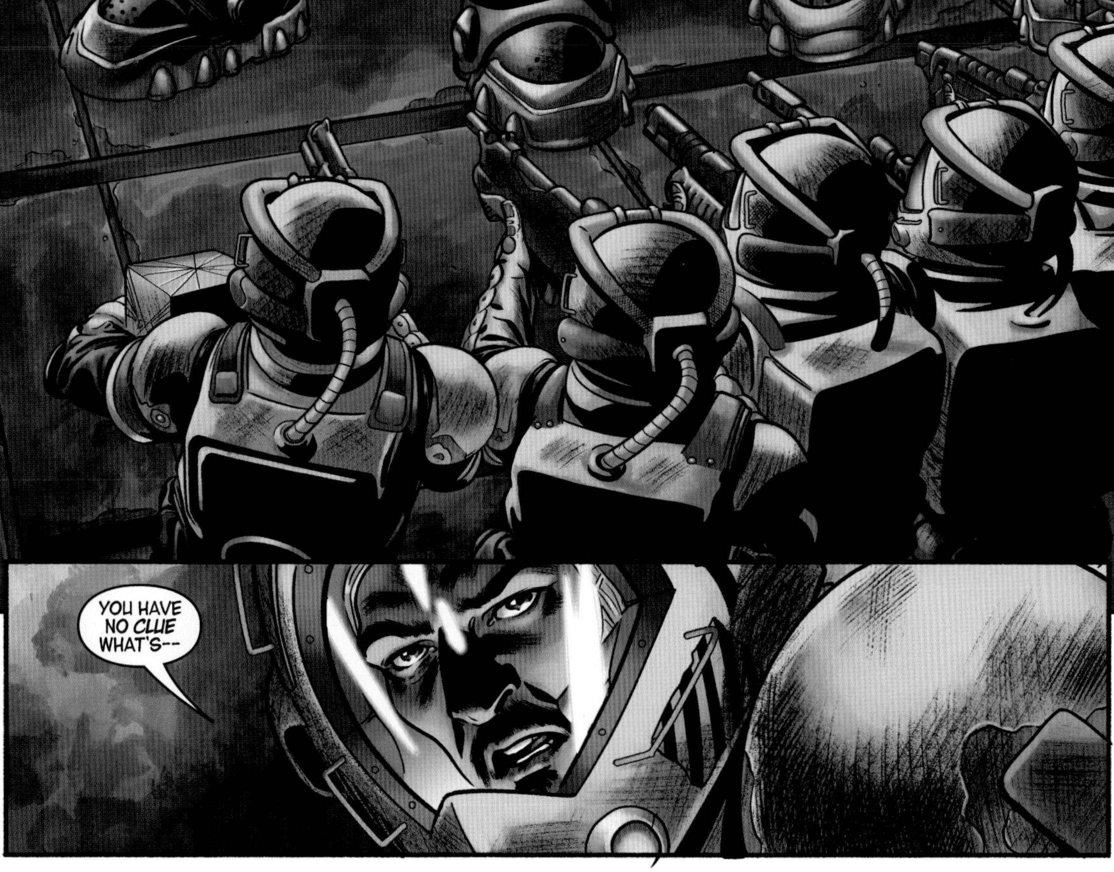
YOU HAVE NO CLUE WHAT'S--

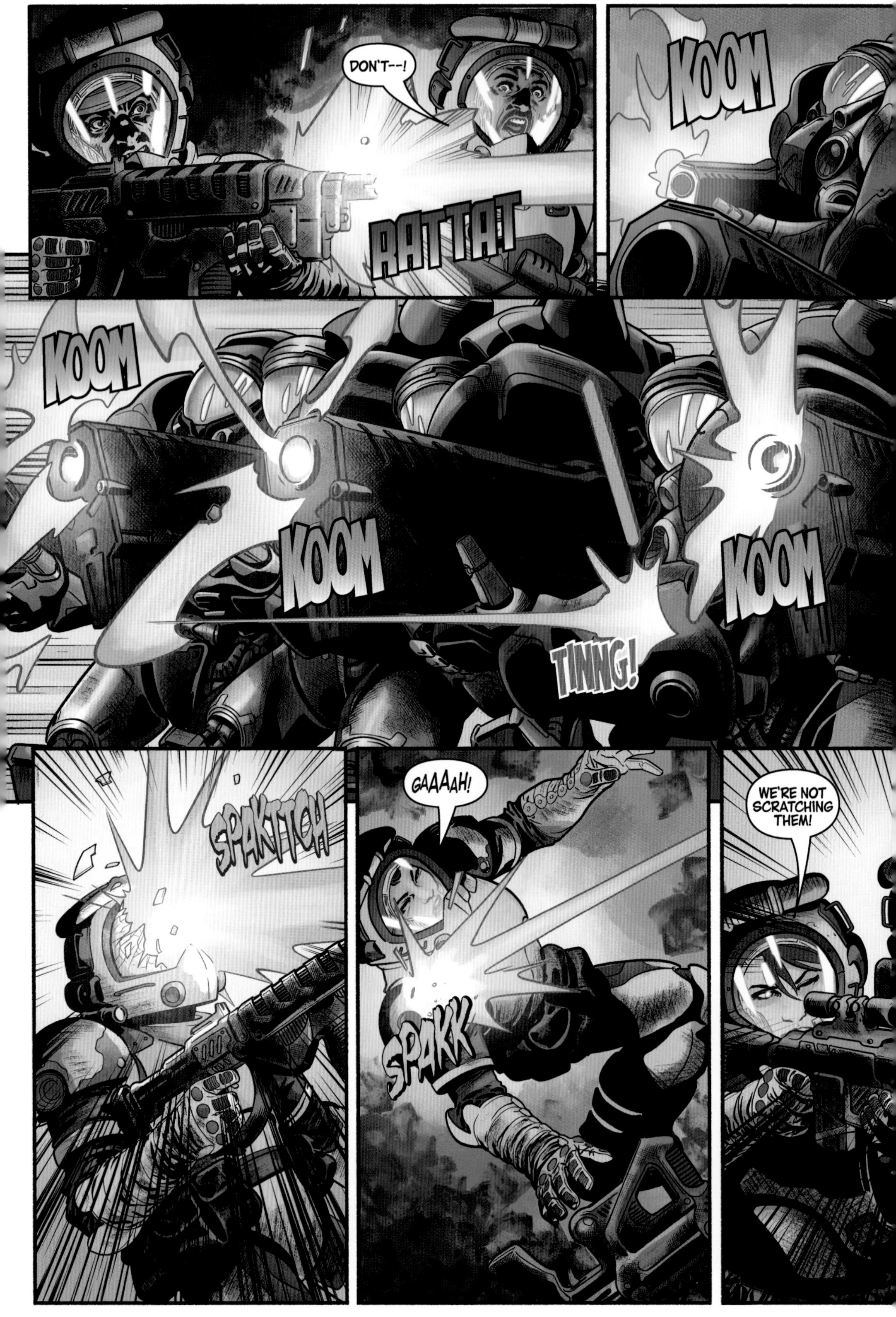

DON'T--!
RATTAT
KOOM
KOOM
KOOM
KOOM
TINNG!
SPAKTTCH
GAAAAH!
SPAKK
WE'RE NOT SCRATCHING THEM!

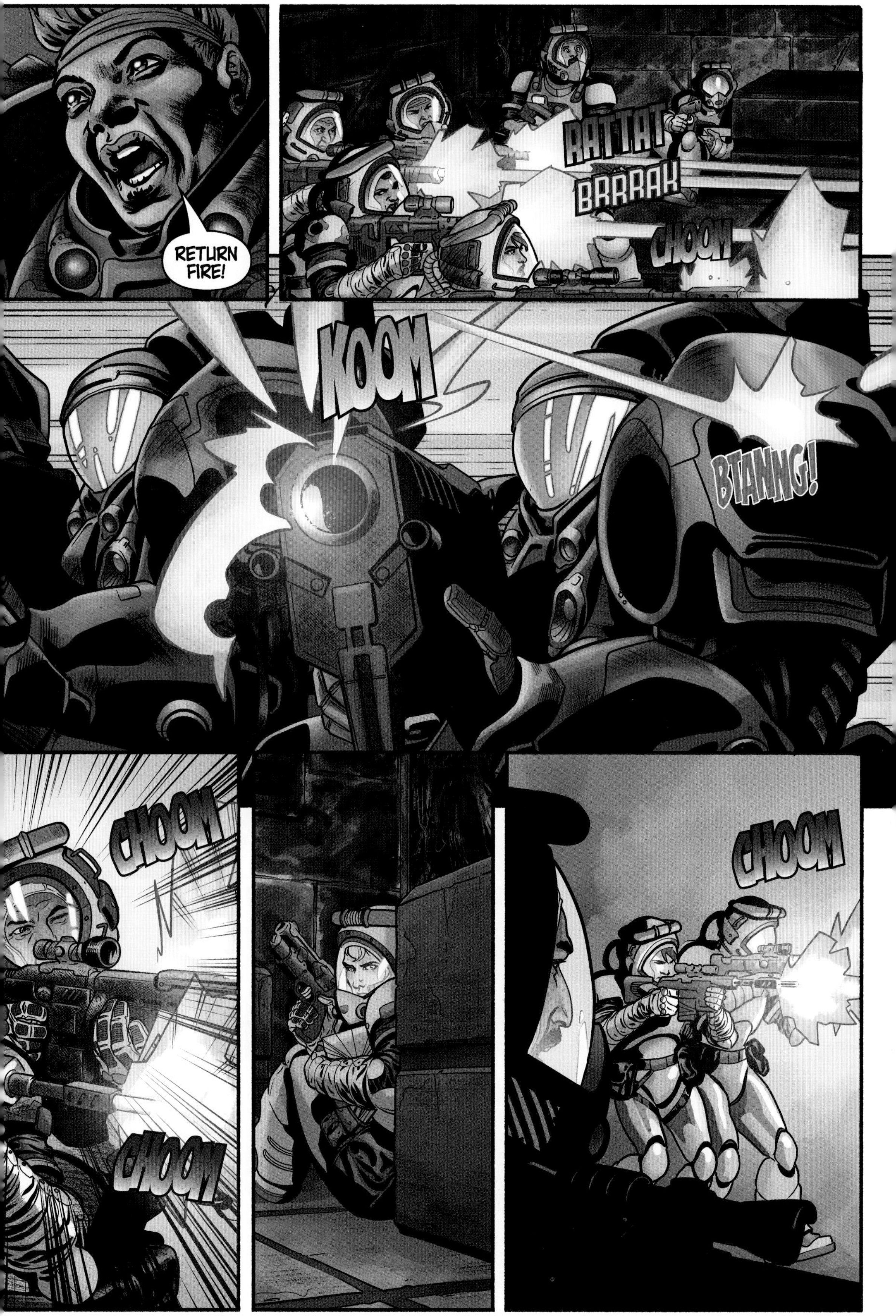
RETURN FIRE!
RATTAT
BRRRAK
CHOOM
KOOM
BTANNG!
CHOOM
CHOOM
CHOOM

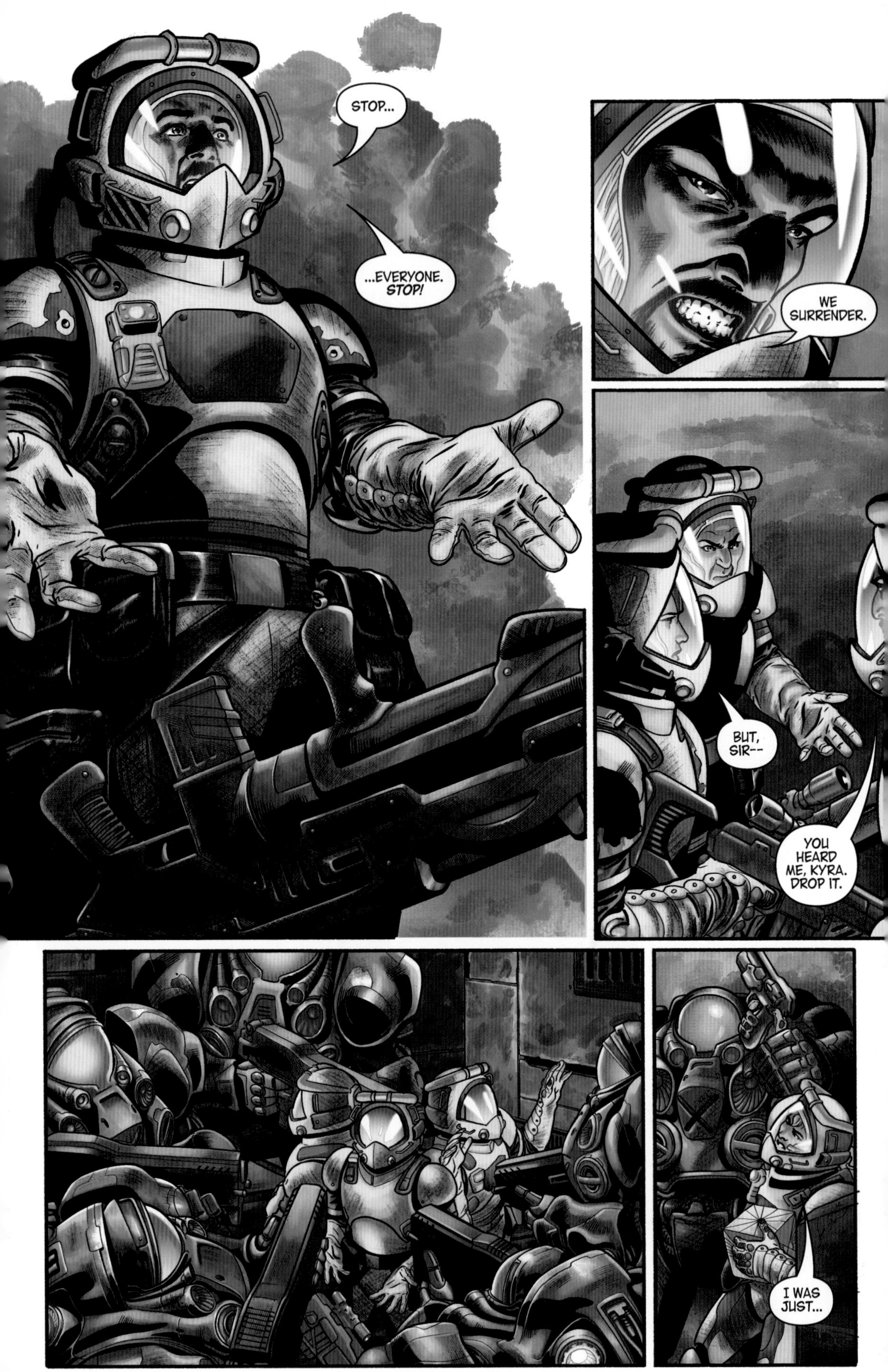
STOP...
...EVERYONE. STOP!
WE SURRENDER.
BUT, SIR--
YOU HEARD ME, KYRA. DROP IT.
I WAS JUST...

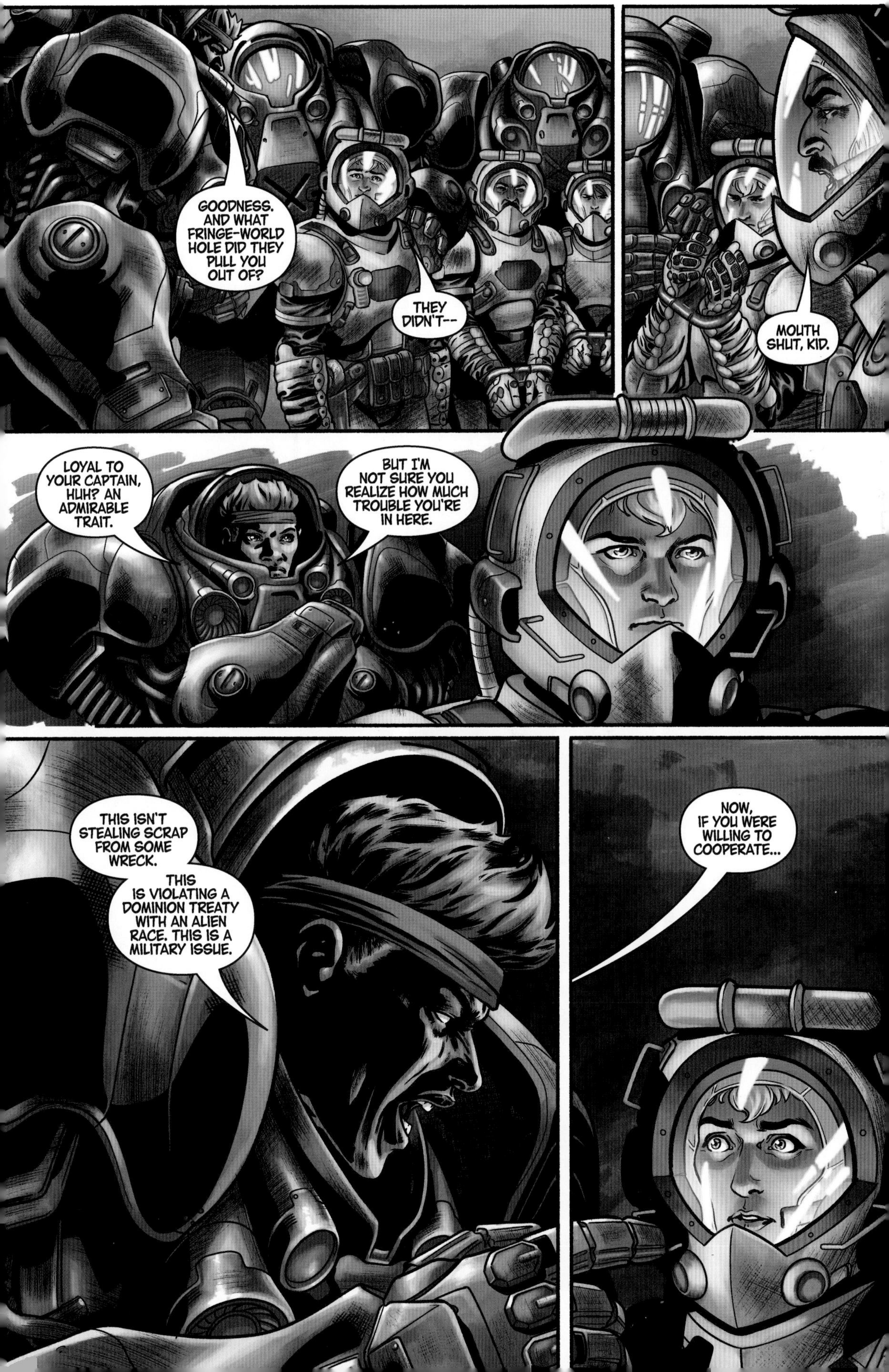
GOODNESS. AND WHAT FRINGE-WORLD HOLE DID THEY PULL YOU OUT OF?
THEY DIDN'T--
MOUTH SHUT, KID.
LOYAL TO YOUR CAPTAIN, HUH? AN ADMIRABLE TRAIT.
BUT I'M NOT SURE YOU REALIZE HOW MUCH TROUBLE YOU'RE IN HERE.
THIS ISN'T STEALING SCRAP FROM SOME WRECK.
THIS IS VIOLATING A DOMINION TREATY WITH AN ALIEN RACE. THIS IS A MILITARY ISSUE.
NOW, IF YOU WERE WILLING TO COOPERATE...

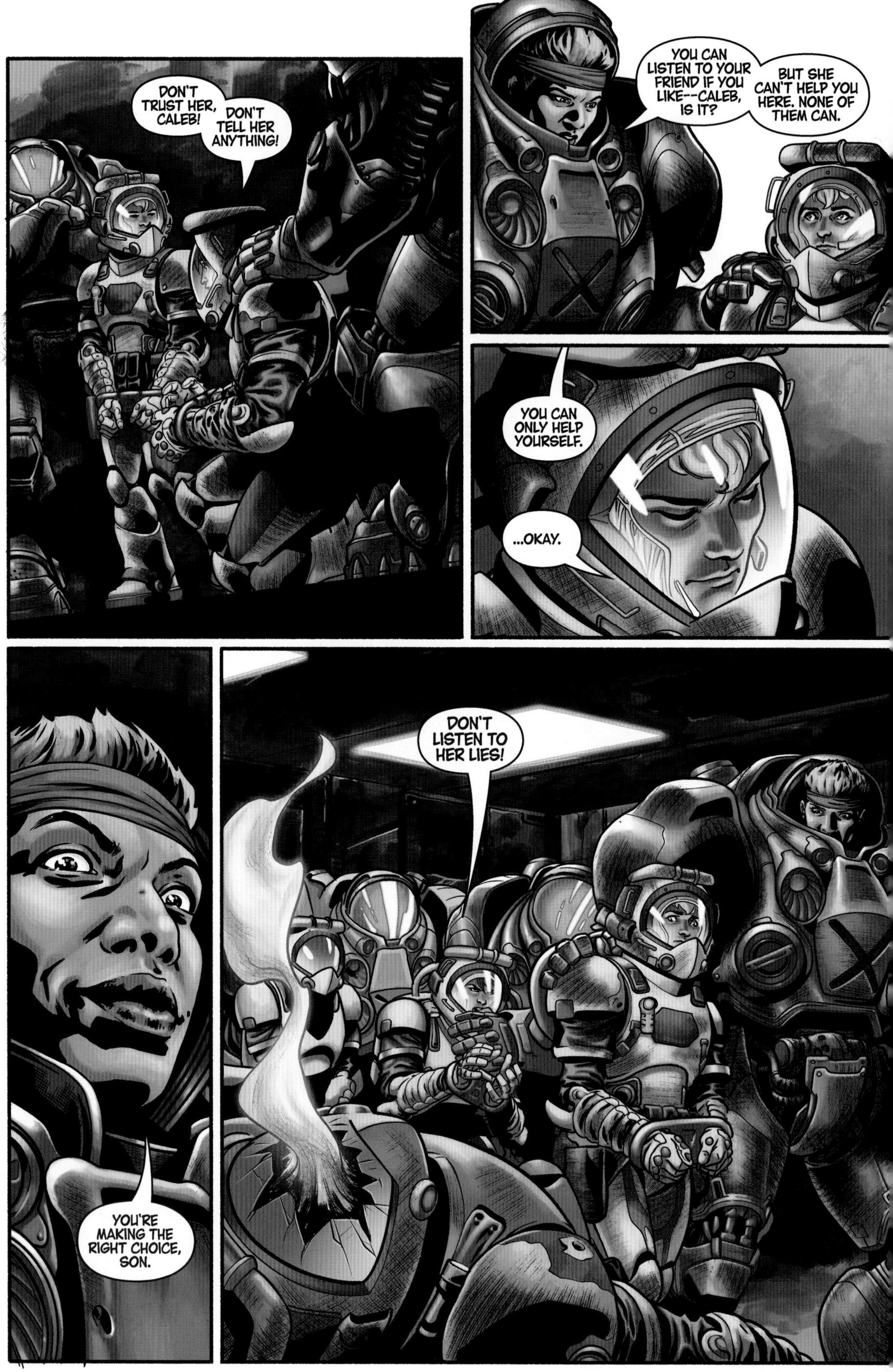
DON'T TRUST HER, CALEB!
DON'T TELL HER ANYTHING!
YOU CAN LISTEN TO YOUR FRIEND IF YOU LIKE--CALEB, IS IT?
BUT SHE CAN'T HELP YOU HERE. NONE OF THEM CAN.
YOU CAN ONLY HELP YOURSELF.
...OKAY.
YOU'RE MAKING THE RIGHT CHOICE, SON.
DON'T LISTEN TO HER LIES!

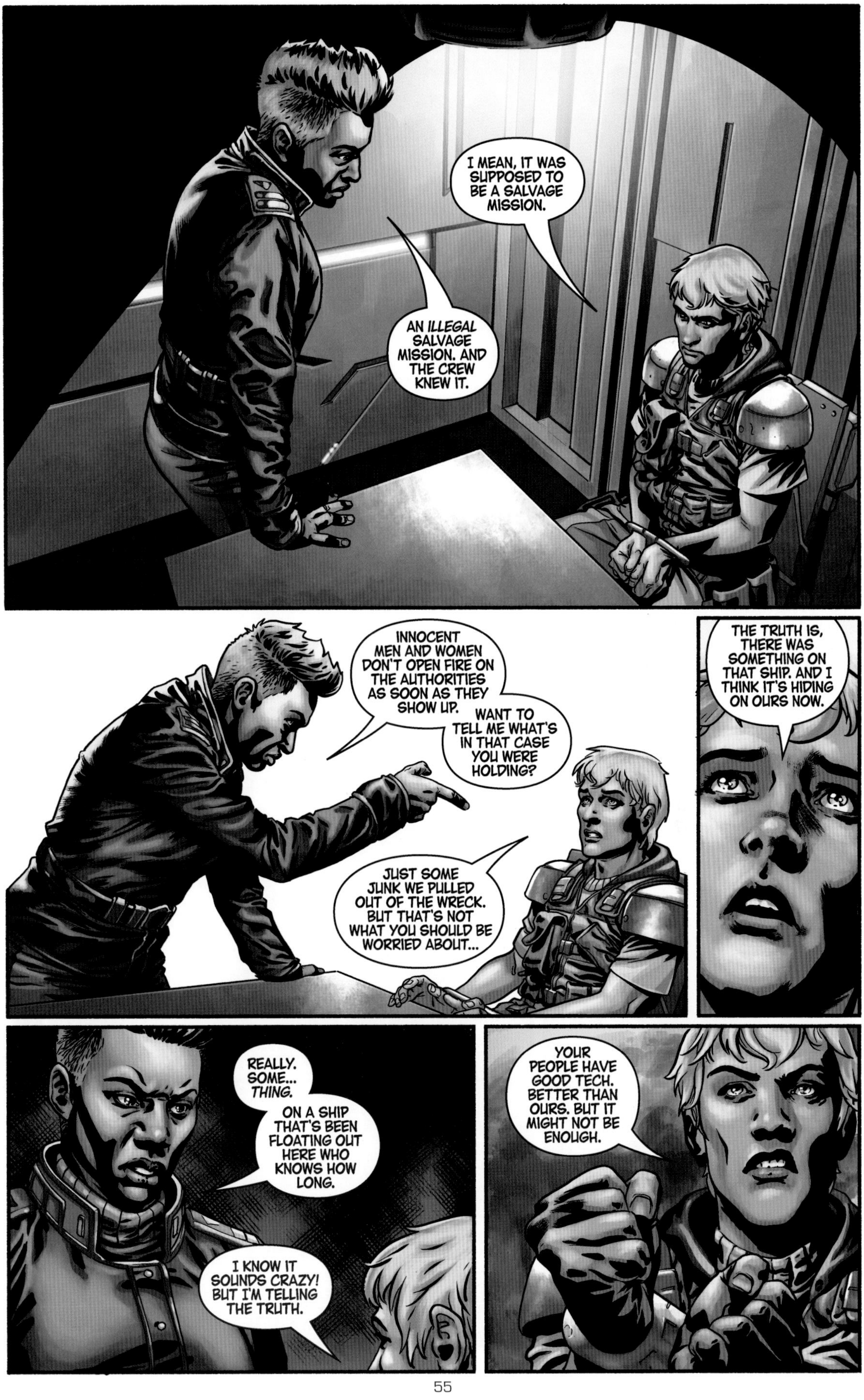
I MEAN, IT WAS SUPPOSED TO BE A SALVAGE MISSION.
AN *ILLEGAL* SALVAGE MISSION. AND THE CREW KNEW IT.
INNOCENT MEN AND WOMEN DON'T OPEN FIRE ON THE AUTHORITIES AS SOON AS THEY SHOW UP.
WANT TO TELL ME WHAT'S IN THAT CASE YOU WERE HOLDING?
JUST SOME JUNK WE PULLED OUT OF THE WRECK. BUT THAT'S NOT WHAT YOU SHOULD BE WORRIED ABOUT...
THE TRUTH IS, THERE WAS SOMETHING ON THAT SHIP. AND I THINK IT'S HIDING ON OURS NOW.
REALLY. SOME... *THING*.
ON A SHIP THAT'S BEEN FLOATING OUT HERE WHO KNOWS HOW LONG.
I KNOW IT SOUNDS CRAZY! BUT I'M TELLING THE TRUTH.
YOUR PEOPLE HAVE GOOD TECH. BETTER THAN OURS. BUT IT MIGHT NOT BE ENOUGH.

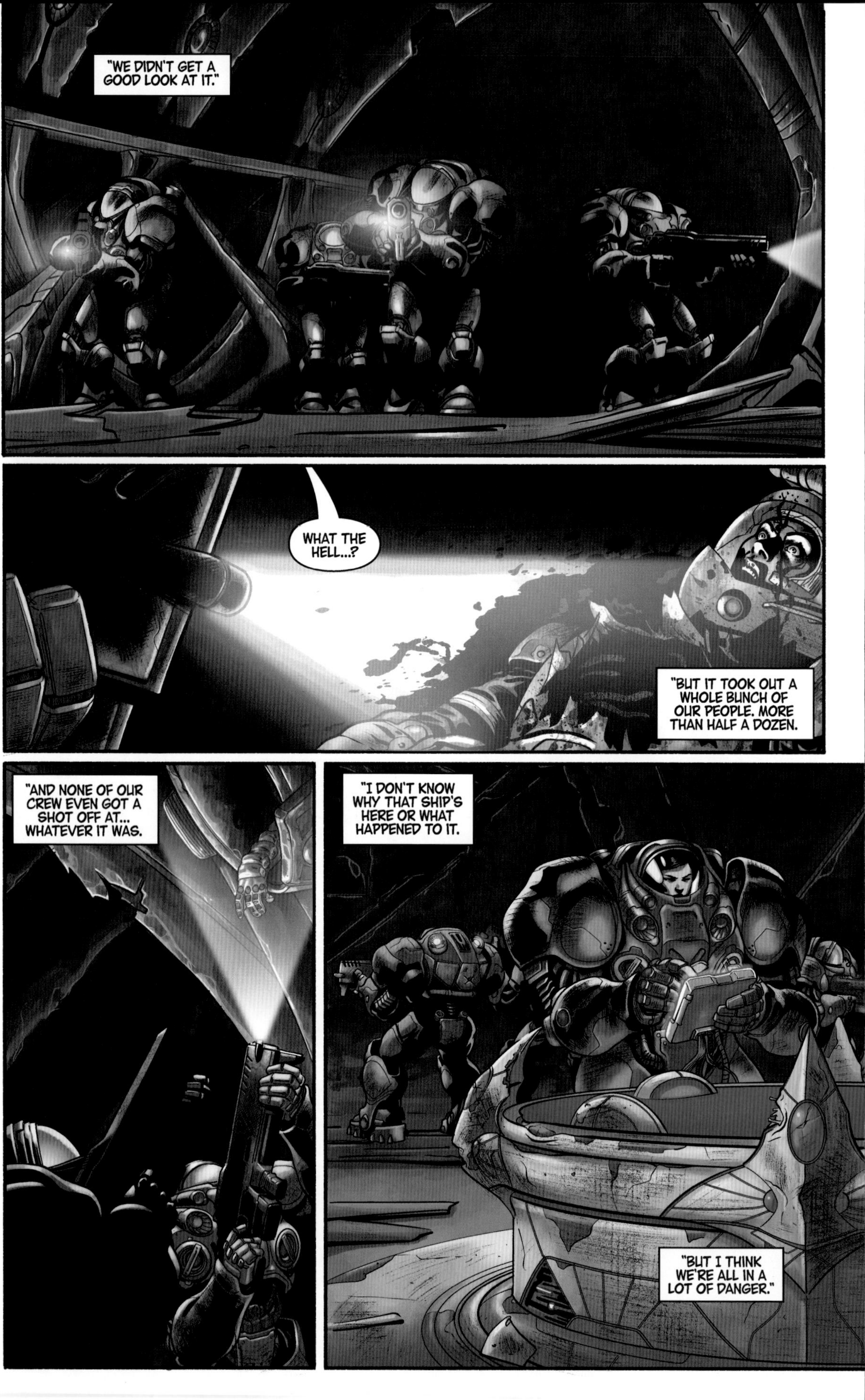
"WE DIDN'T GET A GOOD LOOK AT IT."
WHAT THE HELL...?
"BUT IT TOOK OUT A WHOLE BUNCH OF OUR PEOPLE. MORE THAN HALF A DOZEN.
"AND NONE OF OUR CREW EVEN GOT A SHOT OFF AT... WHATEVER IT WAS.
"I DON'T KNOW WHY THAT SHIP'S HERE OR WHAT HAPPENED TO IT.
"BUT I THINK WE'RE ALL IN A LOT OF DANGER."

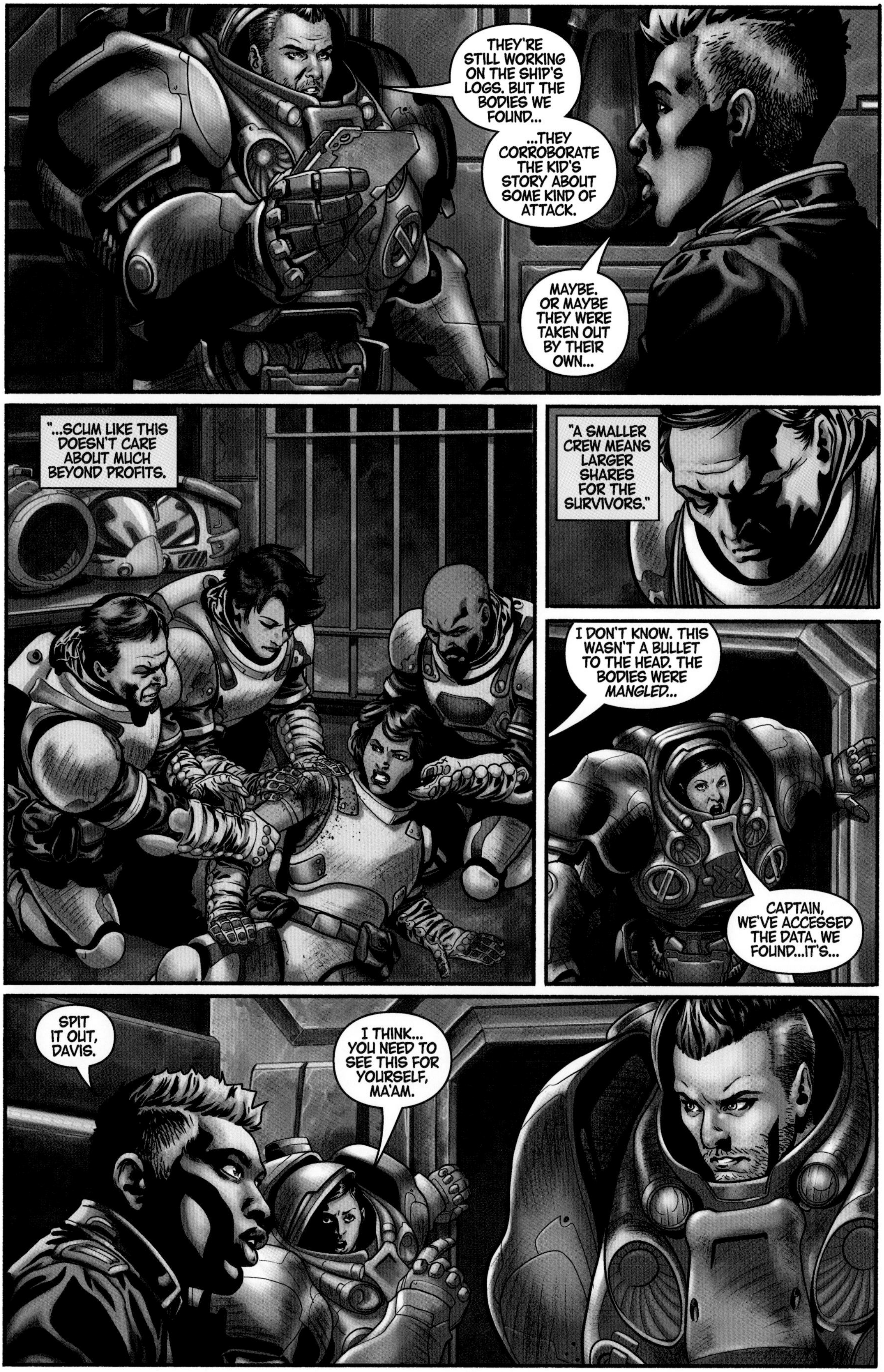
THEY'RE STILL WORKING ON THE SHIP'S LOGS. BUT THE BODIES WE FOUND...
...THEY CORROBORATE THE KID'S STORY ABOUT SOME KIND OF ATTACK.
MAYBE. OR MAYBE THEY WERE TAKEN OUT BY THEIR OWN...
"...SCUM LIKE THIS DOESN'T CARE ABOUT MUCH BEYOND PROFITS.
"A SMALLER CREW MEANS LARGER SHARES FOR THE SURVIVORS."
I DON'T KNOW. THIS WASN'T A BULLET TO THE HEAD. THE BODIES WERE MANGLED...
CAPTAIN, WE'VE ACCESSED THE DATA. WE FOUND...IT'S...
SPIT IT OUT, DAVIS.
I THINK... YOU NEED TO SEE THIS FOR YOURSELF, MA'AM.

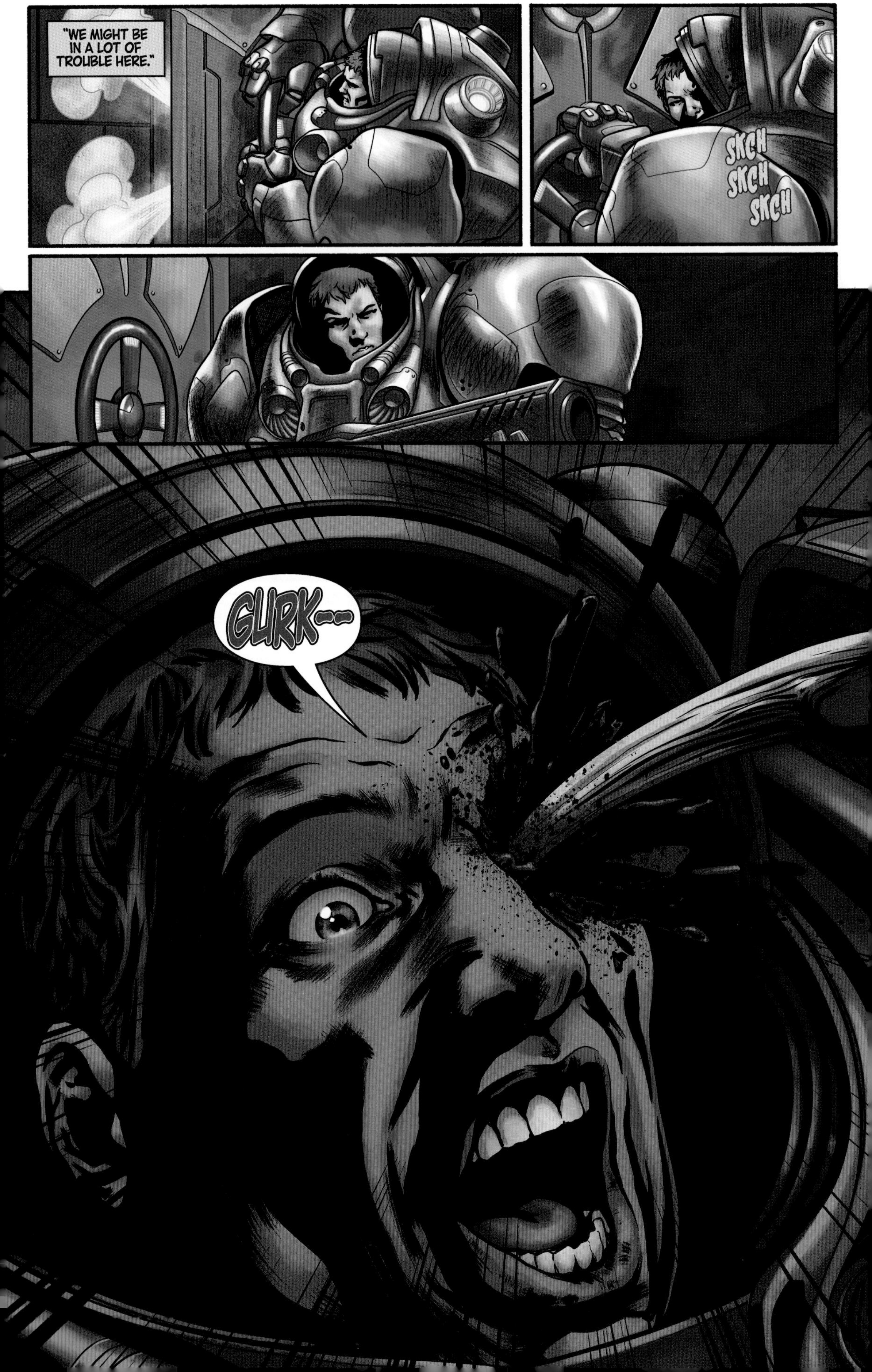
"WE MIGHT BE IN A LOT OF TROUBLE HERE."
SKCH SKCH SKCH
GURK--

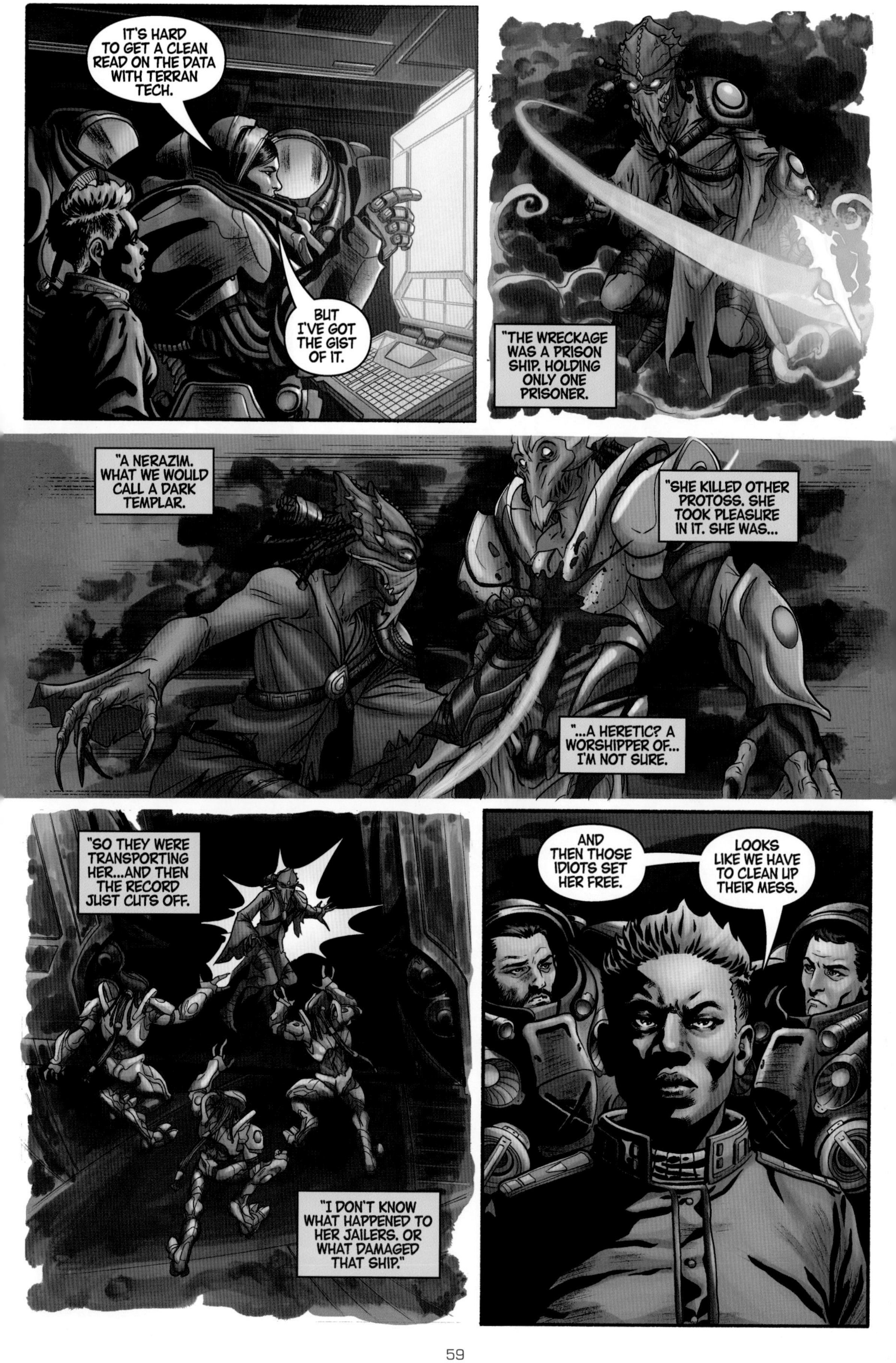
IT'S HARD TO GET A CLEAN READ ON THE DATA WITH TERRAN TECH.
BUT I'VE GOT THE GIST OF IT.
"THE WRECKAGE WAS A PRISON SHIP. HOLDING ONLY ONE PRISONER.
"A NERAZIM. WHAT WE WOULD CALL A DARK TEMPLAR.
"SHE KILLED OTHER PROTOSS. SHE TOOK PLEASURE IN IT. SHE WAS...
"...A HERETIC? A WORSHIPPER OF... I'M NOT SURE.
"SO THEY WERE TRANSPORTING HER...AND THEN THE RECORD JUST CUTS OFF.
"I DON'T KNOW WHAT HAPPENED TO HER JAILERS. OR WHAT DAMAGED THAT SHIP."
AND THEN THOSE IDIOTS SET HER FREE.
LOOKS LIKE WE HAVE TO CLEAN UP THEIR MESS.

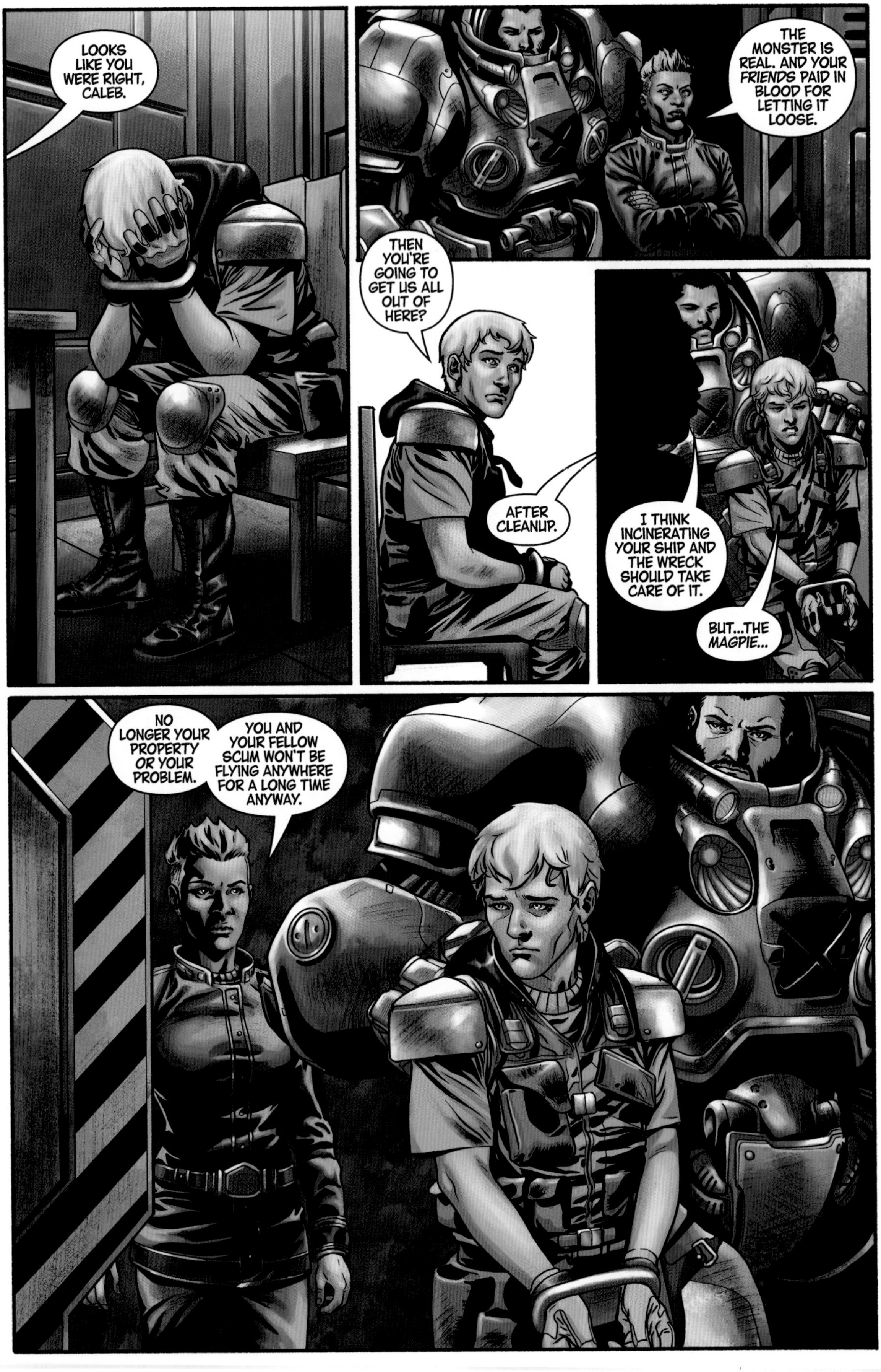

LOOKS LIKE YOU WERE RIGHT, CALEB.
THE MONSTER IS REAL. AND YOUR FRIENDS PAID IN BLOOD FOR LETTING IT LOOSE.
THEN YOU'RE GOING TO GET US ALL OUT OF HERE?
AFTER CLEANUP.
I THINK INCINERATING YOUR SHIP AND THE WRECK SHOULD TAKE CARE OF IT.
BUT...THE MAGPIE...
NO LONGER YOUR PROPERTY OR YOUR PROBLEM.
YOU AND YOUR FELLOW SCUM WON'T BE FLYING ANYWHERE FOR A LONG TIME ANYWAY.

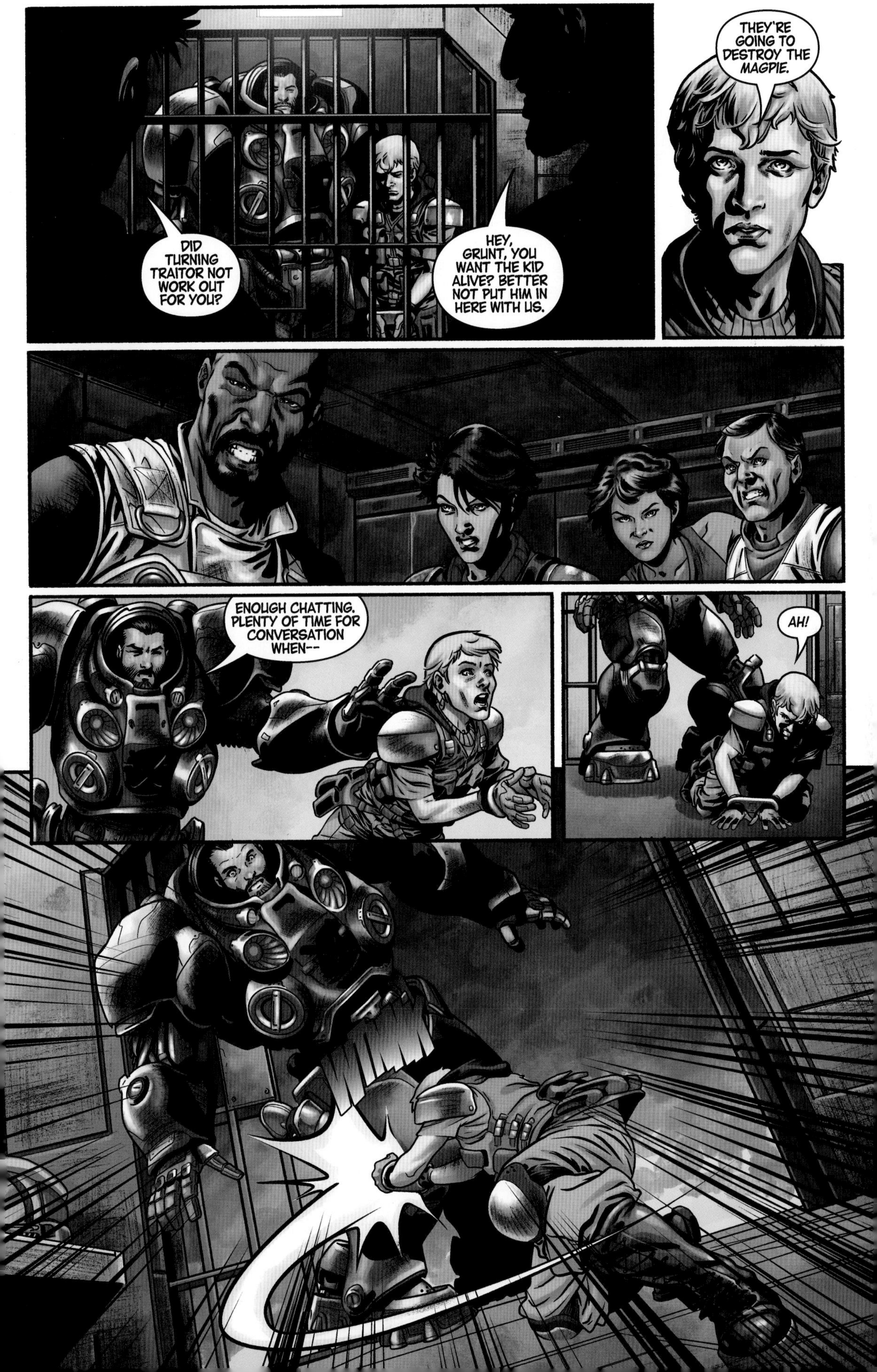
DID TURNING TRAITOR NOT WORK OUT FOR YOU?
HEY, GRUNT, YOU WANT THE KID ALIVE? BETTER NOT PUT HIM IN HERE WITH US.
THEY'RE GOING TO DESTROY THE MAGPIE.
ENOUGH CHATTING. PLENTY OF TIME FOR CONVERSATION WHEN--
AH!

HALT, OR--

GAAH!

DON'T CARE IF YOU HAD A CHANGE OF HEART OR YOU PLANNED THIS ALL ALONG.

BLAM

DON'T BETRAY ME AGAIN.

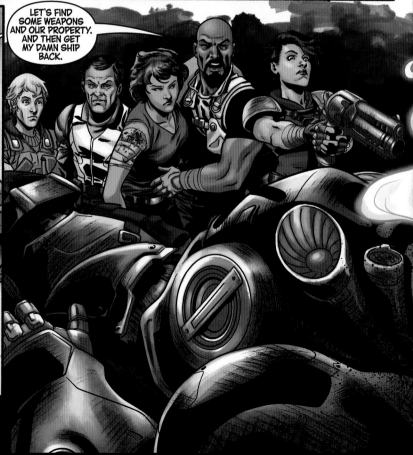

LET'S FIND SOME WEAPONS AND OUR PROPERTY. AND THEN GET MY DAMN SHIP BACK.

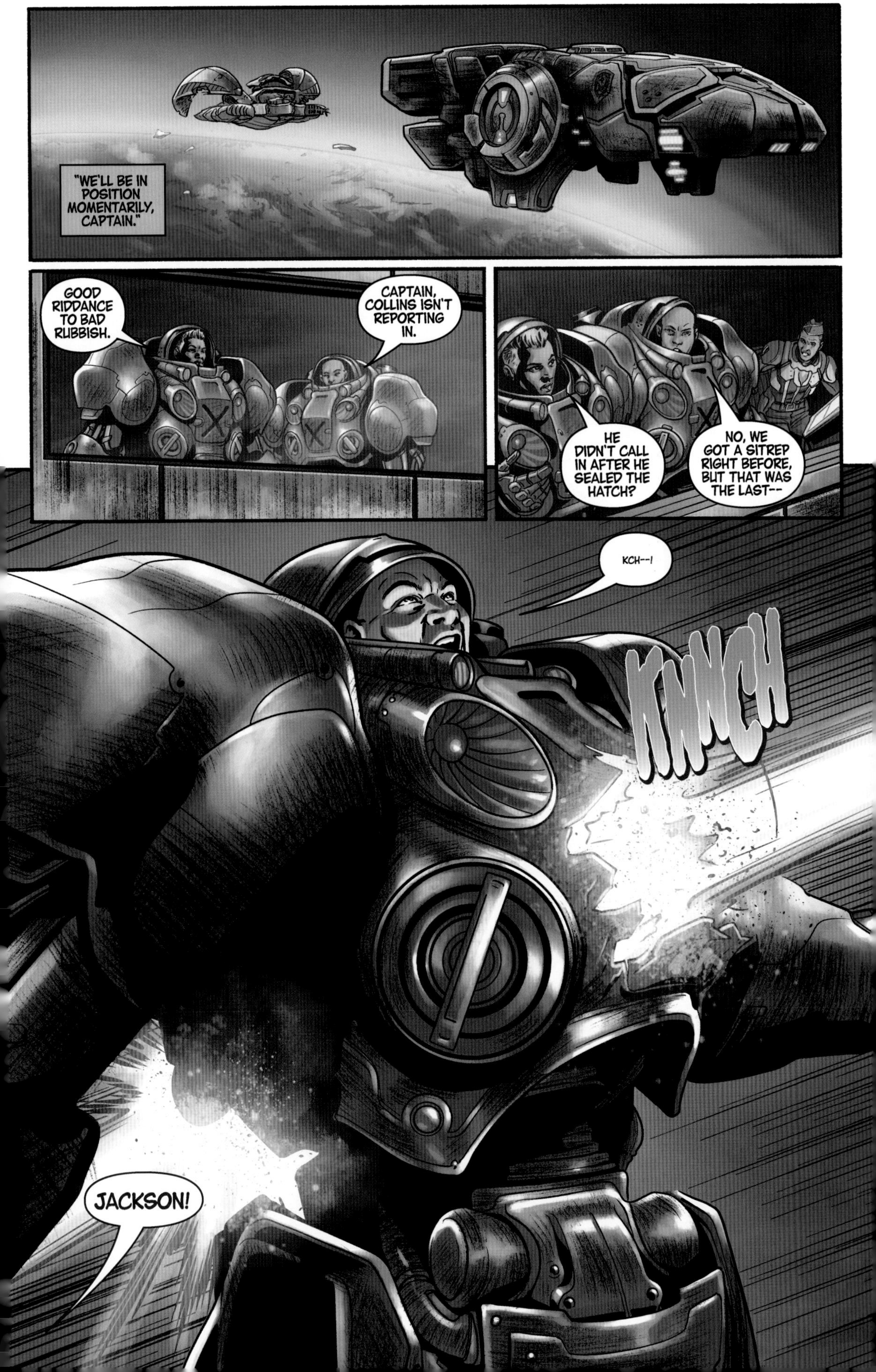
"WE'LL BE IN POSITION MOMENTARILY, CAPTAIN."
GOOD RIDDANCE TO BAD RUBBISH.
CAPTAIN, COLLINS ISN'T REPORTING IN.
HE DIDN'T CALL IN AFTER HE SEALED THE HATCH?
NO, WE GOT A SITREP RIGHT BEFORE, BUT THAT WAS THE LAST--
KCH--!
KNNCH
JACKSON!

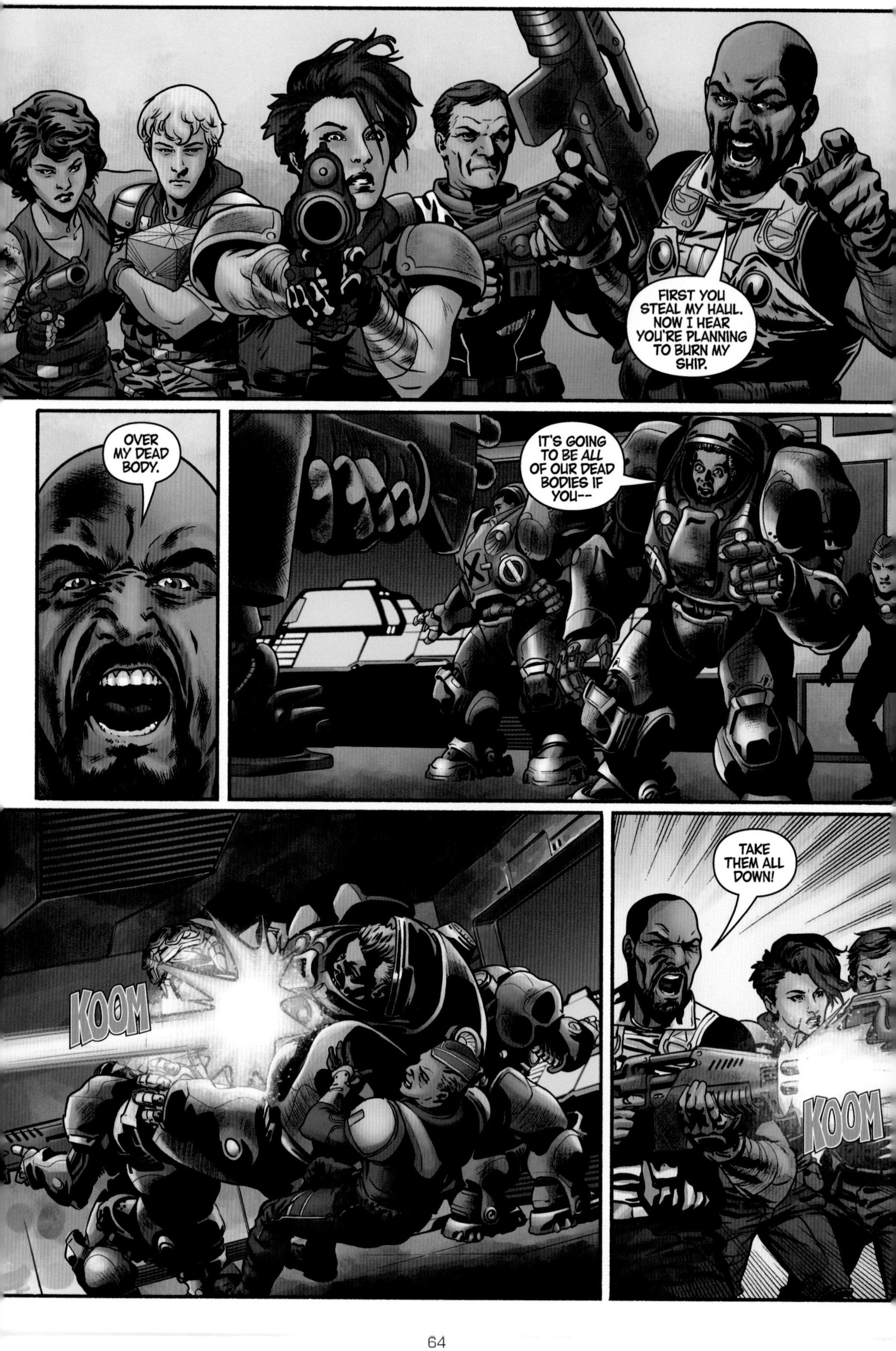
FIRST YOU STEAL MY HAUL. NOW I HEAR YOU'RE PLANNING TO BURN MY SHIP.
OVER MY DEAD BODY.
IT'S GOING TO BE ALL OF OUR DEAD BODIES IF YOU--
KOOM
TAKE THEM ALL DOWN!
KOOM

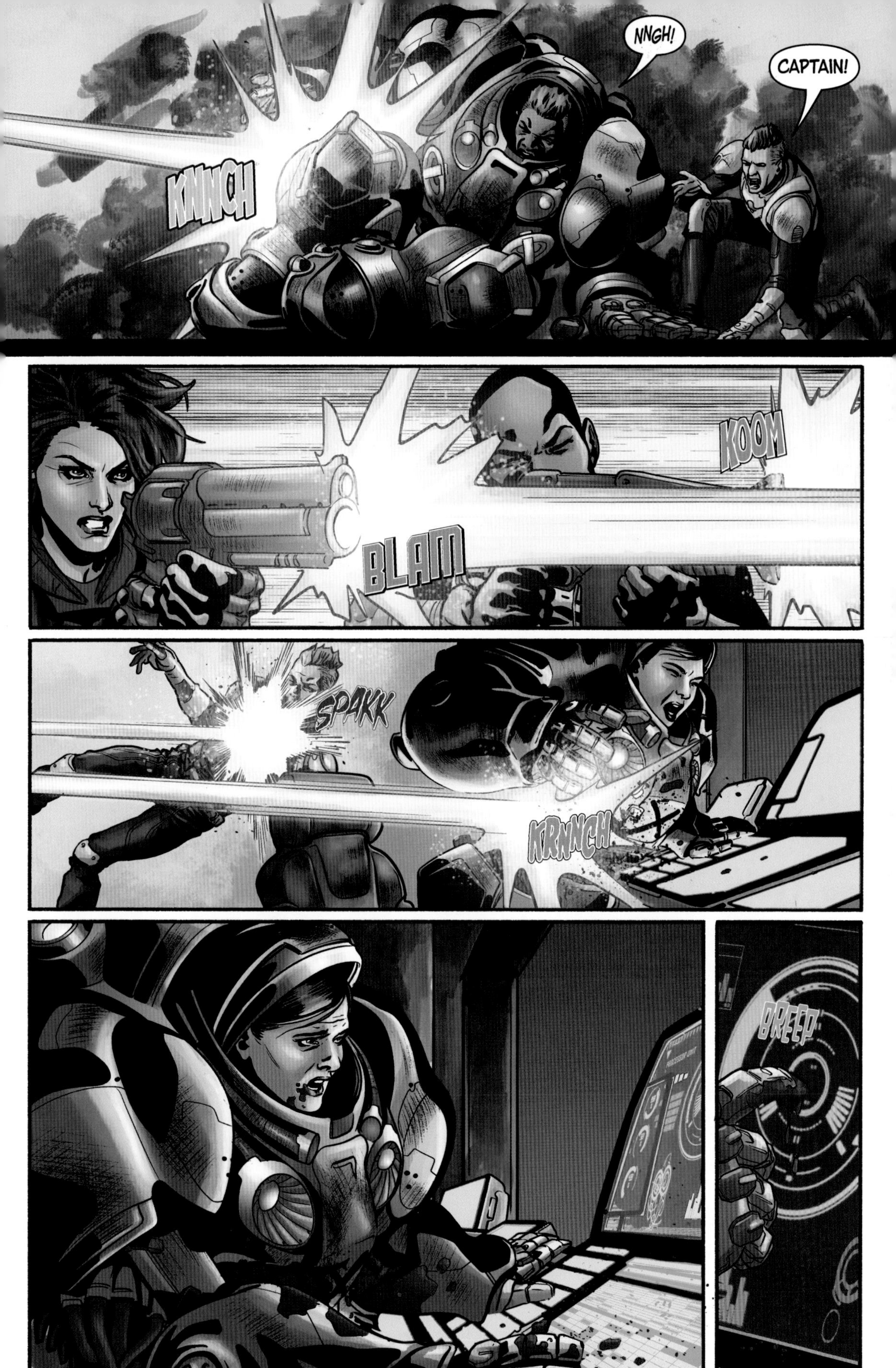
NNGH!
CAPTAIN!
KNNCH
KOOM
BLAM
SPAKK
KRNNCH
BREEP

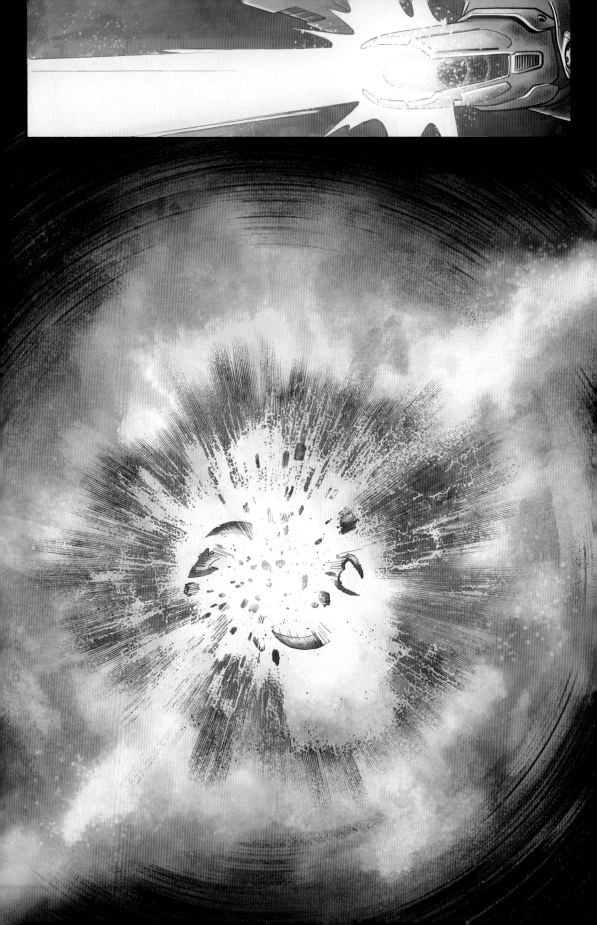

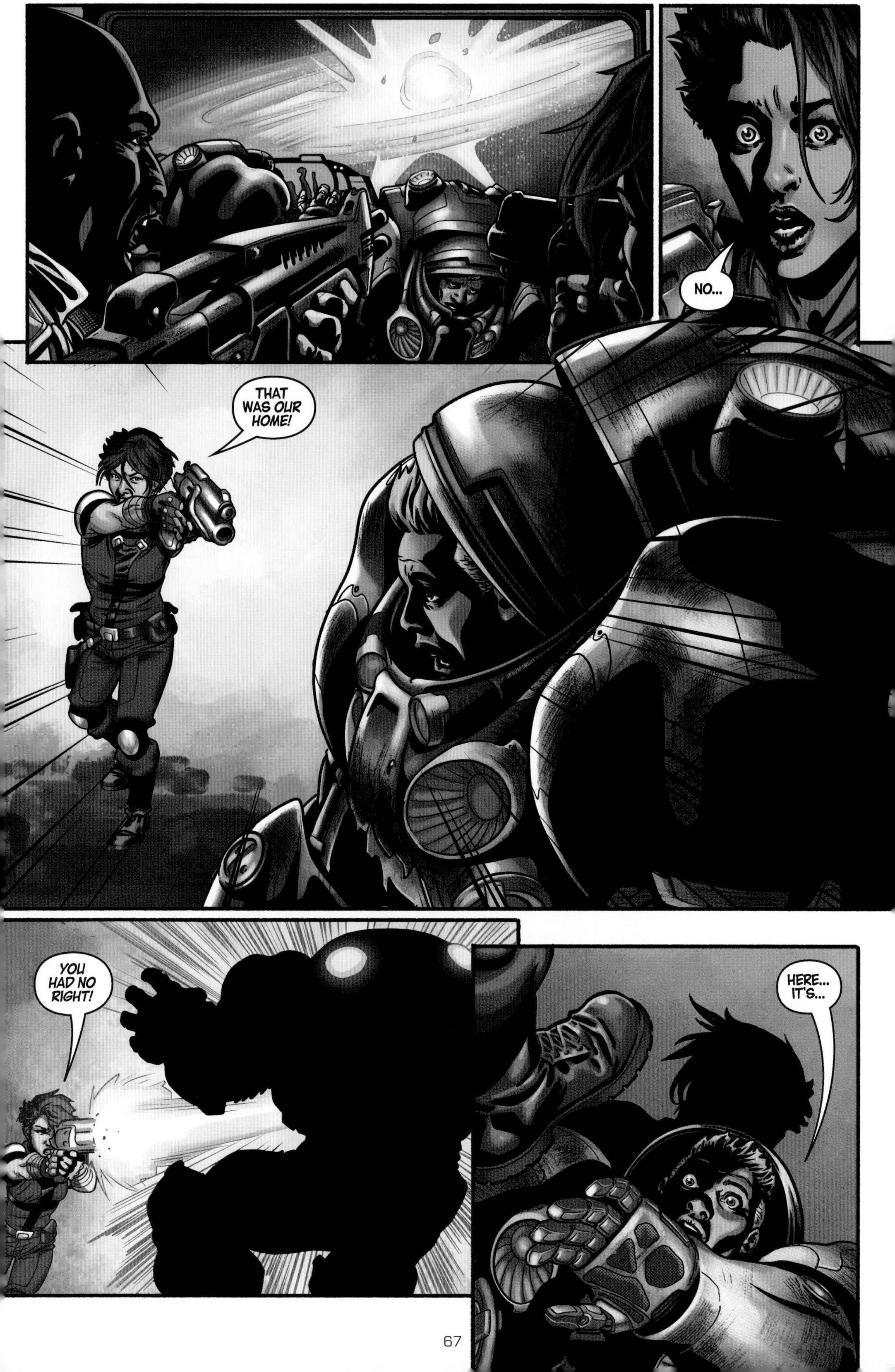
NO...
THAT WAS OUR HOME!
YOU HAD NO RIGHT!
HERE... IT'S...

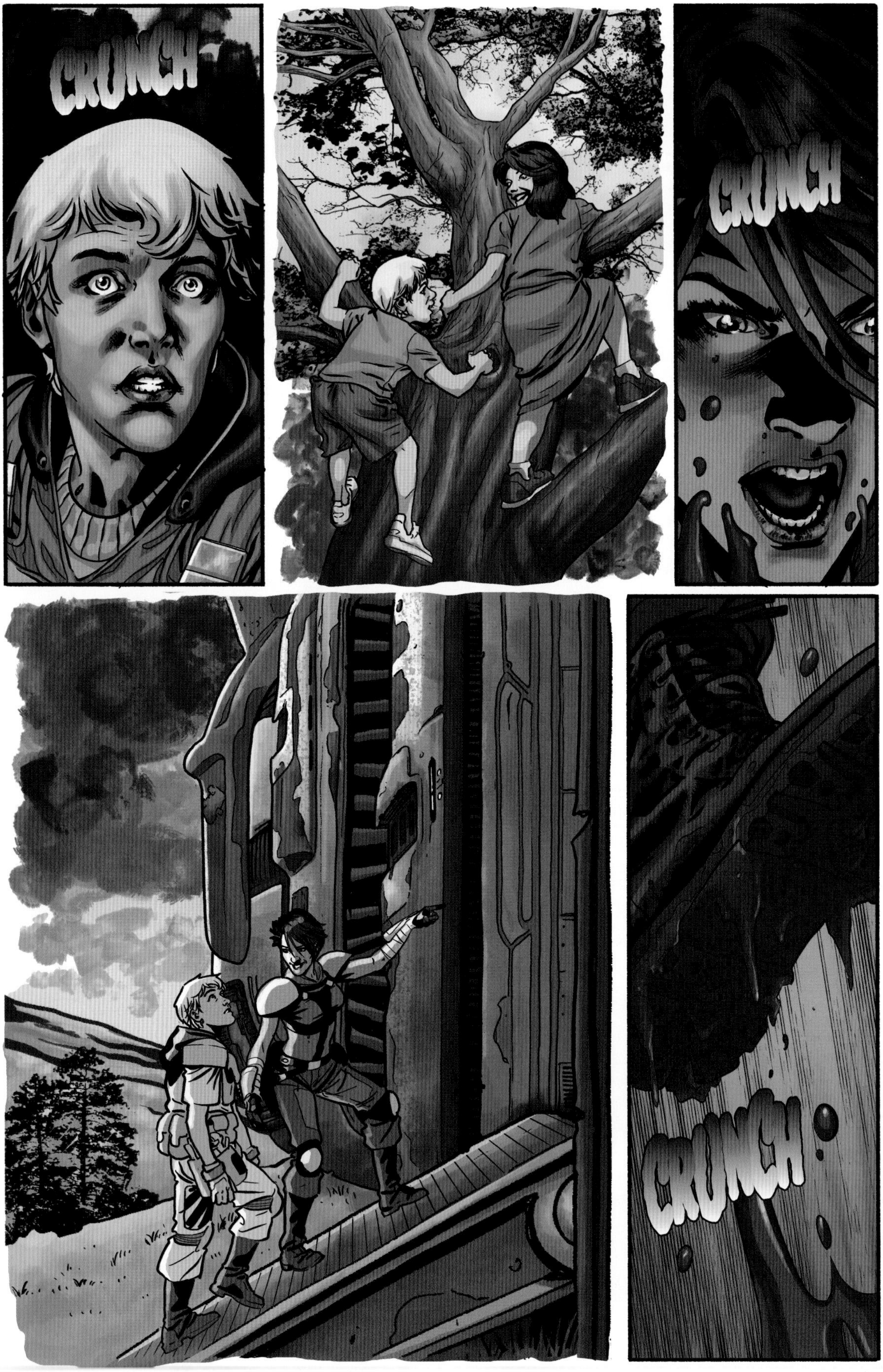
CRUNCH
CRUNCH
CRUNCH

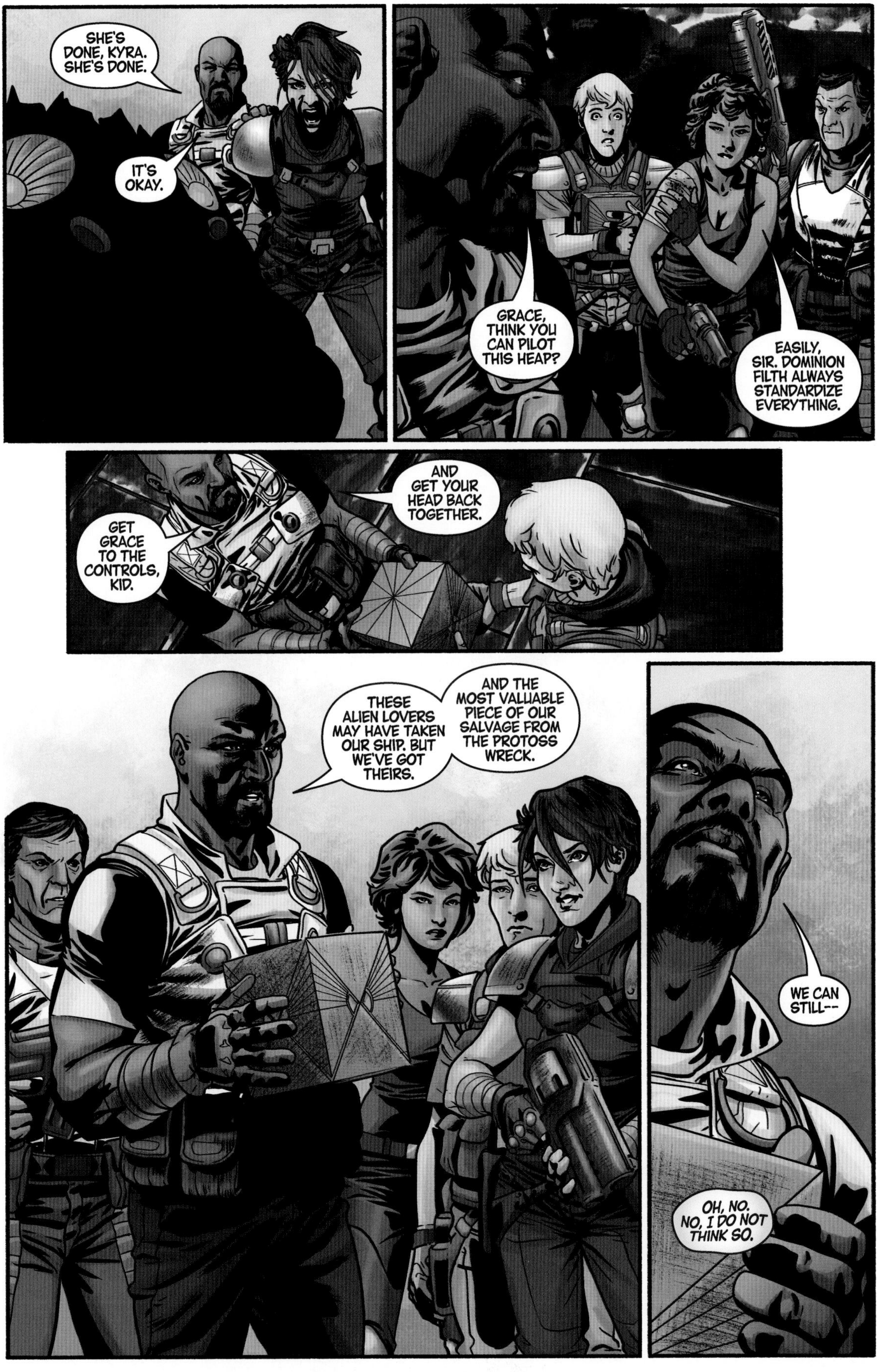
SHE'S DONE, KYRA. SHE'S DONE.
IT'S OKAY.
GRACE, THINK YOU CAN PILOT THIS HEAP?
EASILY, SIR. DOMINION FILTH ALWAYS STANDARDIZE EVERYTHING.
GET GRACE TO THE CONTROLS, KID.
AND GET YOUR HEAD BACK TOGETHER.
THESE ALIEN LOVERS MAY HAVE TAKEN OUR SHIP. BUT WE'VE GOT THEIRS.
AND THE MOST VALUABLE PIECE OF OUR SALVAGE FROM THE PROTOSS WRECK.
WE CAN STILL--
OH, NO. NO, I DO NOT THINK SO.

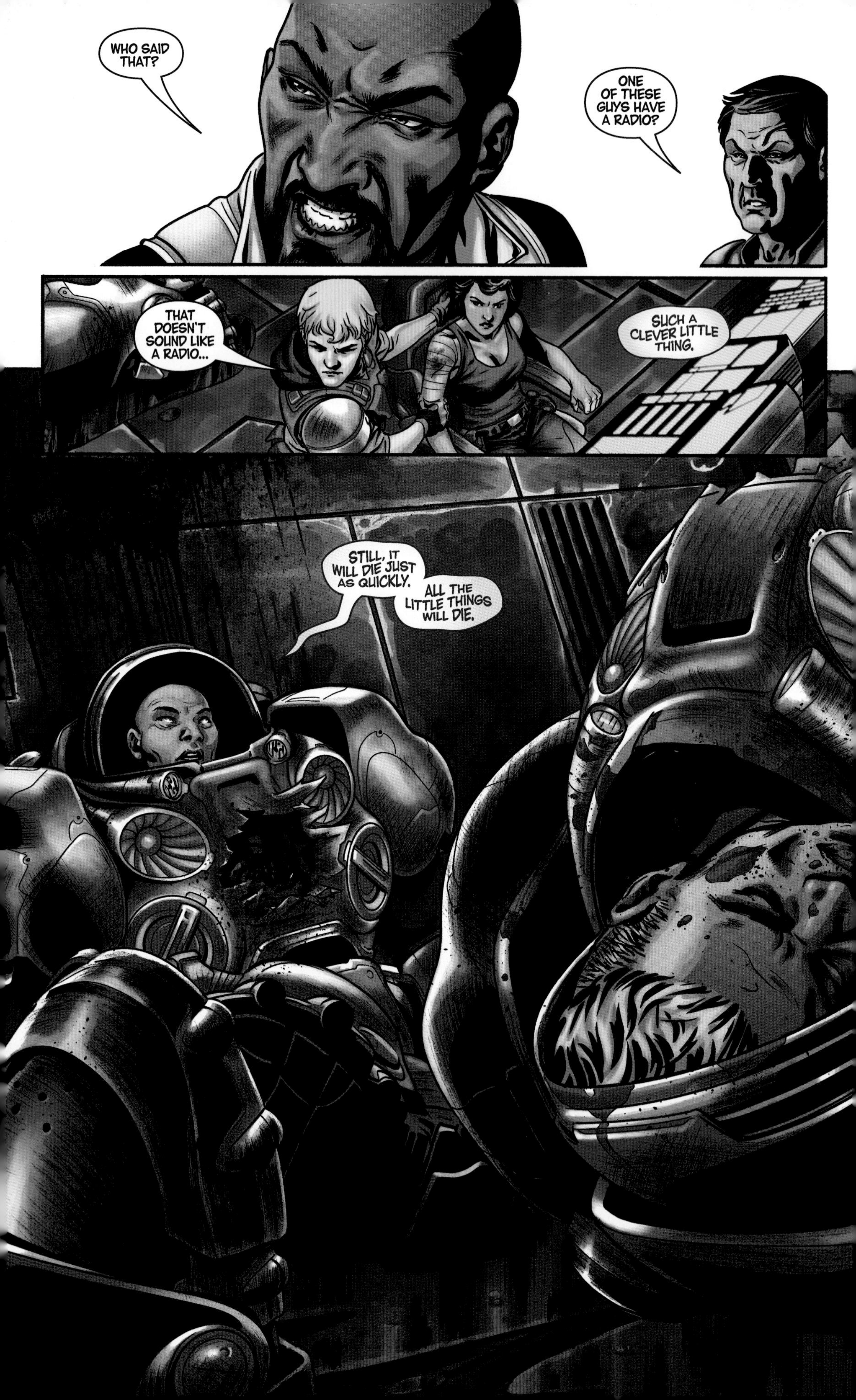
WHO SAID THAT?
ONE OF THESE GUYS HAVE A RADIO?
THAT DOESN'T SOUND LIKE A RADIO...
SUCH A CLEVER LITTLE THING.
STILL, IT WILL DIE JUST AS QUICKLY.
ALL THE LITTLE THINGS WILL DIE.

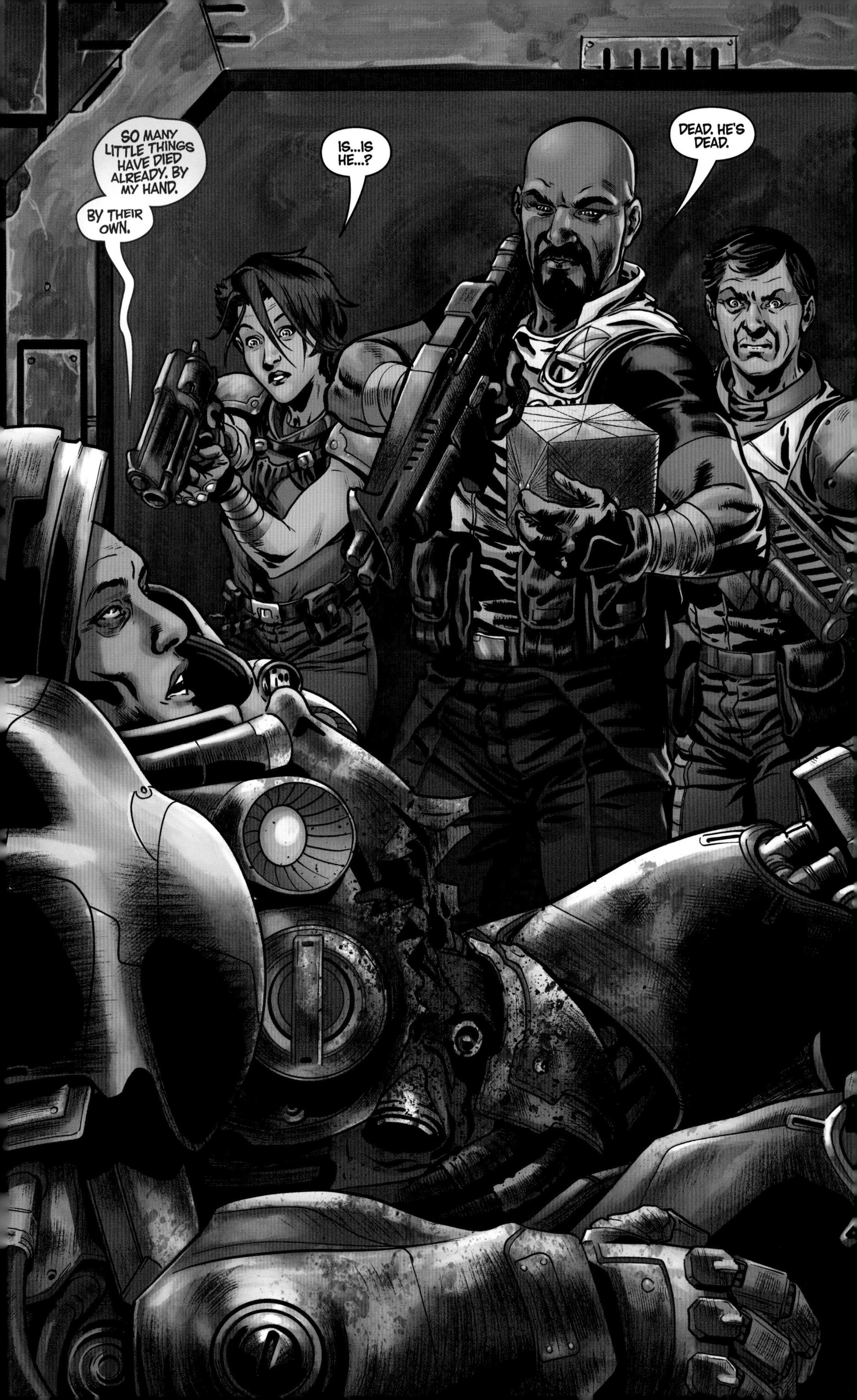
SO MANY LITTLE THINGS HAVE DIED ALREADY. BY MY HAND.
BY THEIR OWN.
IS...IS HE...?
DEAD. HE'S DEAD.

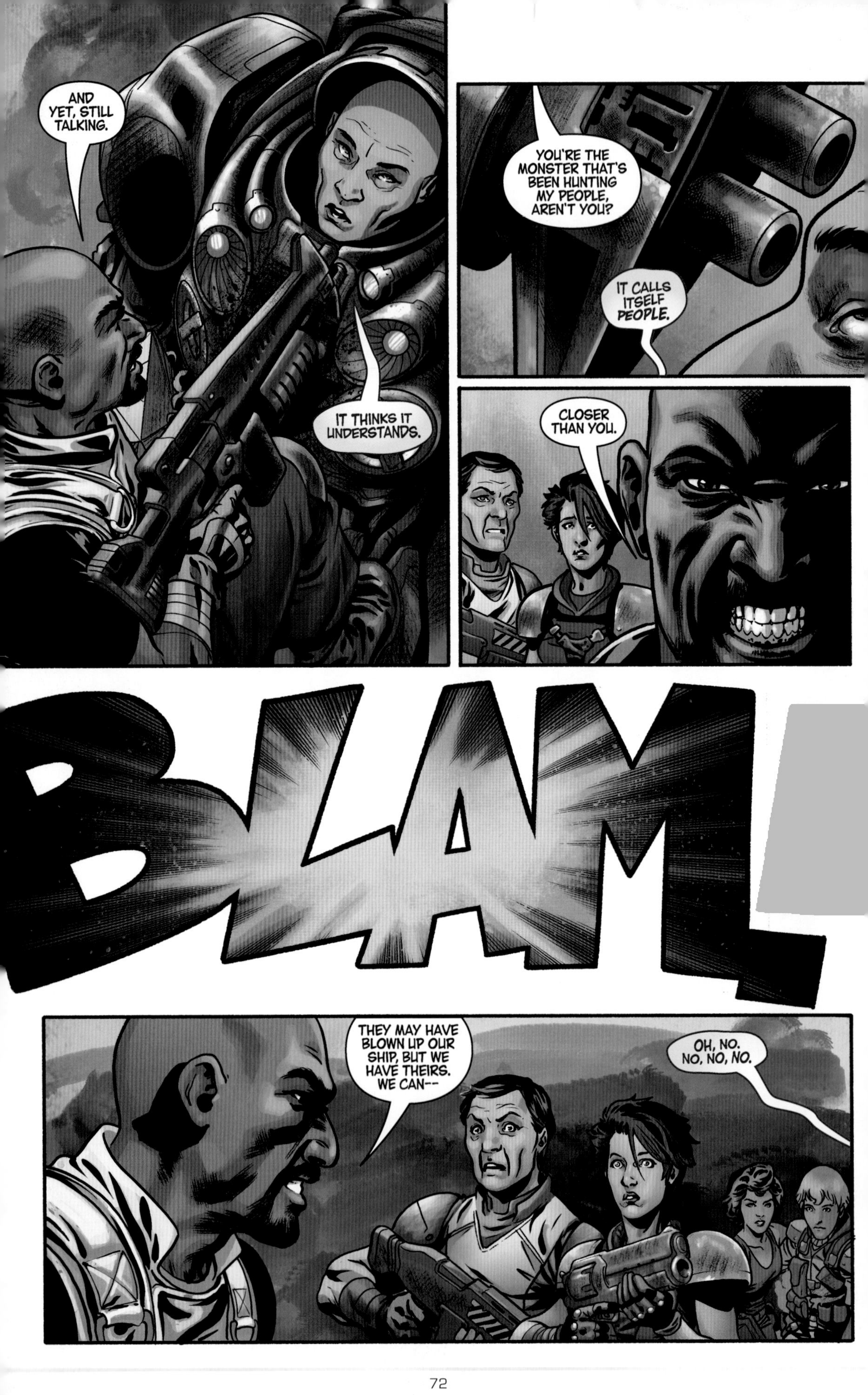
AND YET, STILL TALKING.
IT THINKS IT UNDERSTANDS.
YOU'RE THE MONSTER THAT'S BEEN HUNTING MY PEOPLE, AREN'T YOU?
IT CALLS ITSELF PEOPLE.
CLOSER THAN YOU.
BLAM
THEY MAY HAVE BLOWN UP OUR SHIP, BUT WE HAVE THEIRS. WE CAN--
OH, NO. NO, NO, NO.

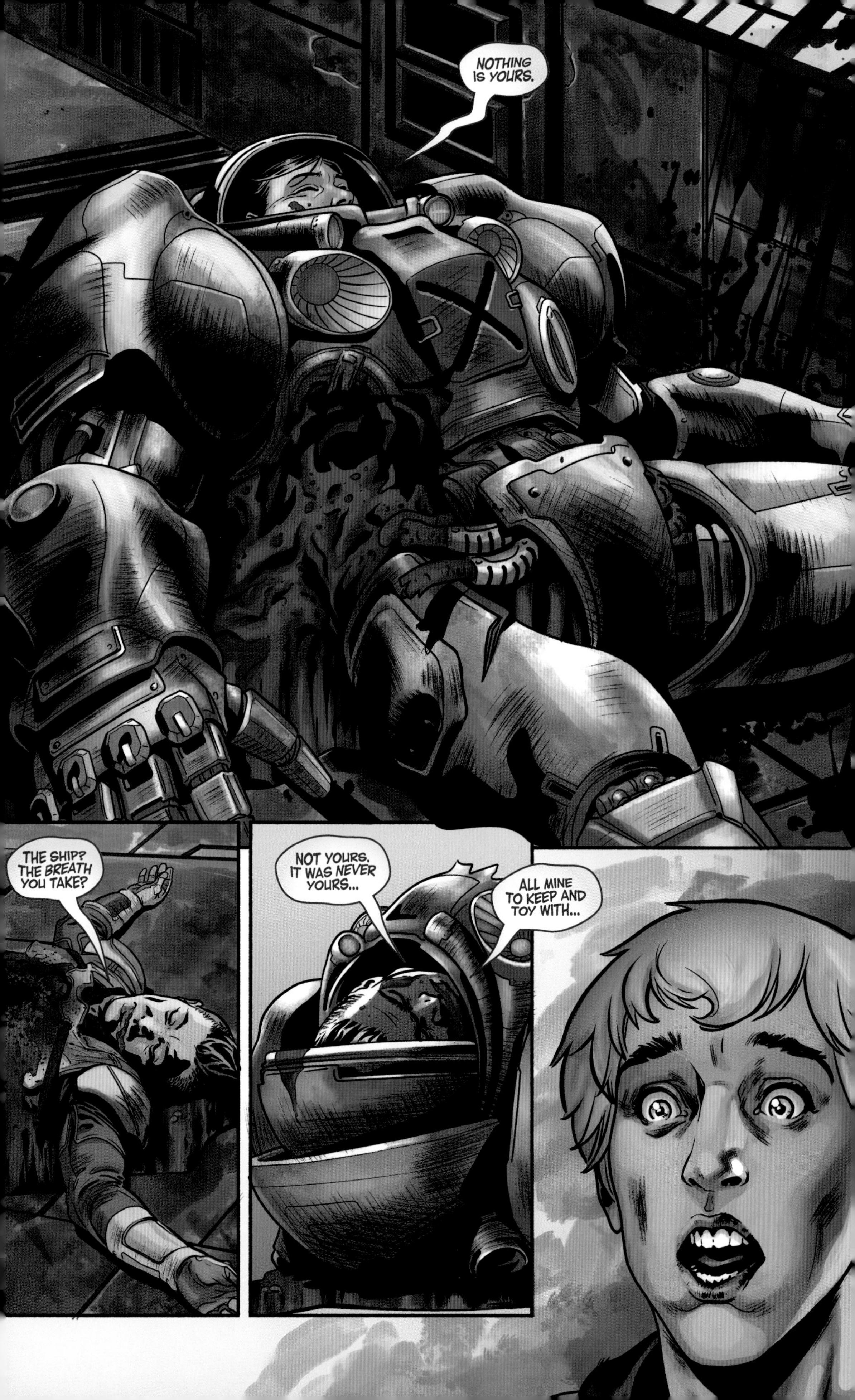
NOTHING IS YOURS.
THE SHIP? THE BREATH YOU TAKE?
NOT YOURS. IT WAS NEVER YOURS...
ALL MINE TO KEEP AND TOY WITH...

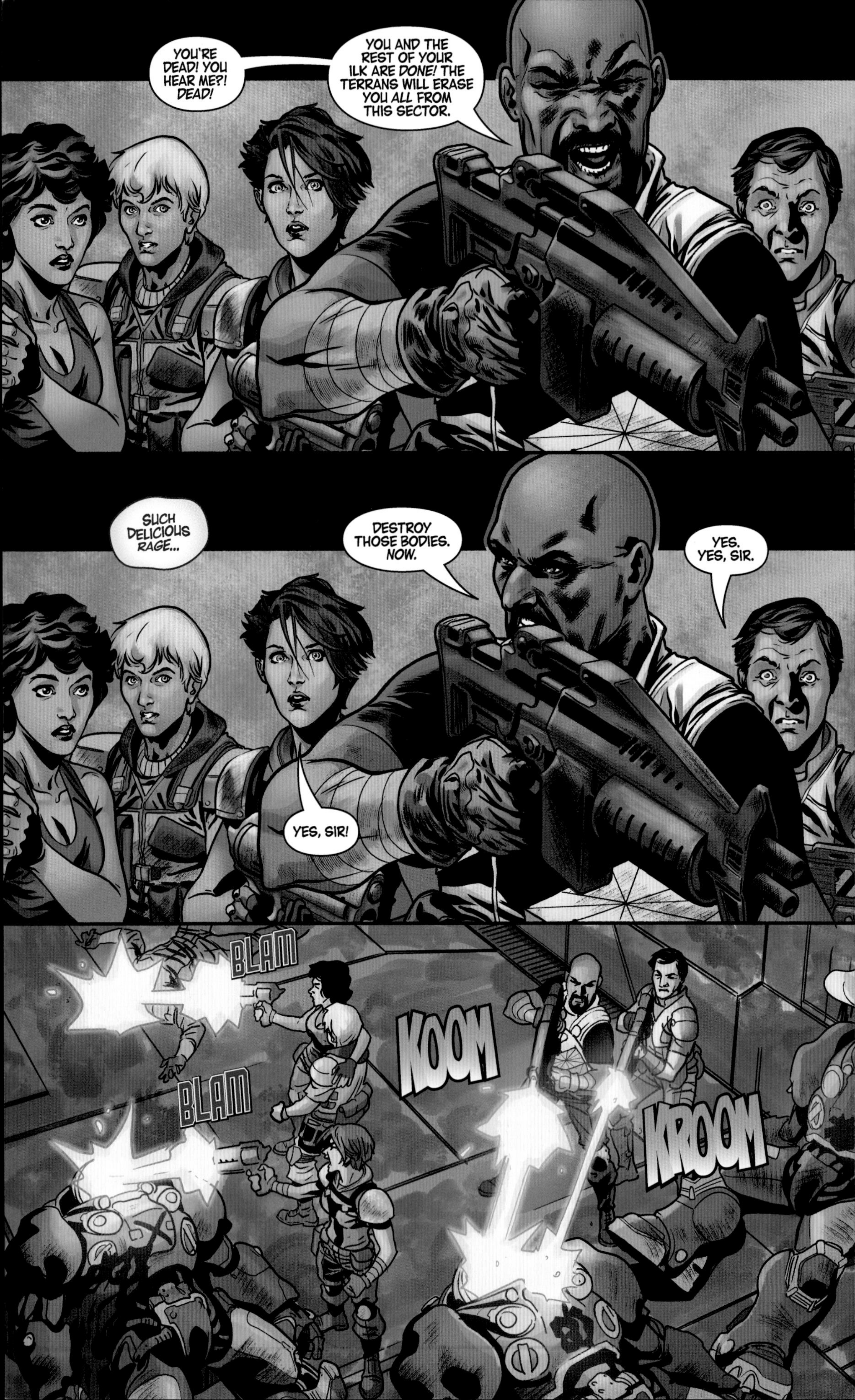
YOU'RE DEAD! YOU HEAR ME?! DEAD!
YOU AND THE REST OF YOUR ILK ARE DONE! THE TERRANS WILL ERASE YOU ALL FROM THIS SECTOR.
SUCH DELICIOUS RAGE...
DESTROY THOSE BODIES. NOW.
YES. YES, SIR.
YES, SIR!
BLAM
BLAM
KOOM
KROOM

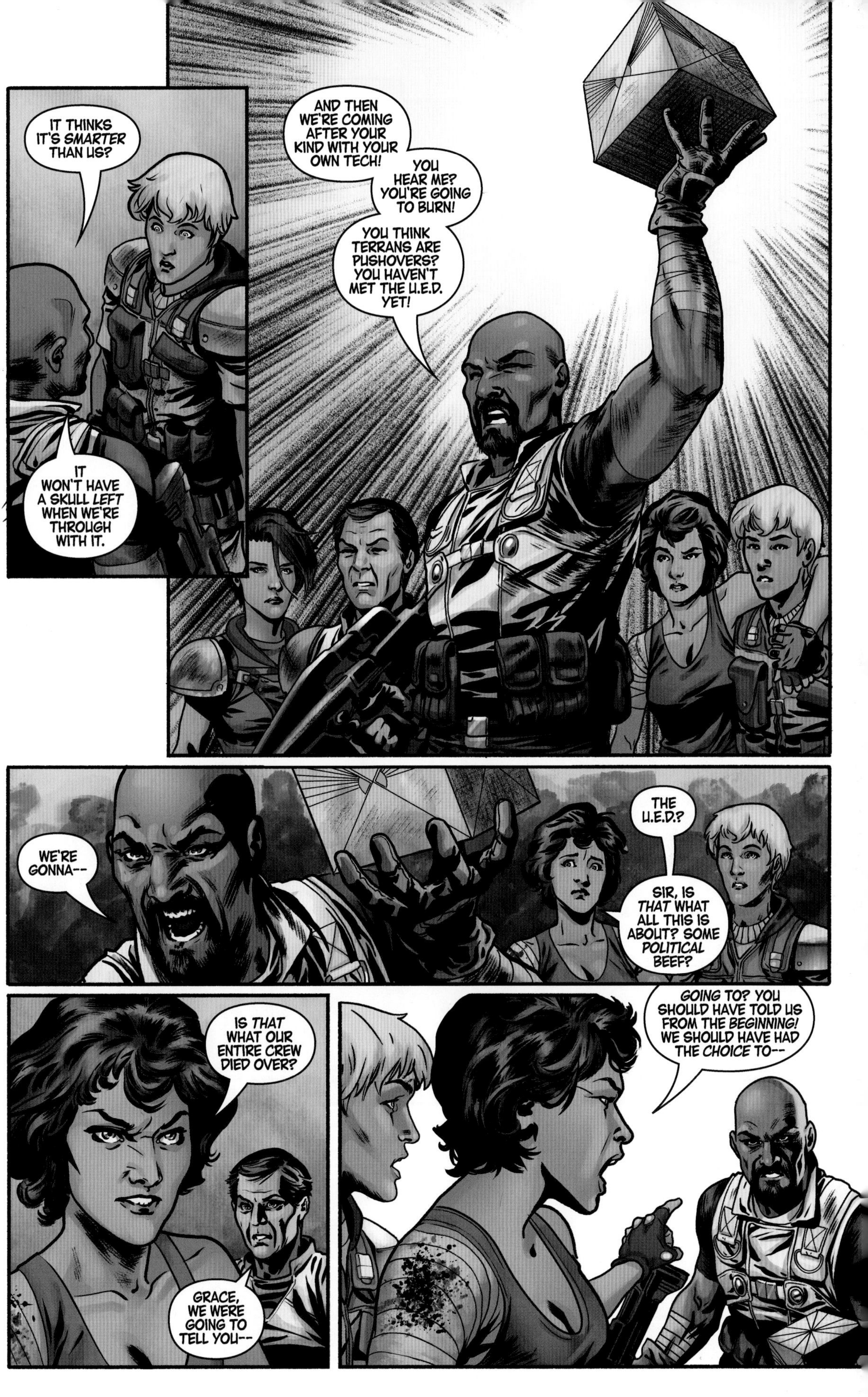

IT THINKS IT'S SMARTER THAN US?
IT WON'T HAVE A SKULL LEFT WHEN WE'RE THROUGH WITH IT.
AND THEN WE'RE COMING AFTER YOUR KIND WITH YOUR OWN TECH!
YOU HEAR ME? YOU'RE GOING TO BURN!
YOU THINK TERRANS ARE PUSHOVERS? YOU HAVEN'T MET THE U.E.D. YET!
WE'RE GONNA--
THE U.E.D.?
SIR, IS THAT WHAT ALL THIS IS ABOUT? SOME POLITICAL BEEF?
IS THAT WHAT OUR ENTIRE CREW DIED OVER?
GRACE, WE WERE GOING TO TELL YOU--
GOING TO? YOU SHOULD HAVE TOLD US FROM THE BEGINNING! WE SHOULD HAVE HAD THE CHOICE TO--

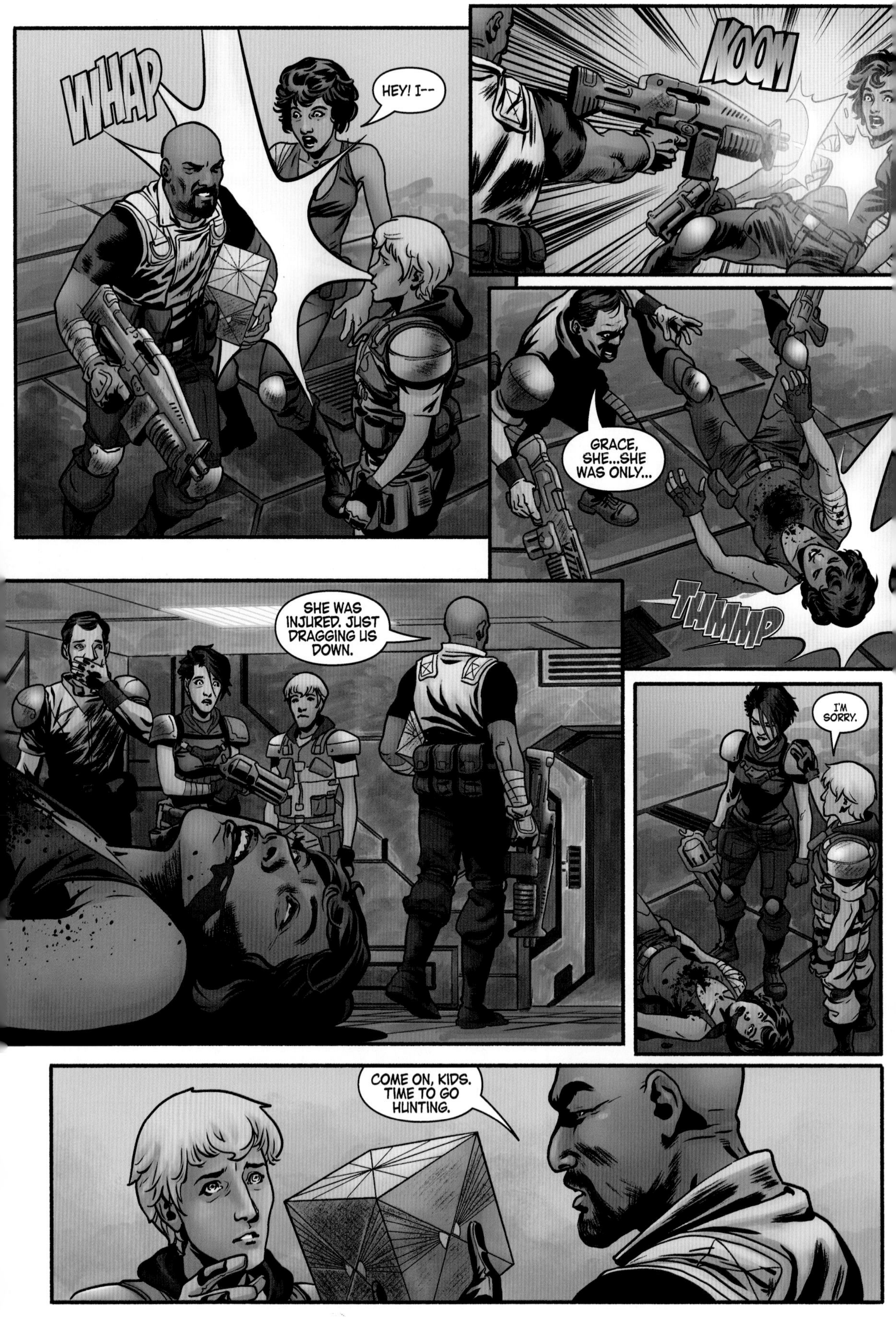

WHAP
HEY! I--
KOOM
GRACE, SHE...SHE WAS ONLY...
THMMP
SHE WAS INJURED. JUST DRAGGING US DOWN.
I'M SORRY.
COME ON, KIDS. TIME TO GO HUNTING.

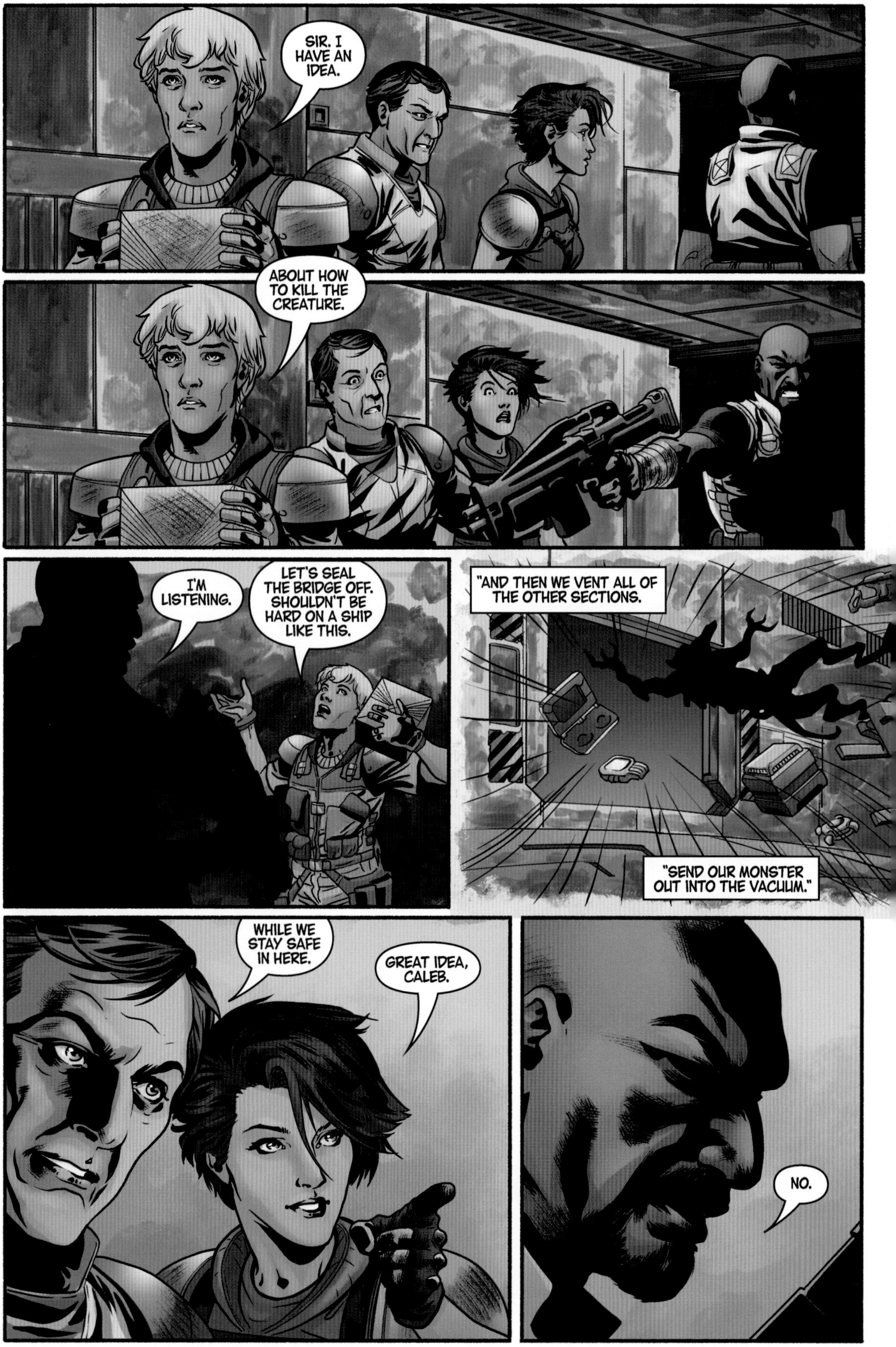
SIR. I HAVE AN IDEA.
ABOUT HOW TO KILL THE CREATURE.
I'M LISTENING.
LET'S SEAL THE BRIDGE OFF. SHOULDN'T BE HARD ON A SHIP LIKE THIS.
"AND THEN WE VENT ALL OF THE OTHER SECTIONS.
"SEND OUR MONSTER OUT INTO THE VACUUM."
WHILE WE STAY SAFE IN HERE.
GREAT IDEA, CALEB.
NO.

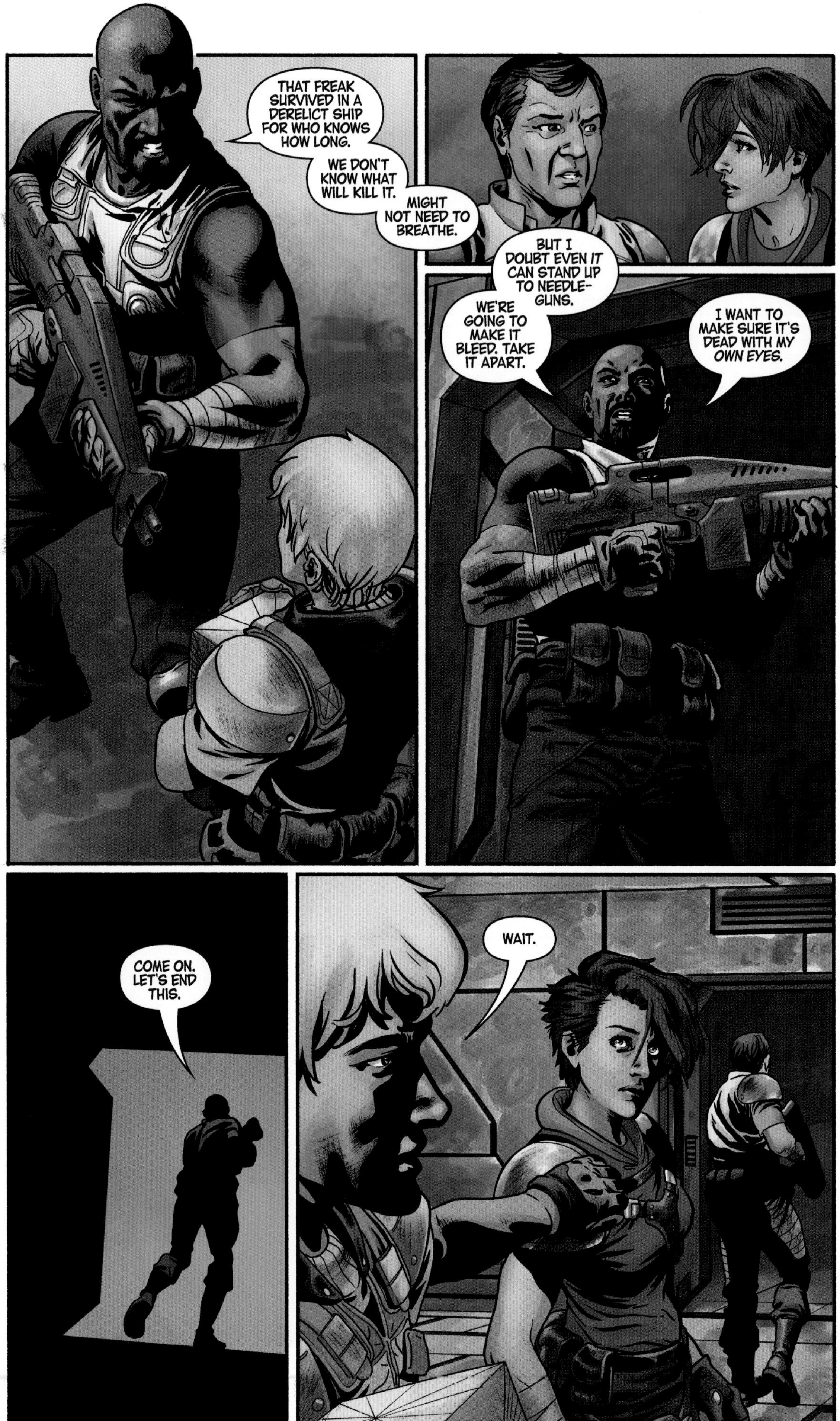
THAT FREAK SURVIVED IN A DERELICT SHIP FOR WHO KNOWS HOW LONG.
WE DON'T KNOW WHAT WILL KILL IT.
MIGHT NOT NEED TO BREATHE.
BUT I DOUBT EVEN IT CAN STAND UP TO NEEDLE-GUNS.
WE'RE GOING TO MAKE IT BLEED. TAKE IT APART.
I WANT TO MAKE SURE IT'S DEAD WITH MY OWN EYES.
COME ON. LET'S END THIS.
WAIT.

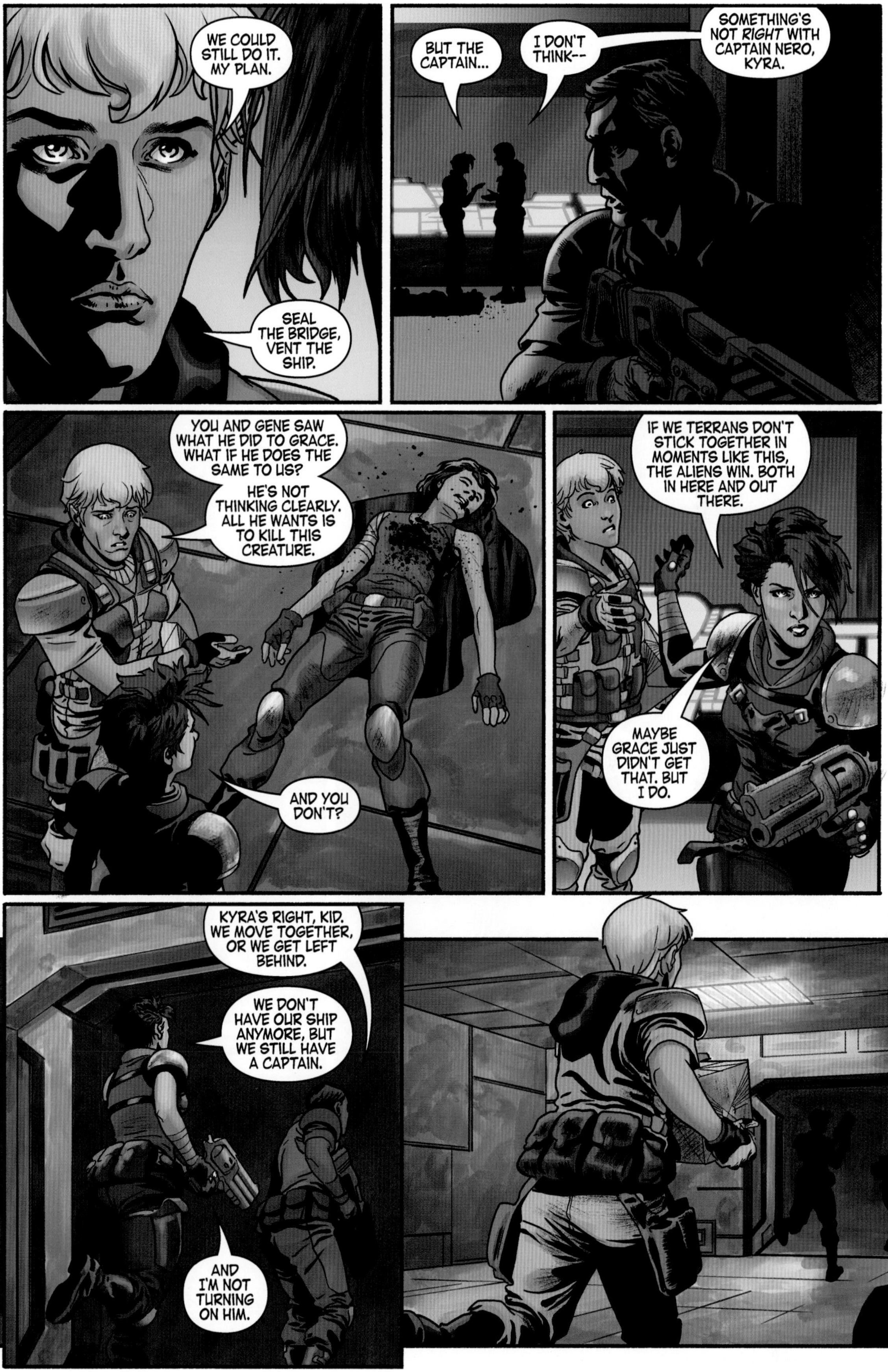
WE COULD STILL DO IT. MY PLAN.
SEAL THE BRIDGE, VENT THE SHIP.
SOMETHING'S NOT RIGHT WITH CAPTAIN NERO, KYRA.
I DON'T THINK--
BUT THE CAPTAIN...
YOU AND GENE SAW WHAT HE DID TO GRACE. WHAT IF HE DOES THE SAME TO US?
HE'S NOT THINKING CLEARLY. ALL HE WANTS IS TO KILL THIS CREATURE.
AND YOU DON'T?
IF WE TERRANS DON'T STICK TOGETHER IN MOMENTS LIKE THIS, THE ALIENS WIN. BOTH IN HERE AND OUT THERE.
MAYBE GRACE JUST DIDN'T GET THAT. BUT I DO.
KYRA'S RIGHT, KID. WE MOVE TOGETHER, OR WE GET LEFT BEHIND.
WE DON'T HAVE OUR SHIP ANYMORE, BUT WE STILL HAVE A CAPTAIN.
AND I'M NOT TURNING ON HIM.

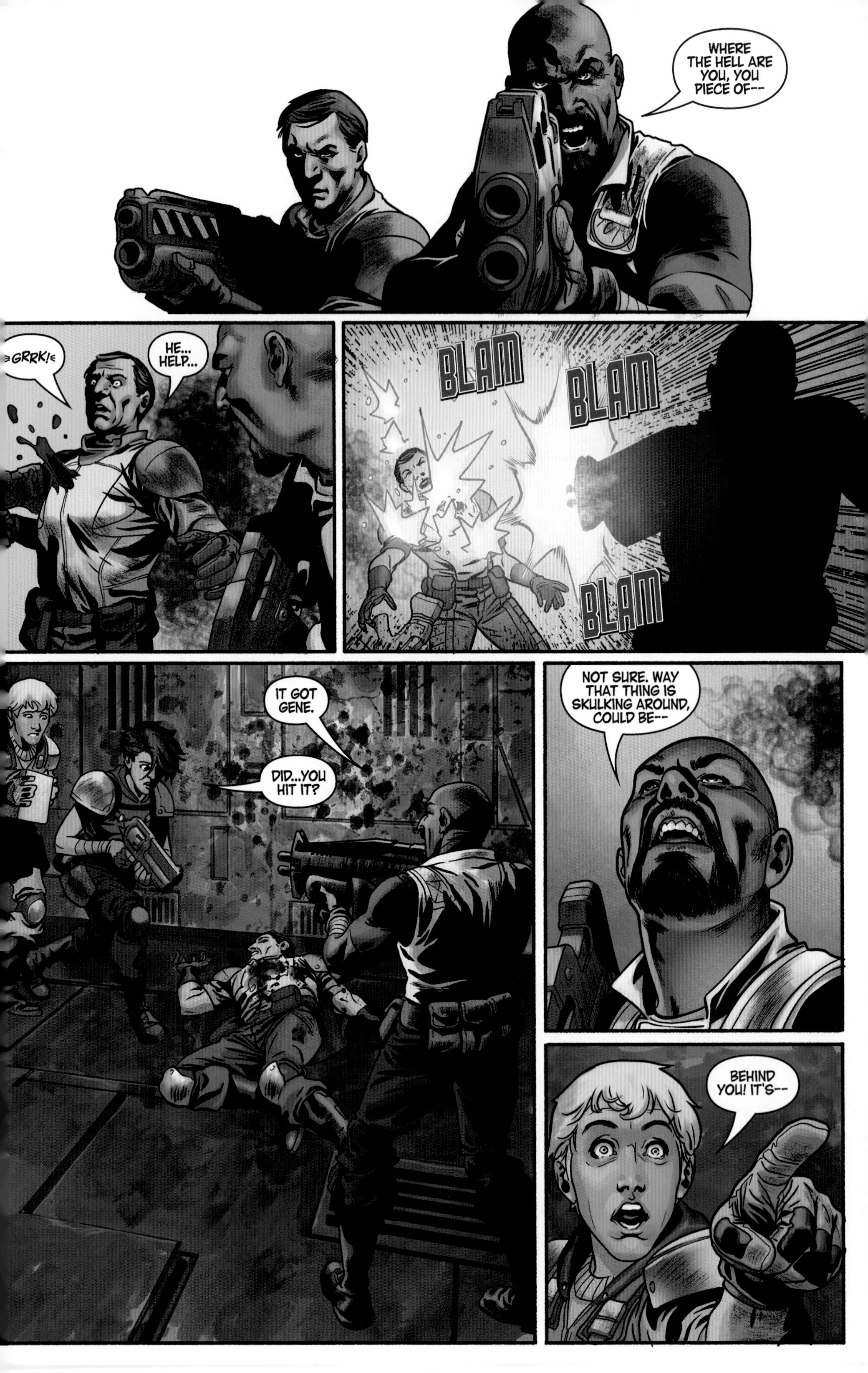
WHERE THE HELL ARE YOU, YOU PIECE OF--
GRRK!
HE... HELP...
BLAM
BLAM
BLAM
IT GOT GENE.
DID...YOU HIT IT?
NOT SURE. WAY THAT THING IS SKULKING AROUND, COULD BE--
BEHIND YOU! IT'S--

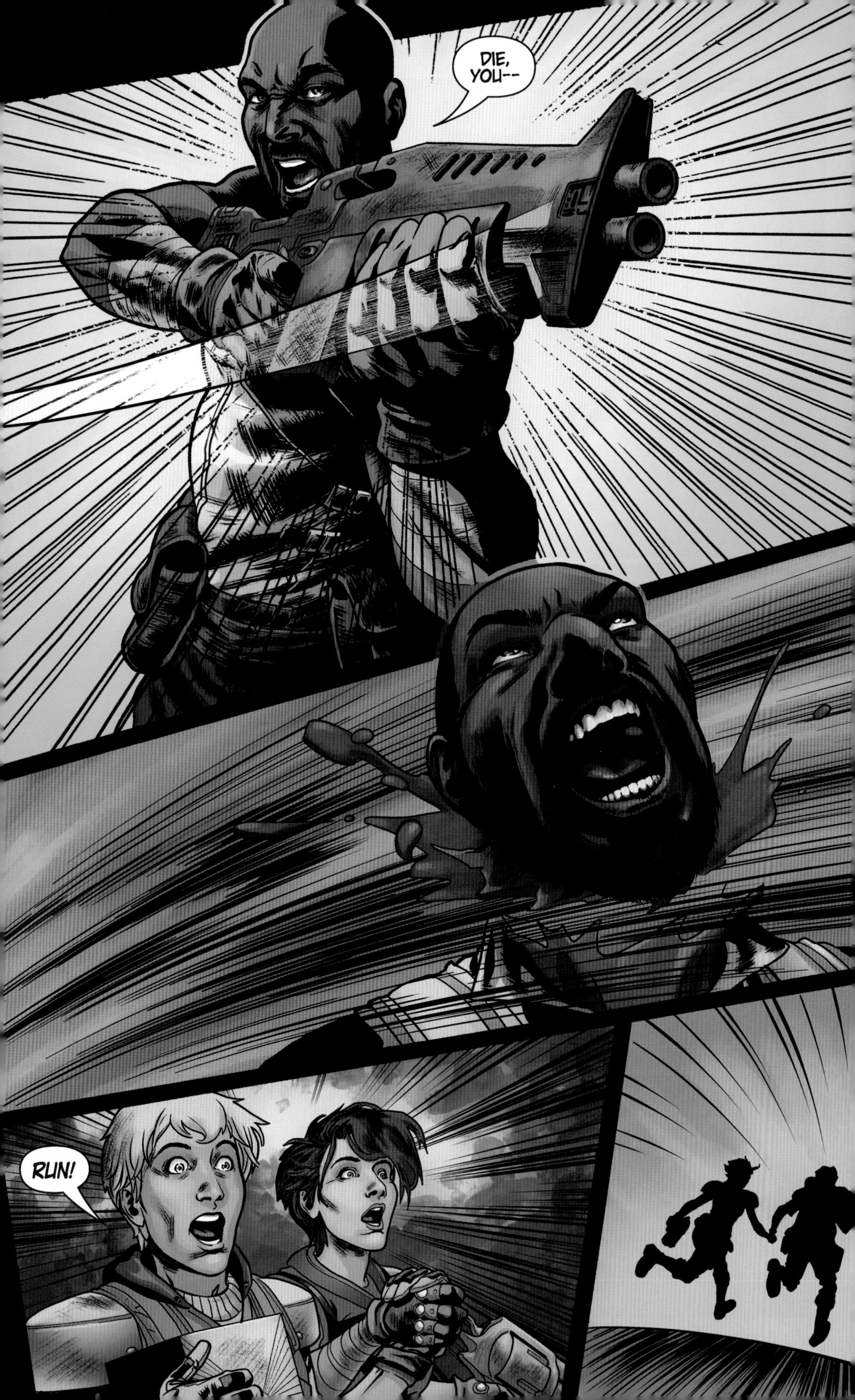
DIE, YOU--
RUN!

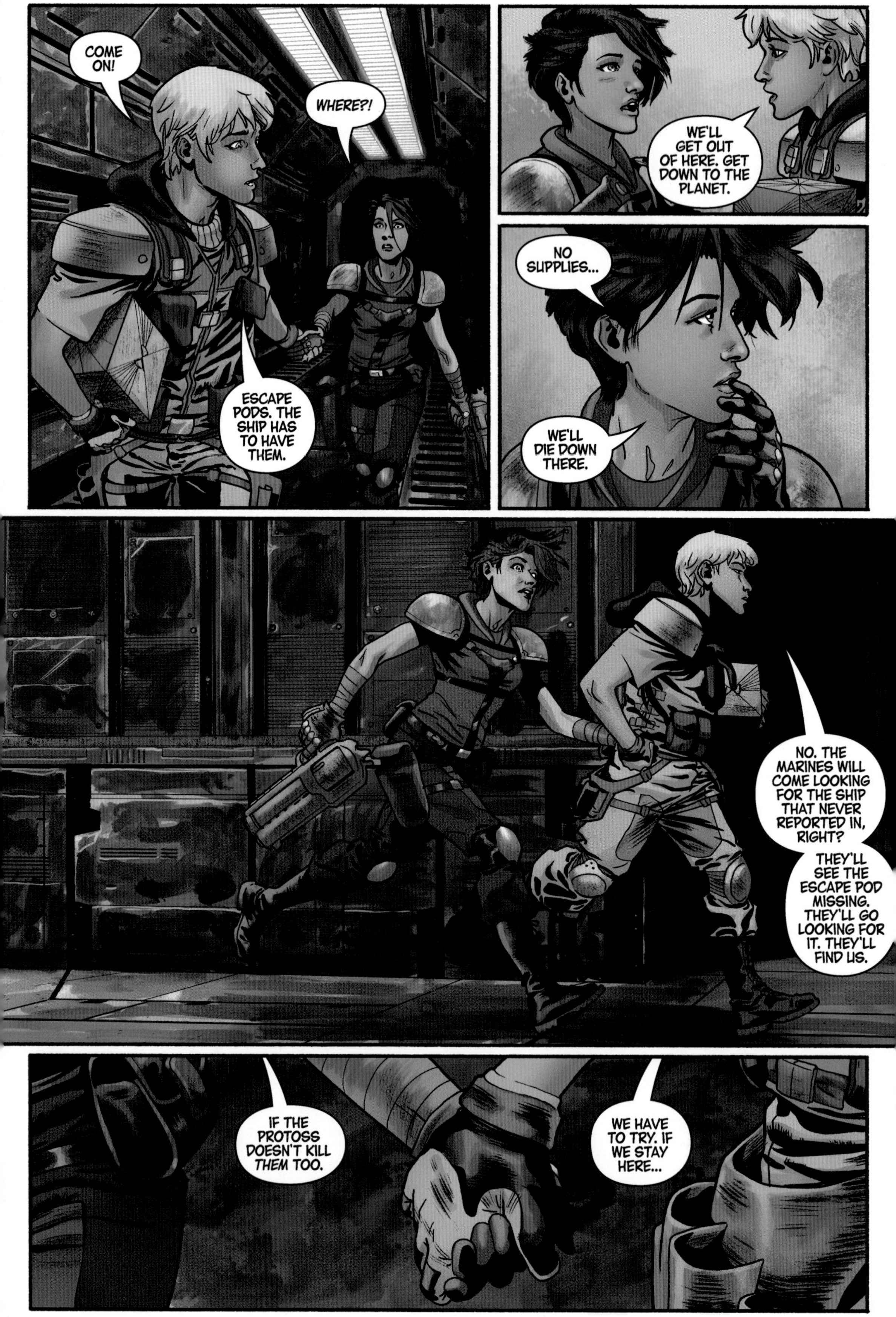
COME ON!
WHERE?!
ESCAPE PODS. THE SHIP HAS TO HAVE THEM.
WE'LL GET OUT OF HERE. GET DOWN TO THE PLANET.
NO SUPPLIES...
WE'LL DIE DOWN THERE.
NO. THE MARINES WILL COME LOOKING FOR THE SHIP THAT NEVER REPORTED IN, RIGHT?
THEY'LL SEE THE ESCAPE POD MISSING. THEY'LL GO LOOKING FOR IT. THEY'LL FIND US.
IF THE PROTOSS DOESN'T KILL THEM TOO.
WE HAVE TO TRY. IF WE STAY HERE...

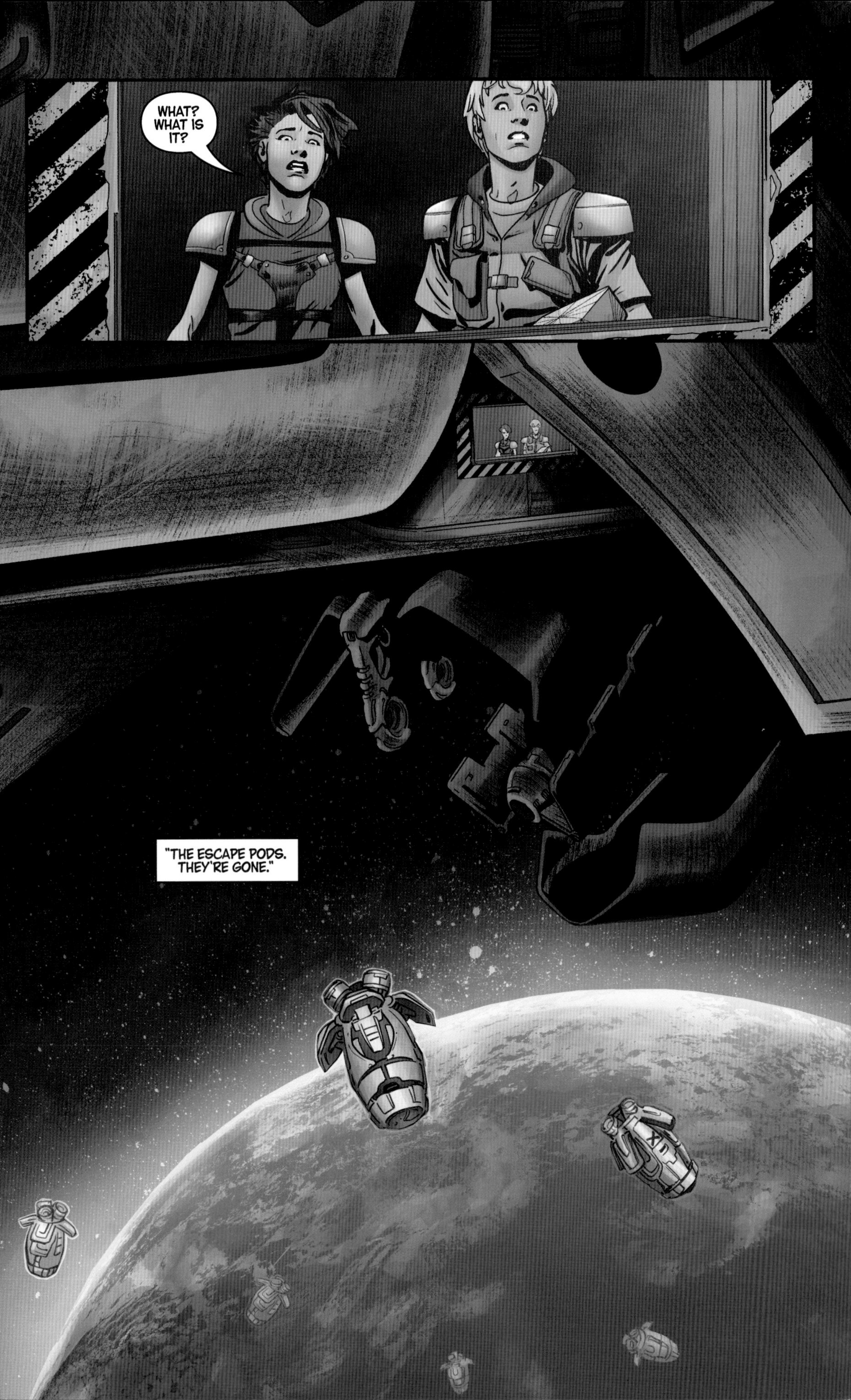
WHAT? WHAT IS IT?
"THE ESCAPE PODS. THEY'RE GONE."

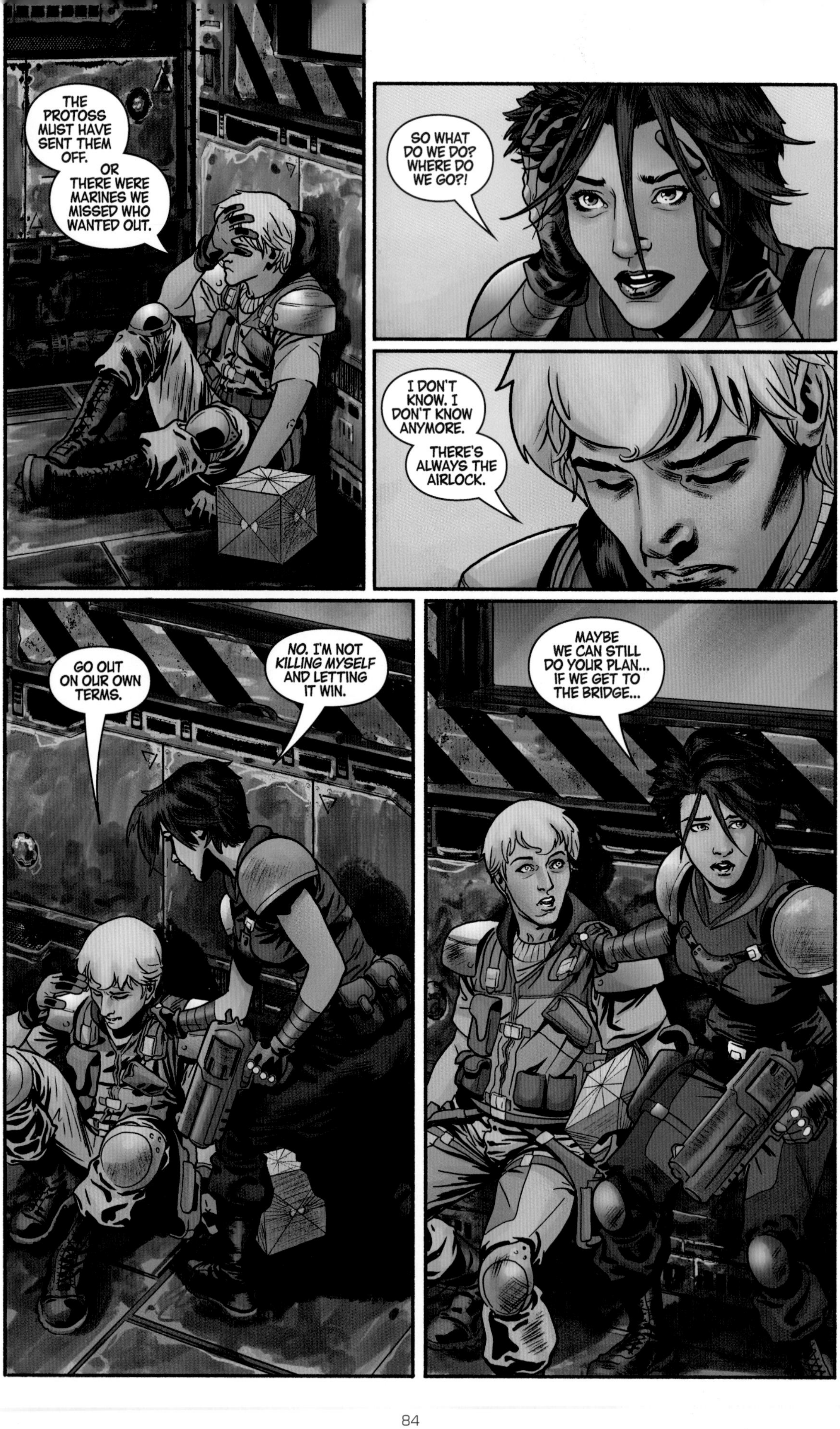
THE PROTOSS MUST HAVE SENT THEM OFF.
OR THERE WERE MARINES WE MISSED WHO WANTED OUT.
SO WHAT DO WE DO? WHERE DO WE GO?!
I DON'T KNOW. I DON'T KNOW ANYMORE.
THERE'S ALWAYS THE AIRLOCK.
GO OUT ON OUR OWN TERMS.
NO. I'M NOT KILLING MYSELF AND LETTING IT WIN.
MAYBE WE CAN STILL DO YOUR PLAN... IF WE GET TO THE BRIDGE...

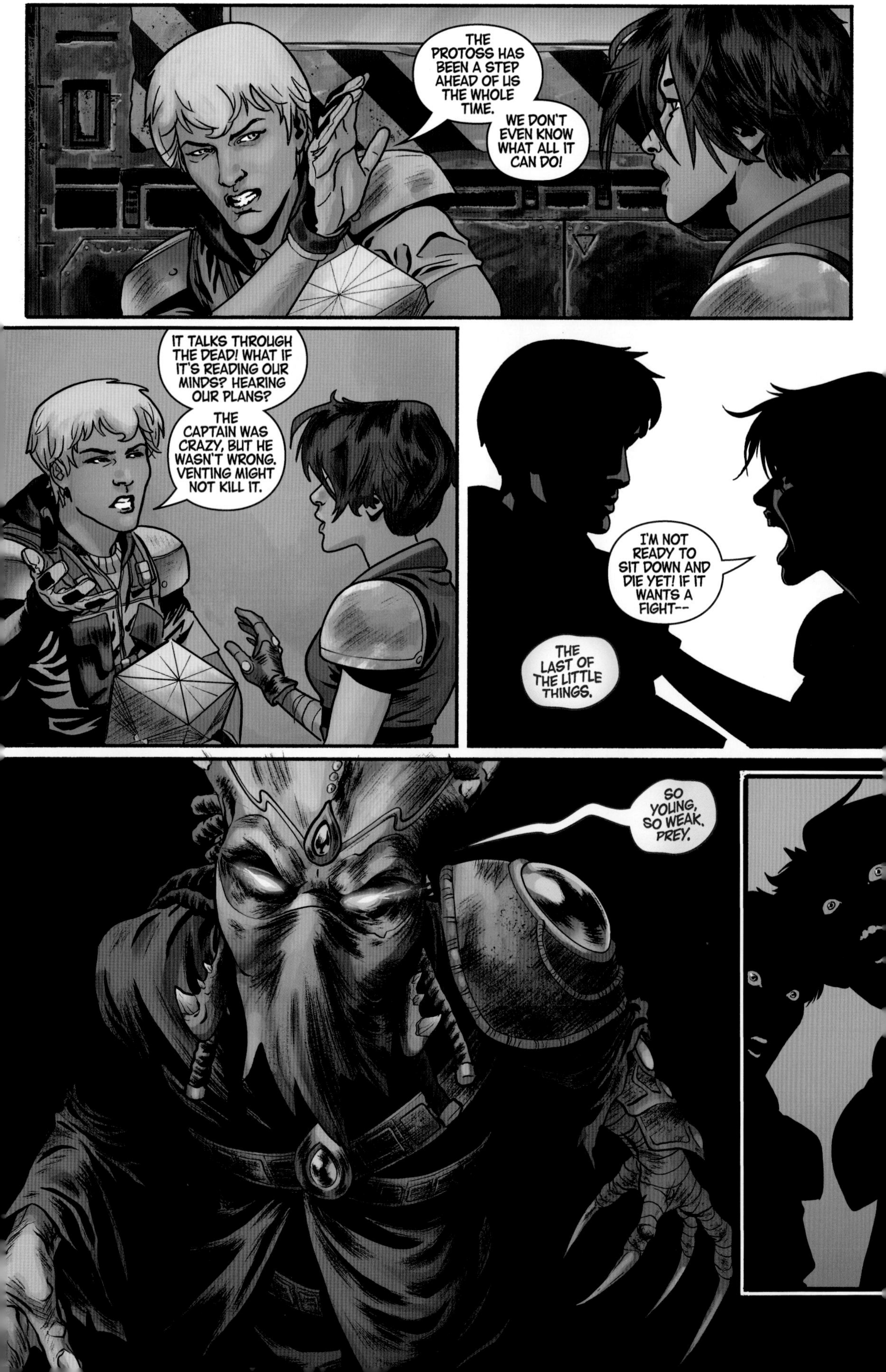
THE PROTOSS HAS BEEN A STEP AHEAD OF US THE WHOLE TIME.
WE DON'T EVEN KNOW WHAT ALL IT CAN DO!
IT TALKS THROUGH THE DEAD! WHAT IF IT'S READING OUR MINDS? HEARING OUR PLANS?
THE CAPTAIN WAS CRAZY, BUT HE WASN'T WRONG. VENTING MIGHT NOT KILL IT.
I'M NOT READY TO SIT DOWN AND DIE YET! IF IT WANTS A FIGHT--
THE LAST OF THE LITTLE THINGS.
SO YOUNG, SO WEAK. PREY.

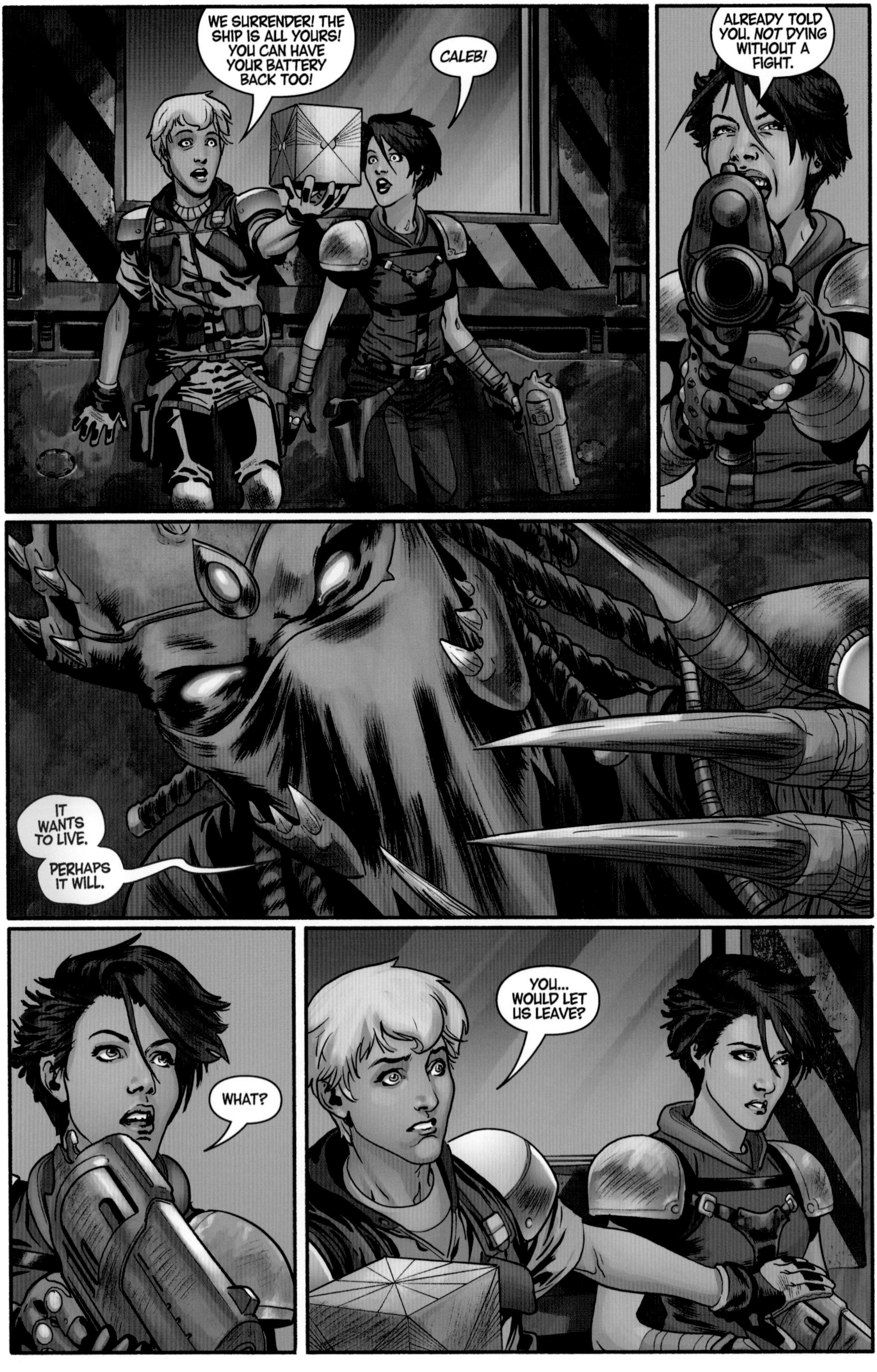
WE SURRENDER! THE SHIP IS ALL YOURS! YOU CAN HAVE YOUR BATTERY BACK TOO!
CALEB!
ALREADY TOLD YOU. *NOT* DYING WITHOUT A FIGHT.
IT WANTS TO LIVE.
PERHAPS IT WILL.
WHAT?
YOU... WOULD LET US LEAVE?

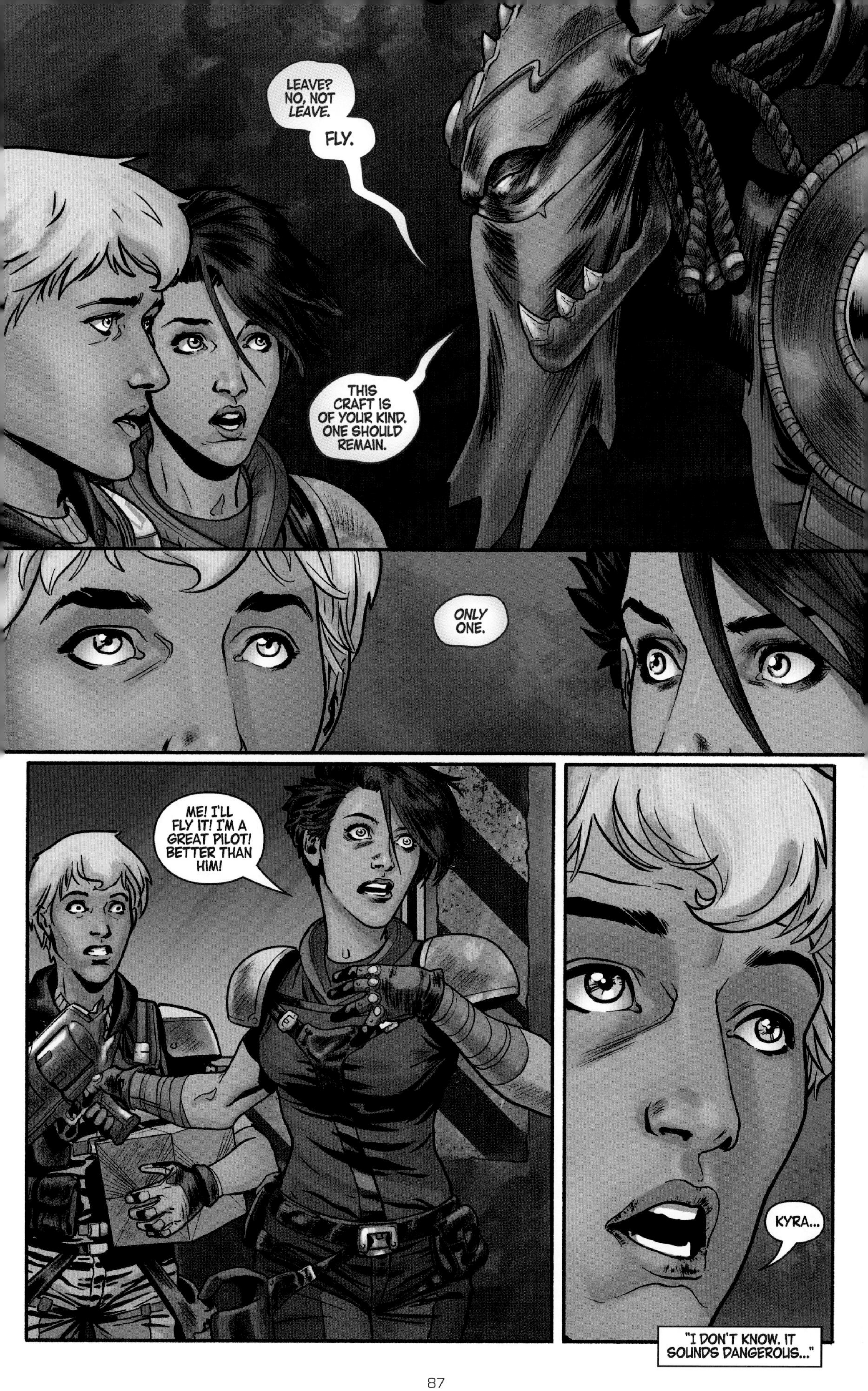
LEAVE? NO, NOT LEAVE.
FLY.
THIS CRAFT IS OF YOUR KIND. ONE SHOULD REMAIN.
ONLY ONE.
ME! I'LL FLY IT! I'M A GREAT PILOT! BETTER THAN HIM!
KYRA...
"I DON'T KNOW. IT SOUNDS DANGEROUS..."

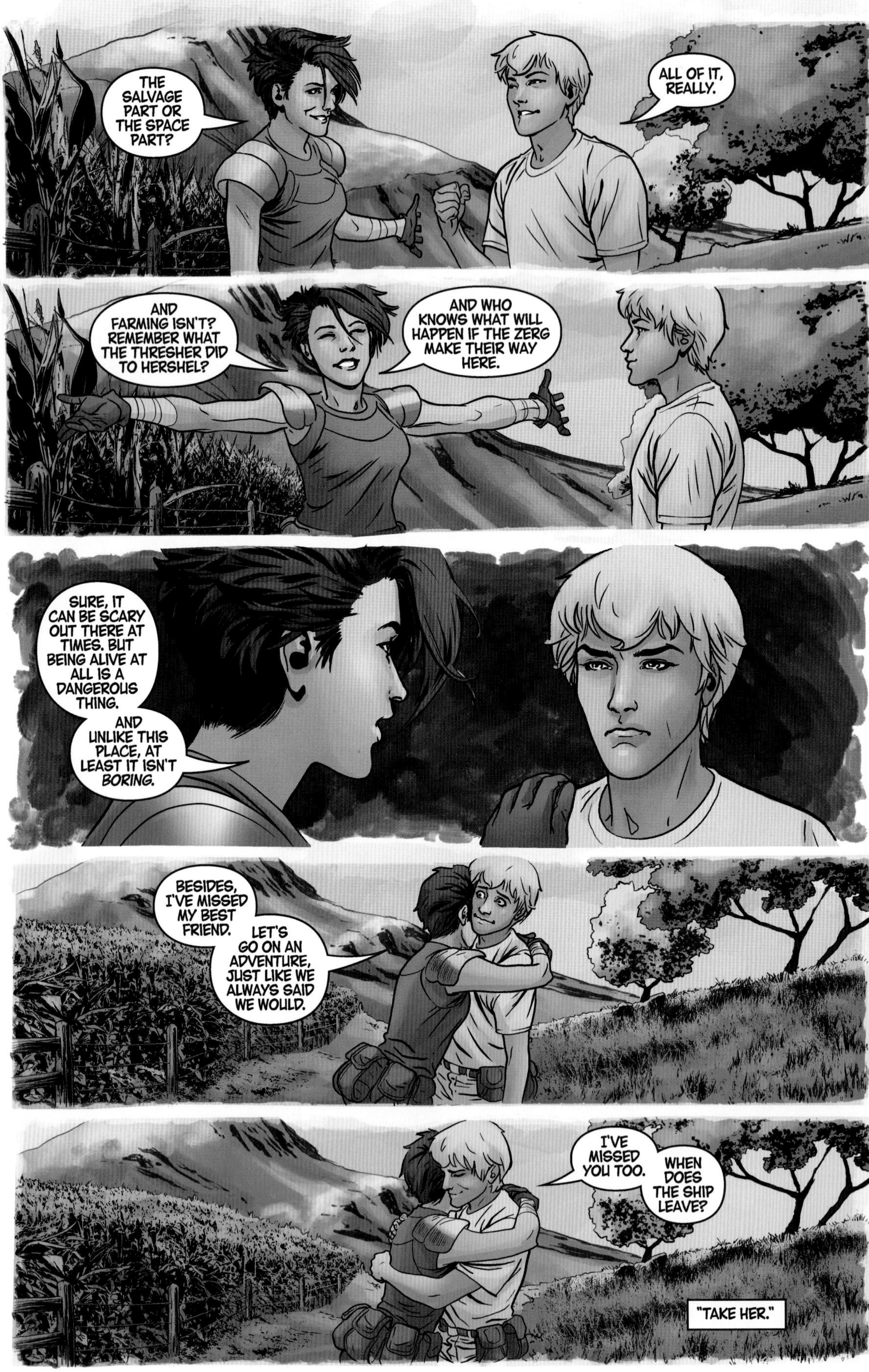
THE SALVAGE PART OR THE SPACE PART?
ALL OF IT, REALLY.
AND FARMING ISN'T? REMEMBER WHAT THE THRESHER DID TO HERSHEL?
AND WHO KNOWS WHAT WILL HAPPEN IF THE ZERG MAKE THEIR WAY HERE.
SURE, IT CAN BE SCARY OUT THERE AT TIMES. BUT BEING ALIVE AT ALL IS A DANGEROUS THING.
AND UNLIKE THIS PLACE, AT LEAST IT ISN'T BORING.
BESIDES, I'VE MISSED MY BEST FRIEND.
LET'S GO ON AN ADVENTURE, JUST LIKE WE ALWAYS SAID WE WOULD.
I'VE MISSED YOU TOO.
WHEN DOES THE SHIP LEAVE?
"TAKE HER."

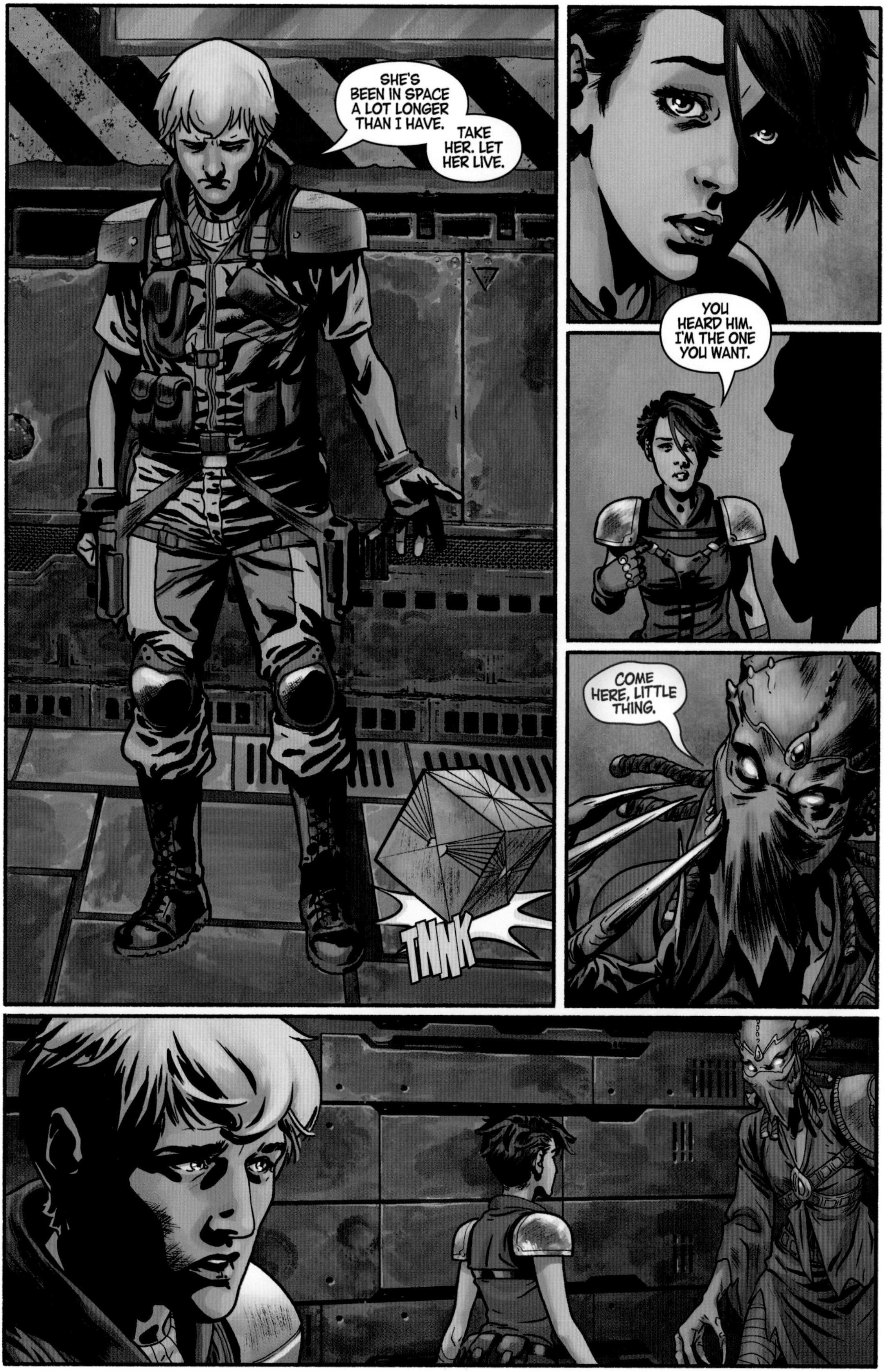
SHE'S BEEN IN SPACE A LOT LONGER THAN I HAVE.
TAKE HER. LET HER LIVE.
TNNK
YOU HEARD HIM. I'M THE ONE YOU WANT.
COME HERE, LITTLE THING.

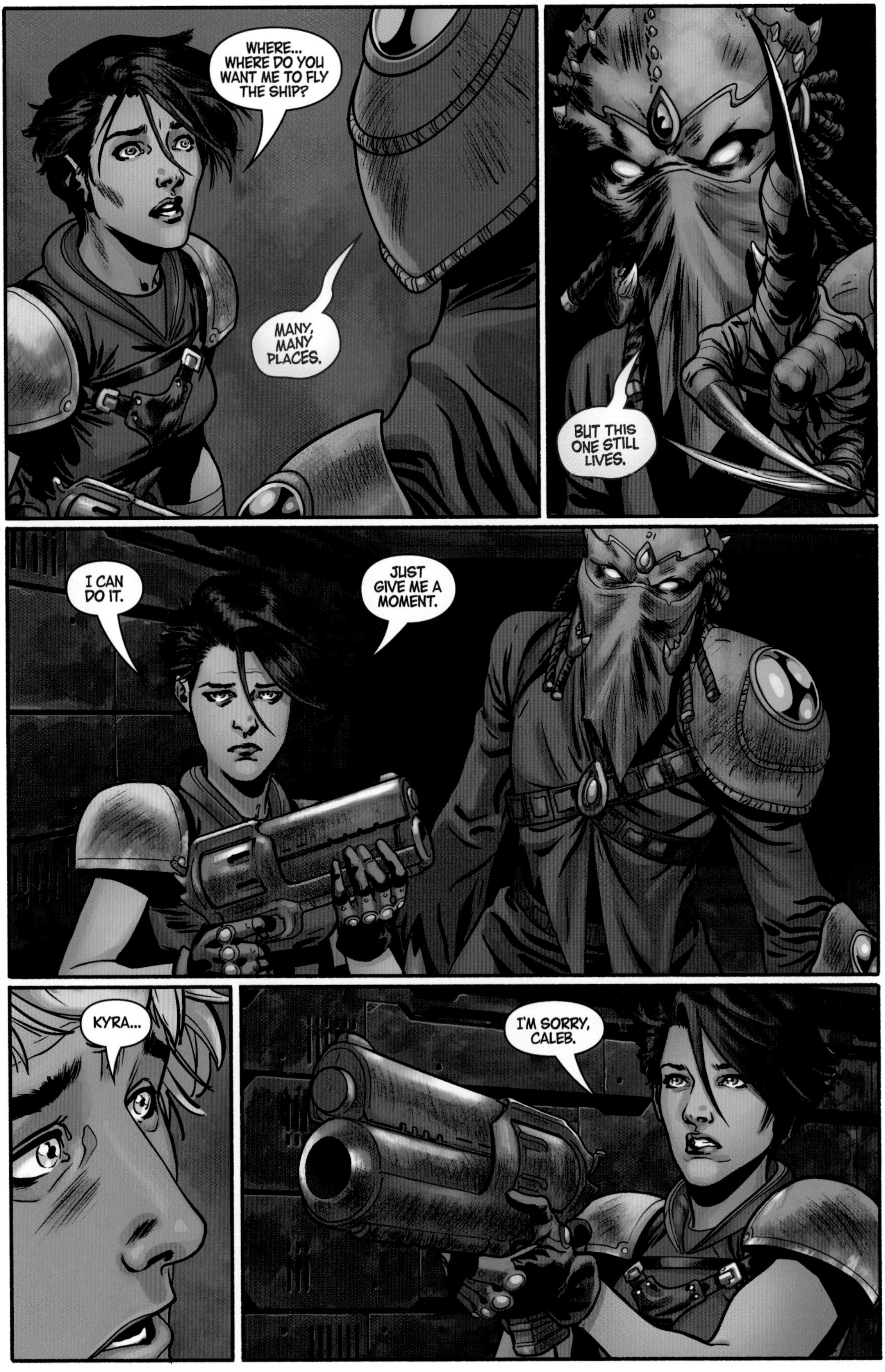
WHERE... WHERE DO YOU WANT ME TO FLY THE SHIP?
MANY, MANY PLACES.
BUT THIS ONE STILL LIVES.
I CAN DO IT.
JUST GIVE ME A MOMENT.
KYRA...
I'M SORRY, CALEB.

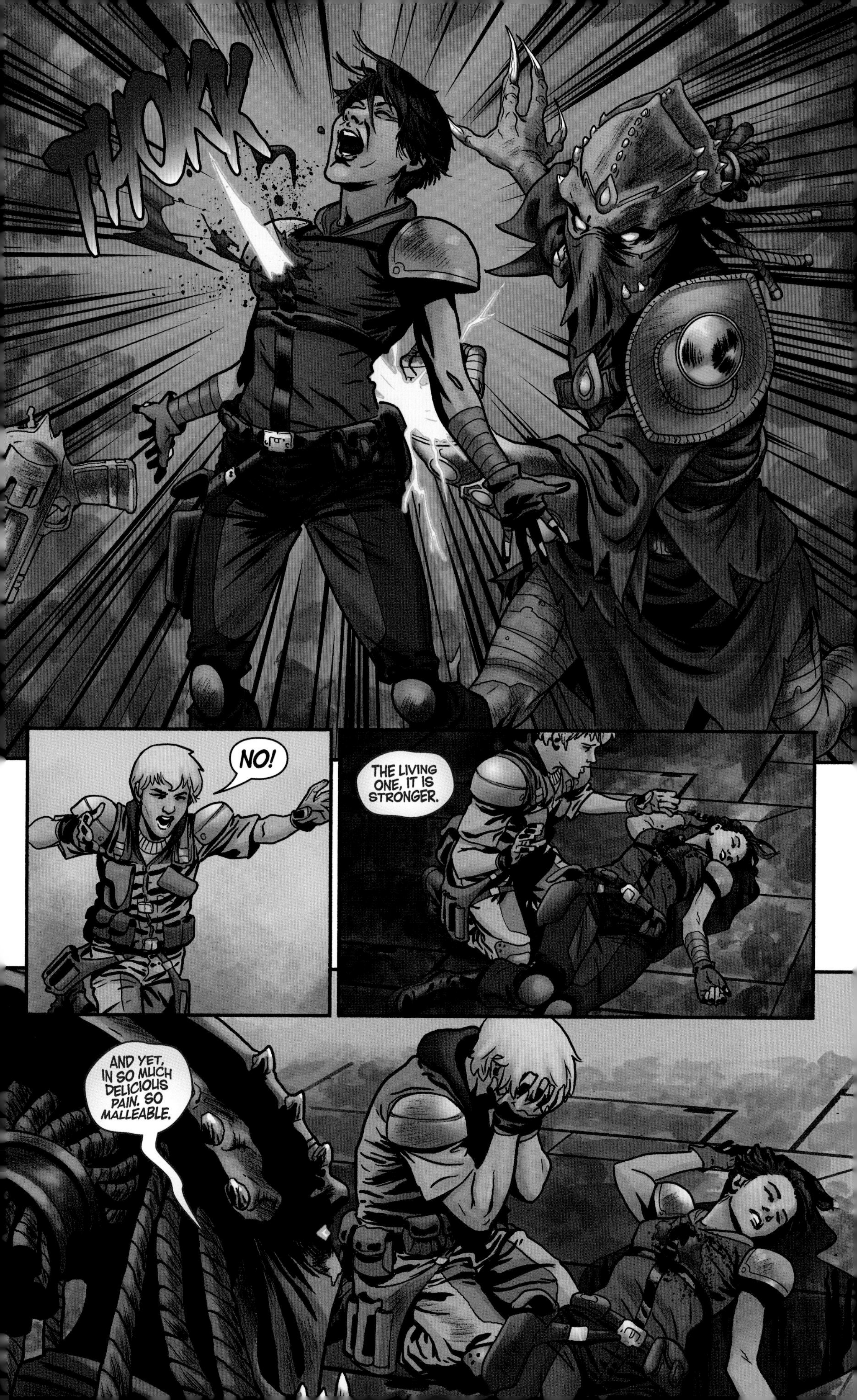
THOKK
NO!
THE LIVING ONE, IT IS STRONGER.
AND YET, IN SO MUCH DELICIOUS PAIN. SO MALLEABLE.

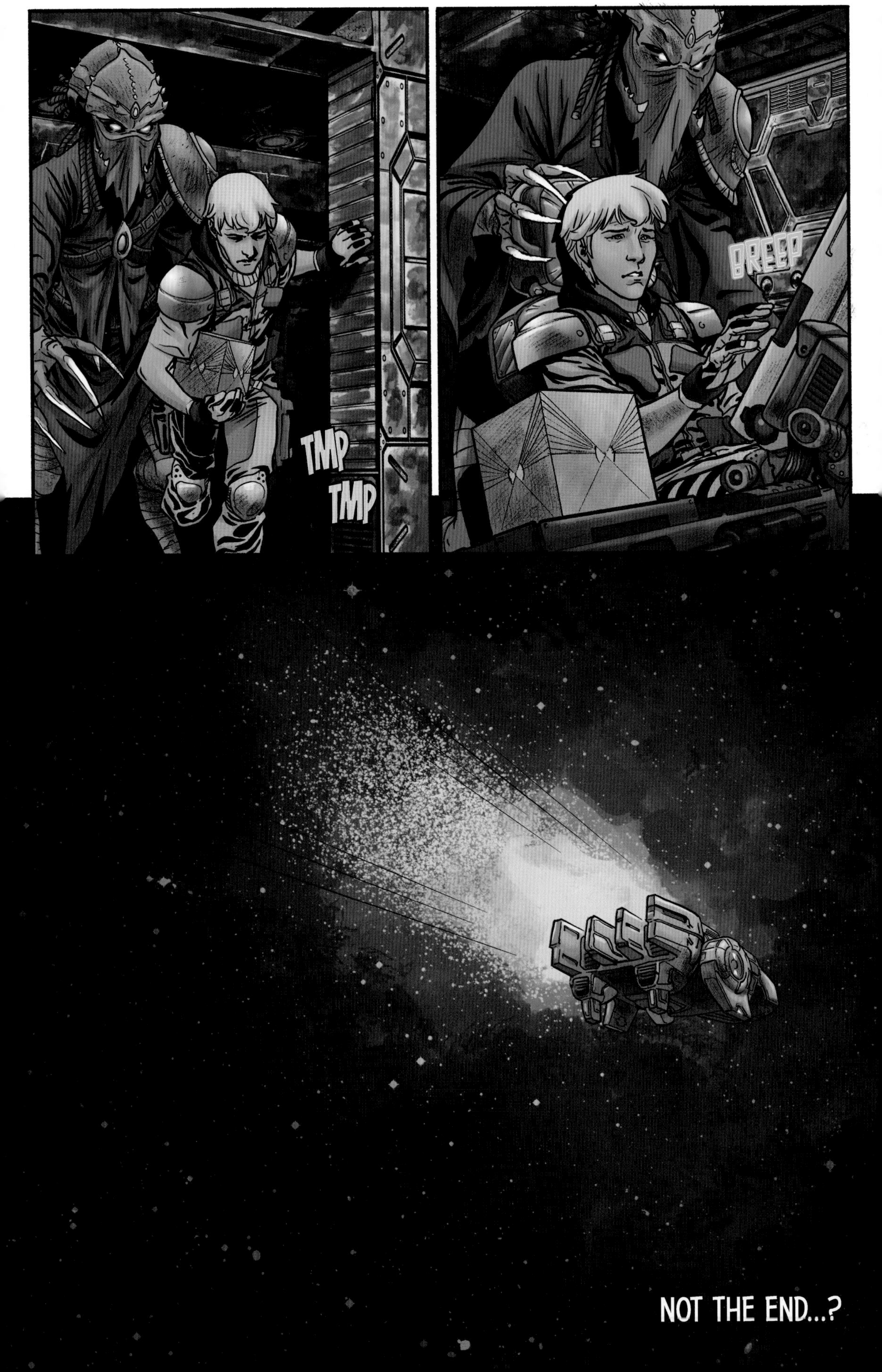
TMP
TMP
BREEP
NOT THE END...?

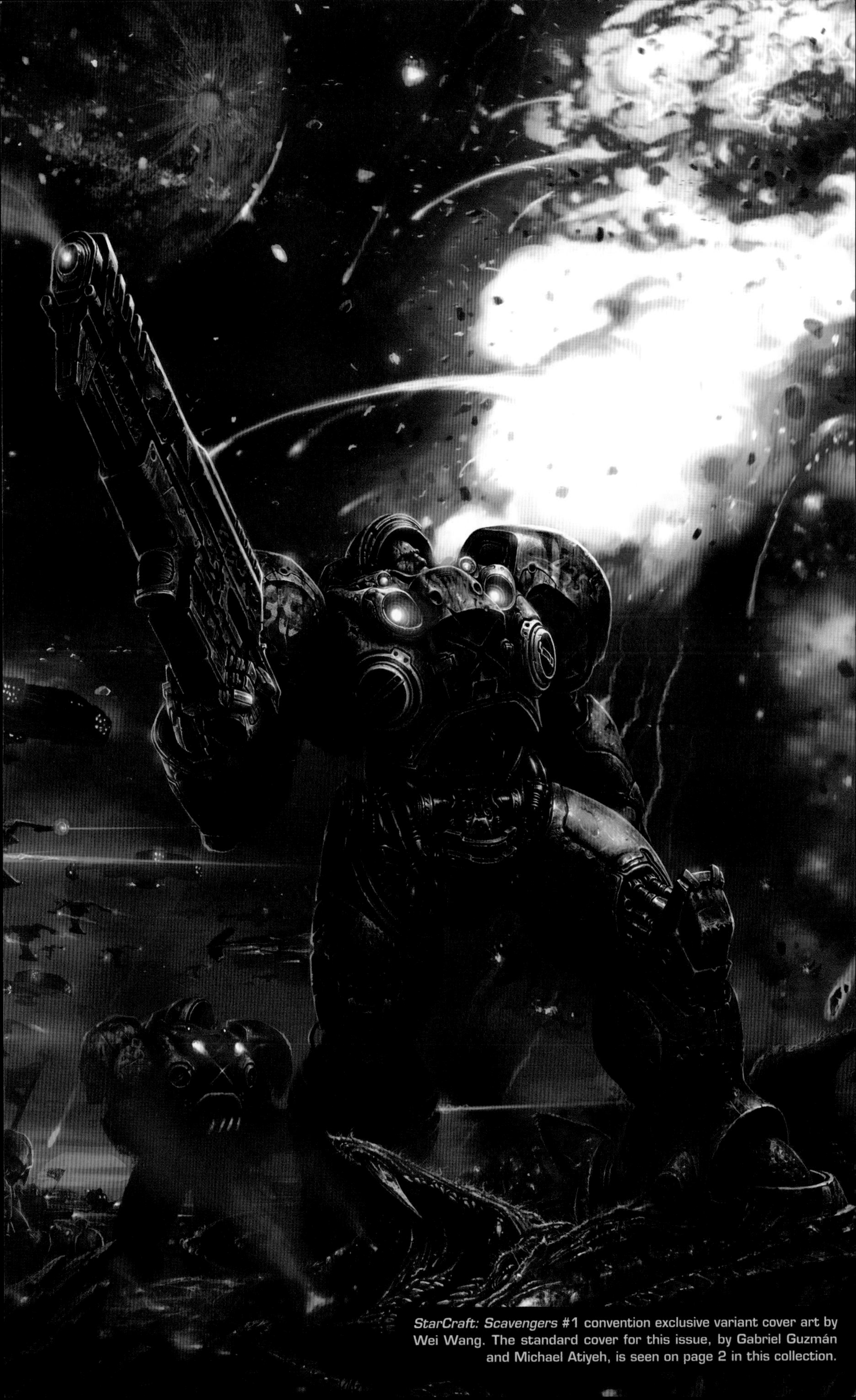

StarCraft: Scavengers #1 convention exclusive variant cover art by Wei Wang. The standard cover for this issue, by Gabriel Guzmán and Michael Atiyeh, is seen on page 2 in this collection.

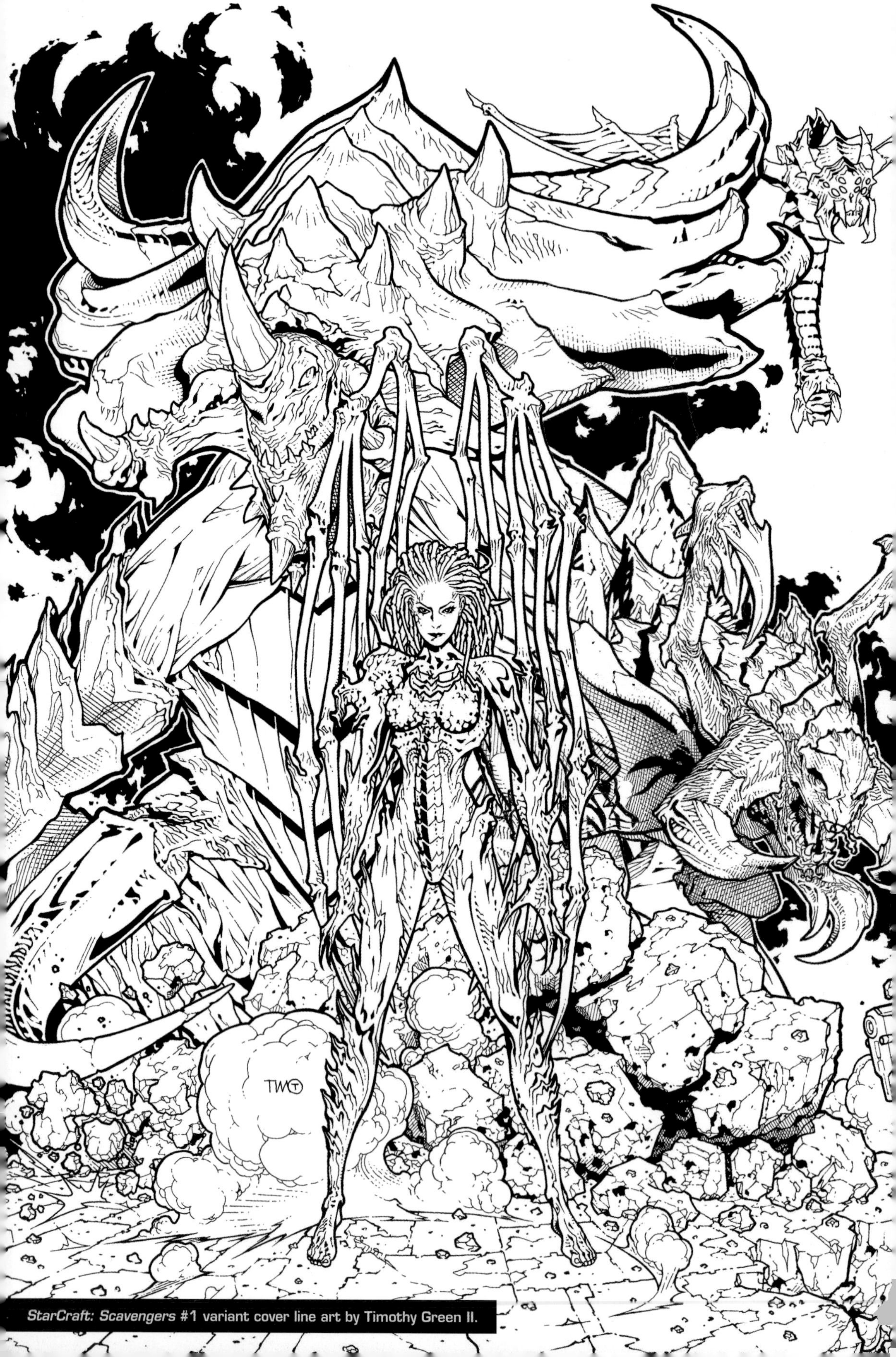

StarCraft: Scavengers #1 variant cover line art by Timothy Green II.

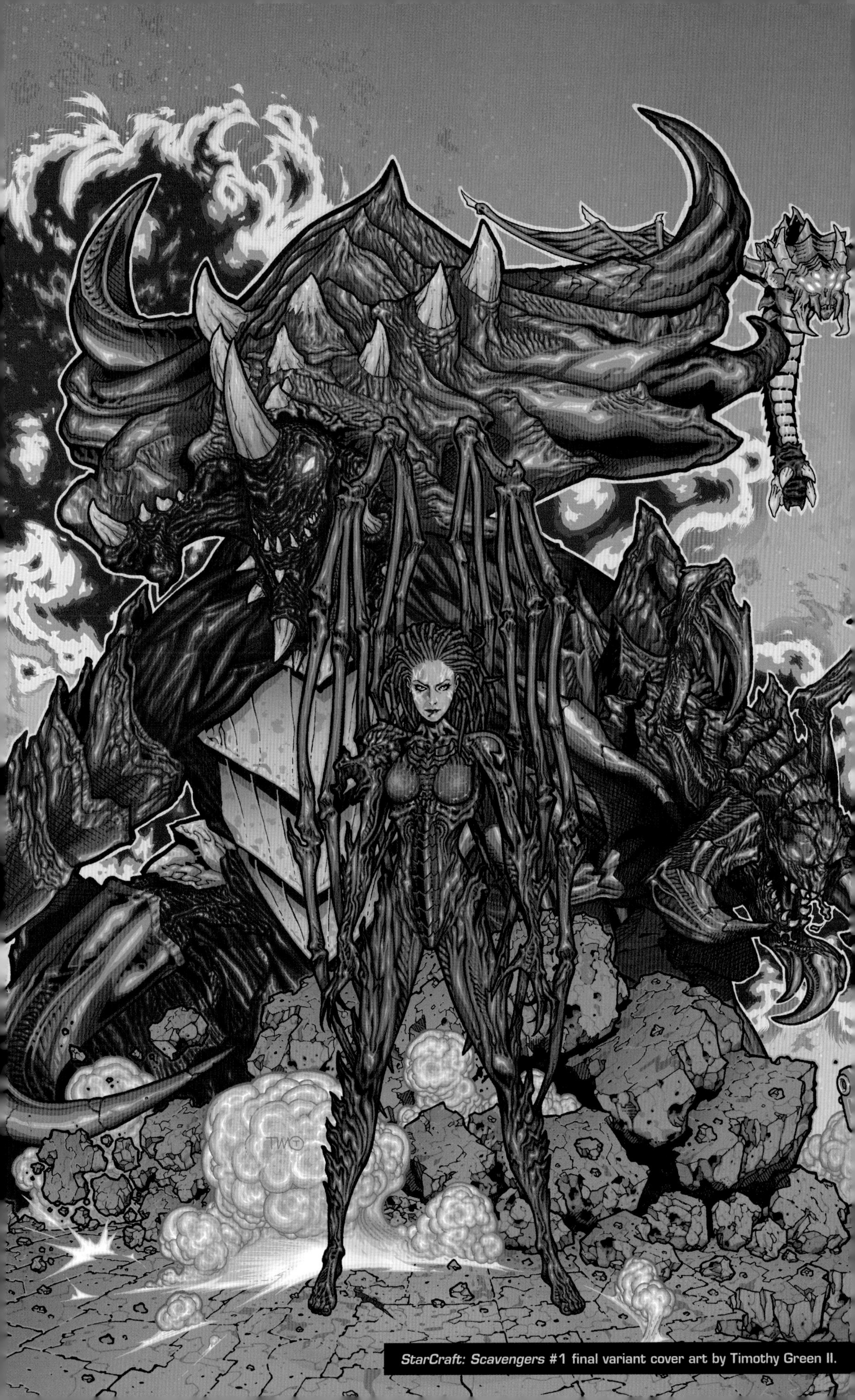

StarCraft: Scavengers #1 final variant cover art by Timothy Green II.

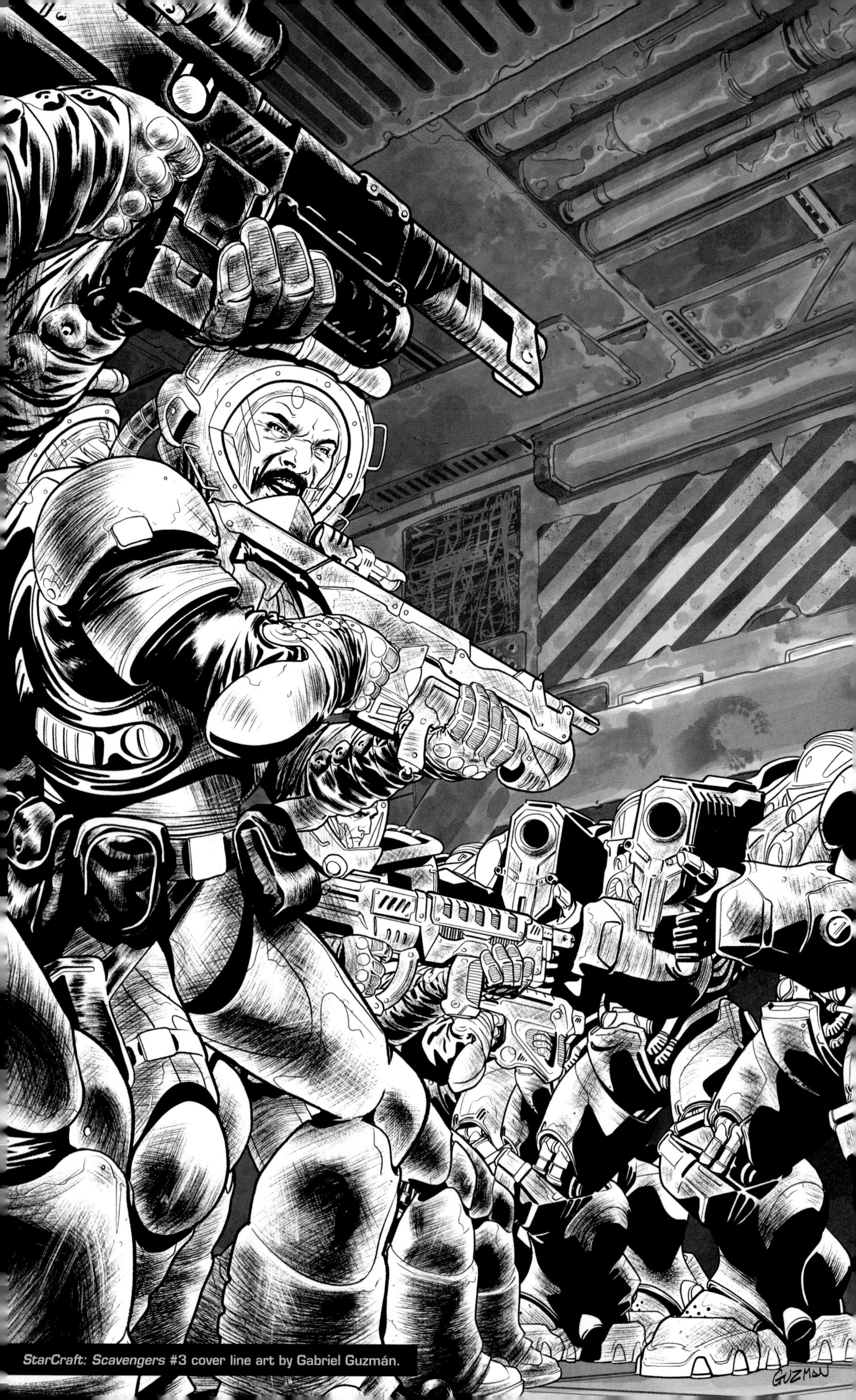
GUZMAN

StarCraft: Scavengers #3 cover line art by Gabriel Guzmán.

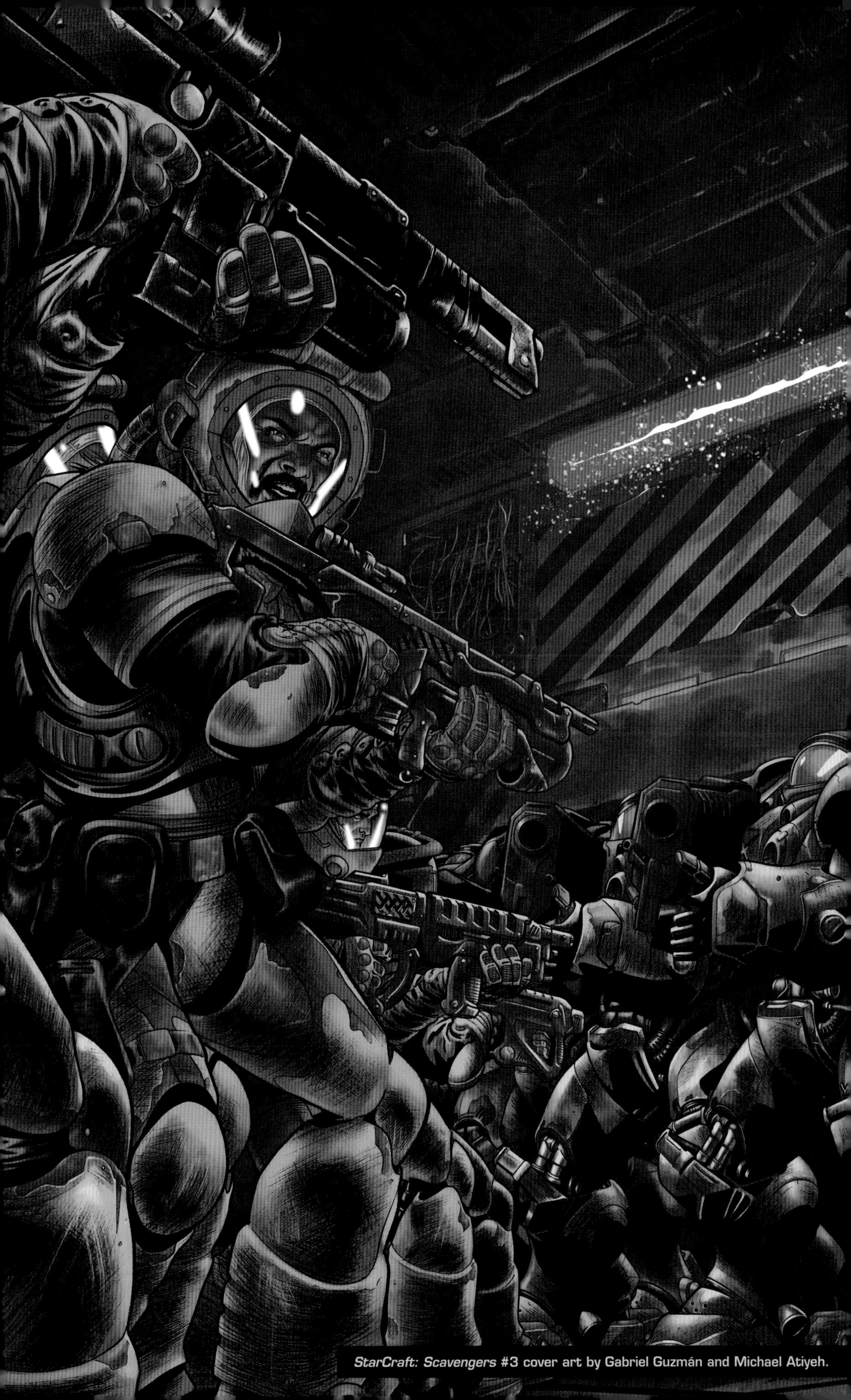

StarCraft: Scavengers #3 cover art by Gabriel Guzmán and Michael Atiyeh.

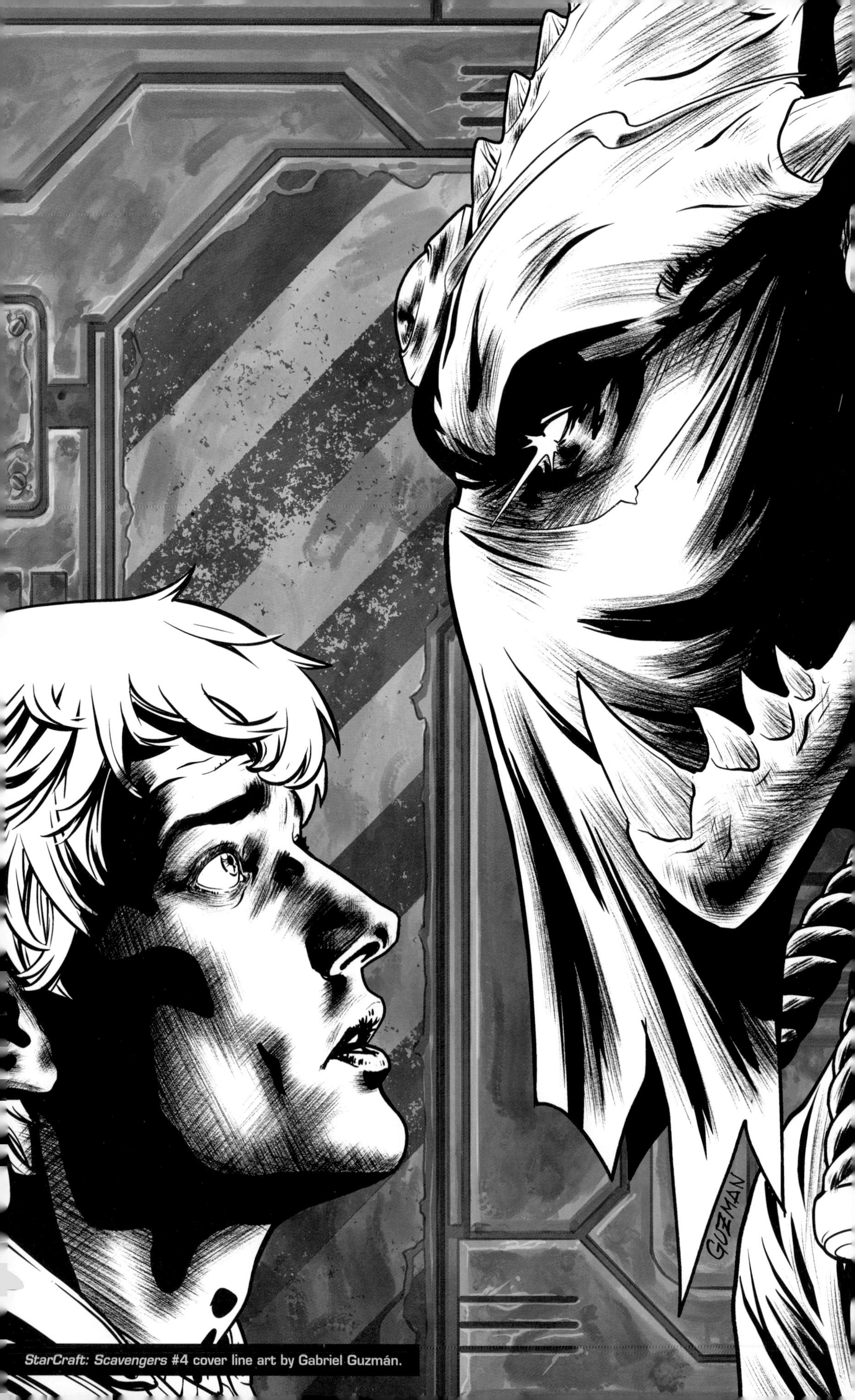
GUZMAN

StarCraft: Scavengers #4 cover line art by Gabriel Guzmán.

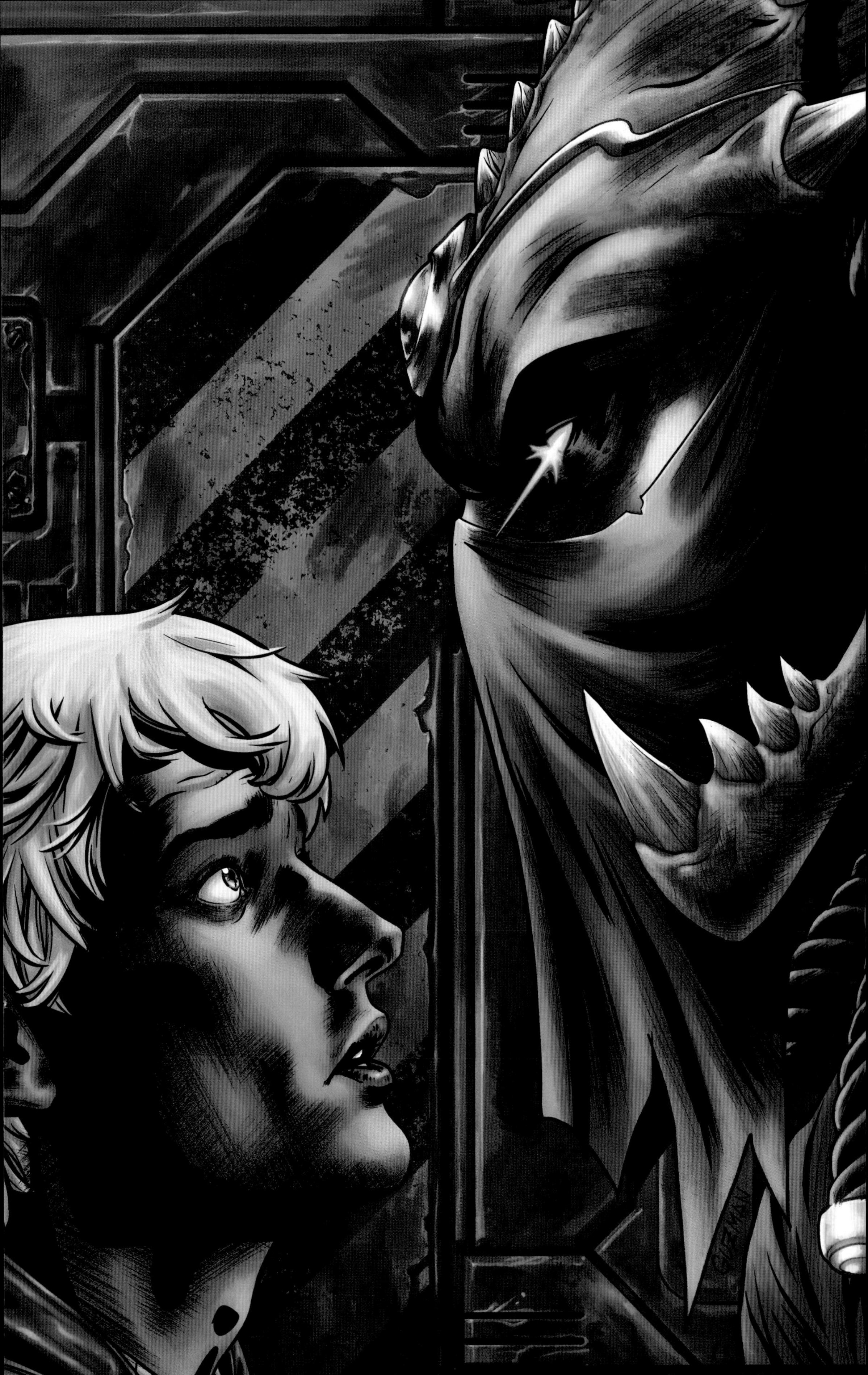

StarCraft: Scavengers #4 cover art by Gabriel Guzmán and Michael Atiyeh.

OVERWATCH®

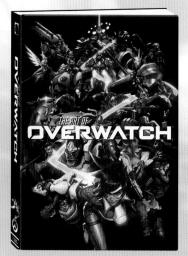

Blizzard Entertainment reveals the creative process behind one of the most popular FPS games of all time! Filled with never-before-seen art as well as commentary provided by the game's development team, this book is sure to please any *Overwatch* fan! The deluxe limited edition comes packaged in a beautiful clamshell box with magnetic closure and includes an acetate slipcover featuring the game's most popular hero, Tracer, as well as two portfolios containing a total of three prints chosen by the *Overwatch* team!

THE ART OF OVERWATCH

ISBN 978-1-50670-367-1
$49.99 US

THE ART OF
OVERWATCH
LIMITED EDITION

ISBN 978-1-50670-553-8
$100.00 US

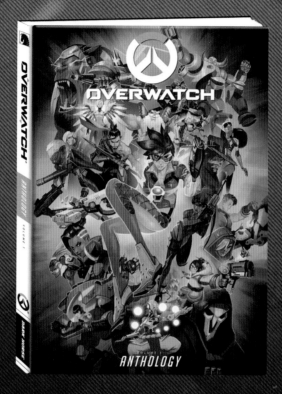

OVERWATCH: ANTHOLOGY VOLUME 1
ISBN 978-1-50670-540-8
$19.99 US

Your favorite *Overwatch* heroes' backstories are revealed in this anthology from
Dark Horse Books and Blizzard Entertainment! This hardcover anthology collects
the first twelve issues of Blizzard Entertainment's digital *Overwatch* comic series
and features an all-star creative team, including Matt Burns, Robert Brooks, Micky
Neilson, Andrew R. Robinson, Nesskain, Bengal, Miki Montlló, and more. Whether
you are a beginner or a Grandmaster, this anthology is an essential companion
to *Overwatch* gameplay!

NEVER-BEFORE-REVEALED SECRETS OF THE WARCRAFT UNIVERSE!

These definitive collections reveal untold stories about the birth of the cosmos, the rise of ancient empires, and the forces that shaped Azeroth. Featuring original art, this multipart series explores the rich lore of the Warcraft universe, from the distant past to the modern era. Showcasing all-new artwork from Peter C. Lee, Stanton Feng, Alex Horley, Wei Wang, Bayard Wu, and other fan-favorite artists, as well as intricately detailed maps and spot art by Joseph Lacroix.

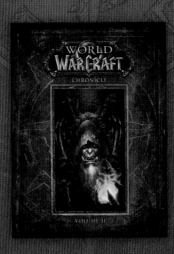

WORLD OF WARCRAFT CHRONICLE: VOLUME I
ISBN 978-1-61655-845-1
$39.99 US

WORLD OF WARCRAFT CHRONICLE: VOLUME II
ISBN 978-1-61655-846-8
$39.99 US

WORLD OF WARCRAFT CHRONICLE: VOLUME III
ISBN 978-1-61655-847-5
$39.99 US

THE ADVENTURE CONTINUES WITH *STARCRAFT: SOLDIERS*!

Newly graduated Lieutenant Shivani Singh wants to defend the Dominion on the front lines, but it will take more than good grades and confidence to survive on the edge of zerg space. After a routine patrol goes awry, Singh launches an investigation to root out threats to the fragile peace between the Dominion and the zerg Swarm. This story is plotted by veteran animation and Blizzard Entertainment comics writer Andrew R. Robinson (*Overwatch Anthology, World of Warcraft*) and the StarCraft game development team, with co-scripting by Jody Houser (*Stranger Things, Star Wars*) and art by Miguel Sepulveda (*Lone Wolf 2100, Green Lantern*).

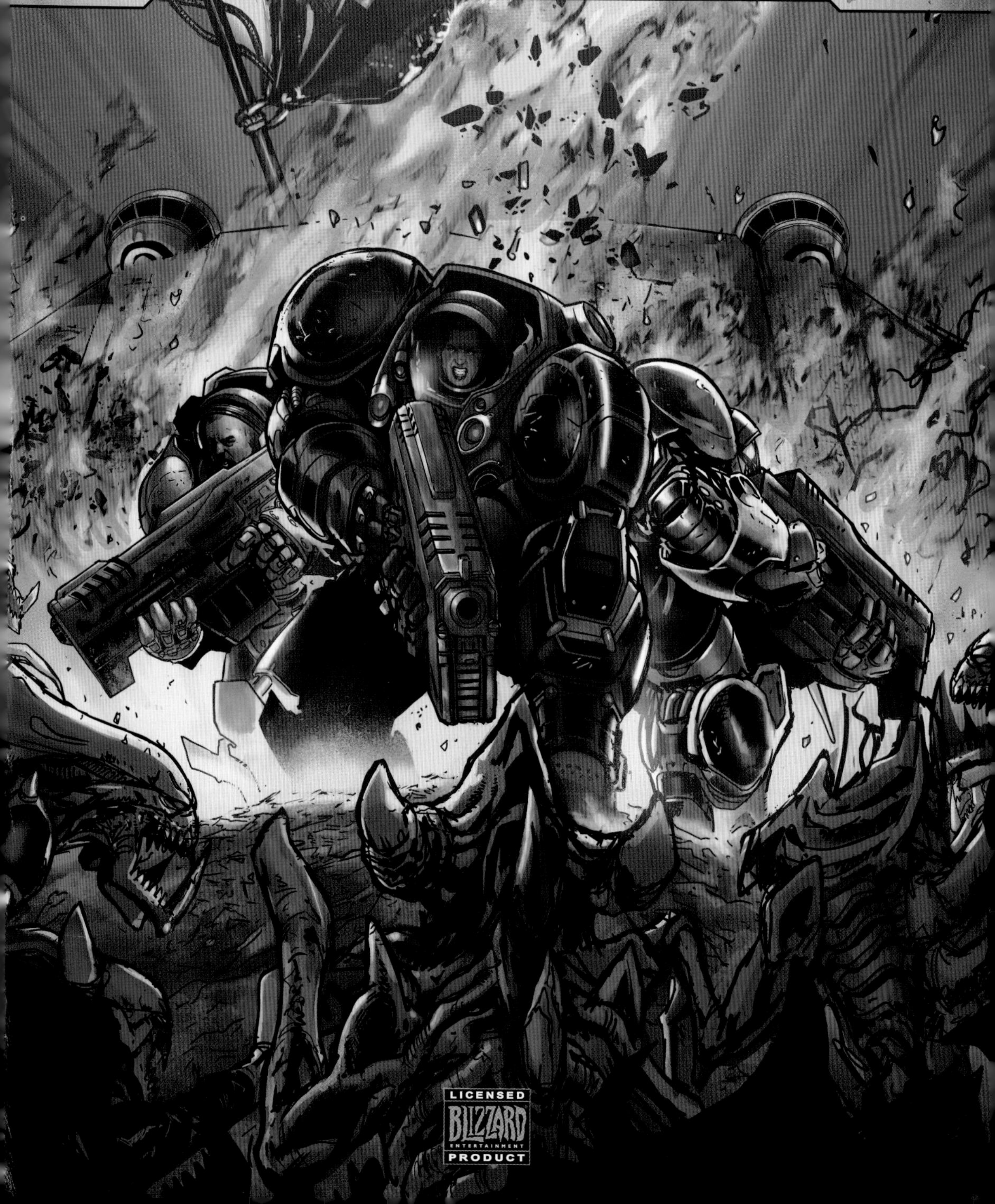

EXIT